Lynn Hershman Leeson: Anti-Bodies

# Lynn Hershman Leeson
# Anti-Bodies

Mit Texten von
George Church
Rudolf Frieling
Sabine Himmelsbach
und Thomas Huber

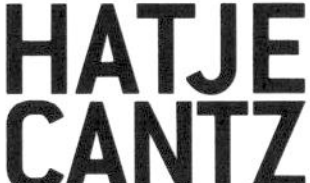

# 6 Sabine Himmelsbach
# Foreword

From May 3 to August 5, 2018 the House of Electronic Arts Basel hosted the exhibition titled *Lynn Hershman Leeson: Anti-Bodies.* It was dedicated to a new cycle of works by the American artist and filmmaker Lynn Hershman Leeson: biotechnologies and their significance for society and people. Throughout her artistic career, Hershman Leeson has focused on the interplay between technologies, media and identity, and the changing relationship between the body and technology. Hershman Leeson has worked with photography, film, video, objects and installations, computer-based art, software and performance. Since the 1960s, her art has been a kind of seismograph, measuring the impact of groundbreaking technological developments on our notions of individual identity and uniqueness. At the outset of her career, she grappled with the concept of the human being as a cyborg, a hybrid being permeated by technology. In the 1970s, she invented *Roberta Breitmore,* a character that functioned as her own alter ego. In 1984 she created *Lorna,* the first interactive videodisk that enabled the audience to intervene in the protagonist's story. In the 1990s, she dedicated many works to the impact of the World Wide Web; she focused on questions about virtual reality and became one of the first to grapple with the impact of artificial intelligence. In the early 1990s, Hershman Leeson's work was marked by the use of the "Anti-body," which referred to her research and works on a virtual identity in cyberspace. After all, one no longer needed a physical body like that of Roberta Breitmore in order to assume a fictional identity in the global network. Hershman Leeson's "Anti-body" saw itself as a viral presence on the Internet; it manifested itself in artificial intelligence, such as her online persona *DiNA.*

Hershman Leeson considers the rapid developments of biotechnologies to be the central challenge of our age. She has traced these developments in numerous works, starting with her 2007 film, *Strange Culture.* The HeK exhibition focused on this confrontation with biotechnologies. For several years, Hershman Leeson worked on her complicated installation, *The Infinity Engine,* segments of which were seen by the public for the first time in her major retrospective, *Civic Radar,* at the ZKM | Center for Art and Media in Karlsruhe; it was then included in the HeK exhibition.

Basel, the center of the Swiss pharmaceutical industry, was the ideal location for such an exploration. In a stroke of luck, Dr. Thomas Huber, senior investigator at the NIBR Biologics Center of Novartis Pharma AG, agreed to take part in an exchange with Hershman Leeson. The fruit of this artistic-scientific brainstorming was the development of the LYNNHERSHMAN antibody by Dr. Huber's research group. The development and testing phase of the new antibody formed a fundamental role in the exhibition, becoming one of the central new spaces in *The Infinity Engine.* Hershman Leeson emphasizes that completion of her complex installation depended on the latest biotechnological developments – from the use of DNA as a biological storage to personalized medicine. The exhibition shows these developments – both the opportunities they offer, and their ethical challenges – through numerous statements by leading researchers. In her staging of the eight rooms of *The Infinity Engine,* Hershman Leeson uses her artistic interpretation and appropriation to draw back the curtains from the scientific laboratory as a place of knowledge production. She shows how the boundaries between natural and artificial life are increasingly dissolving in the age of artificial biology, and how life today can be synthetically formed and manipulated. Our task is to shape this future in the best possible way.

This ambitious project could not have happened without the creative collaboration of Novartis Pharma AG. My thanks go to Dr. Thomas Huber and his team. It was their open-mindedness and willingness that made it possible to break new ground and initiate a mutually inspiring dialogue. I would also like to thank Sandra Schlüchter, Head of NIBR Basel Communications, for her support of the project. The generous financial support of Novartis Pharma AG made it possible for us to publish this documentation of the exhibition. My thanks go to Martin Furler Bassand, Global Art Curator of the Novartis Art Collection.

Additional thanks go to the Ernst and Olga Gubler-Hablützel Foundation for their generous support of the exhibition.

And my gratitude also goes to those who loaned works to the exhibition, particularly the ZKM | Center for Art and Media in Karlsruhe, and the artist's galleries: Waldburger Wouters in Brussels, Bridget Donahue in New York, and Anglim Gilbert Gallery in San Francisco.

Most importantly, I want to thank Lynn Hershman Leeson for the dedication and passion with which she brought this project to fruition. Working with her on this unique exhibition was an inspiring and enriching experience.

Sabine Himmelsbach, Director, HeK

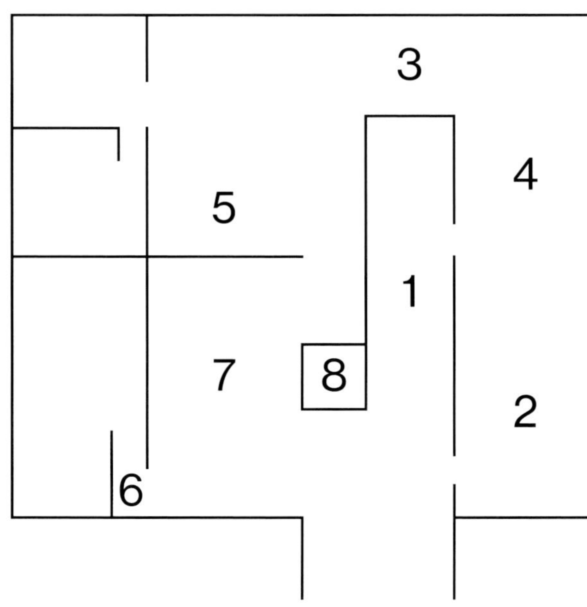
3
4
5
1
7
8
2
6

# The Infinity Engine
Room 1

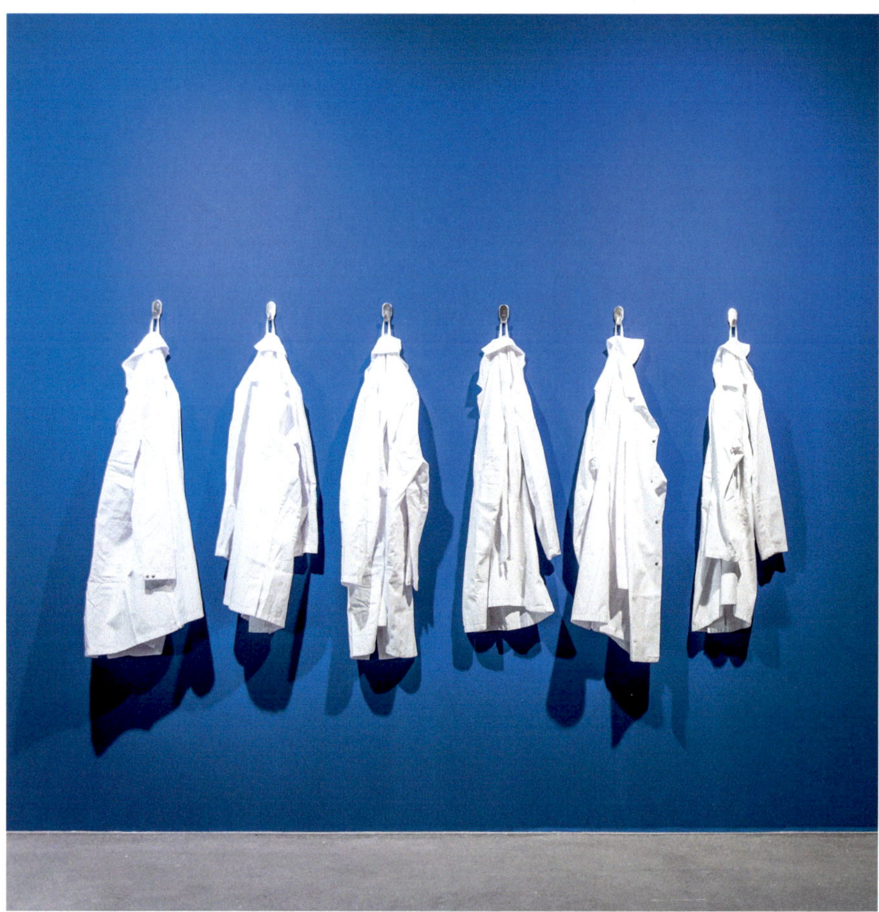

Installation view HeK, House of Electronic Arts Basel, 2018

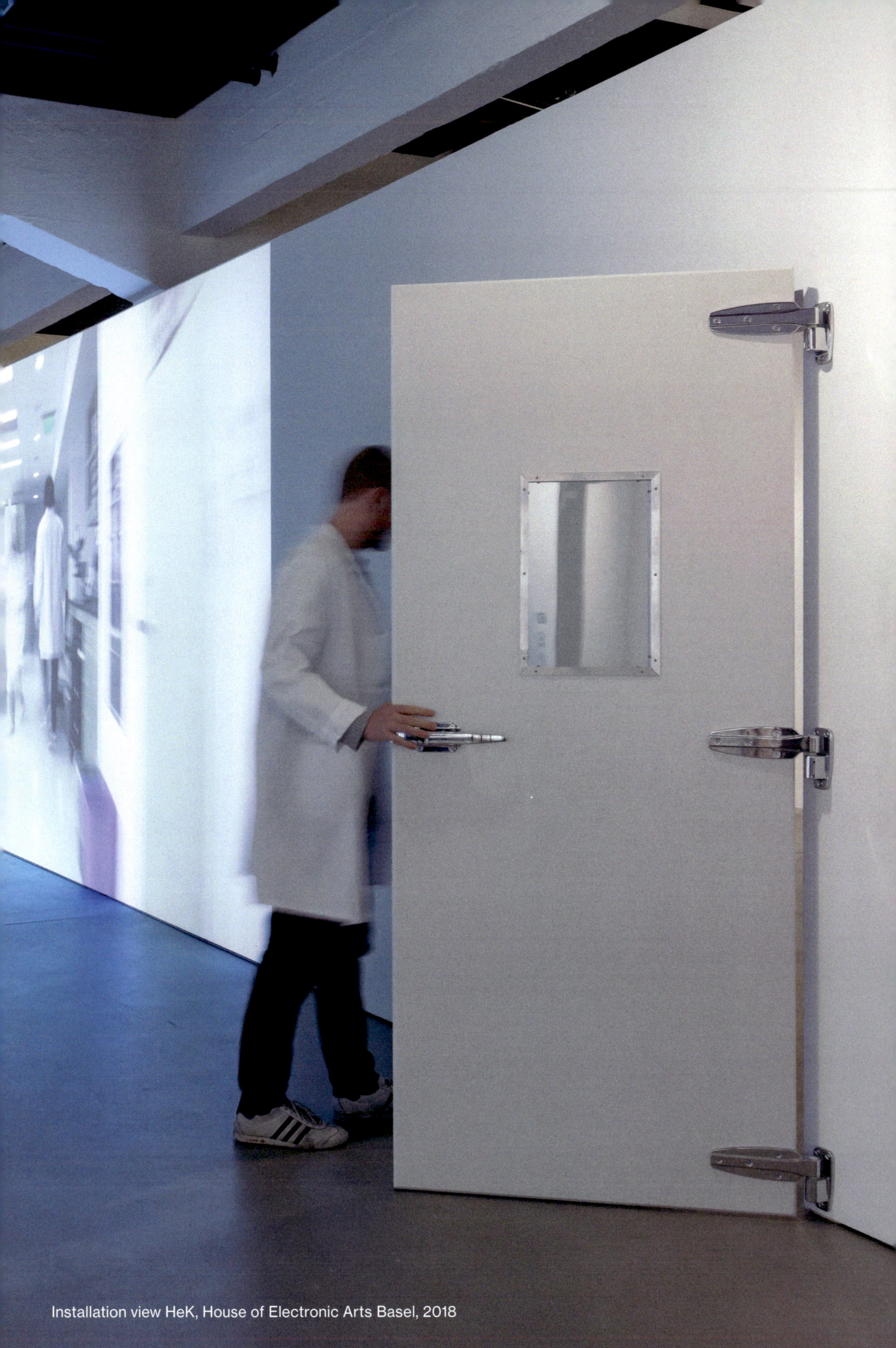

Installation view HeK, House of Electronic Arts Basel, 2018

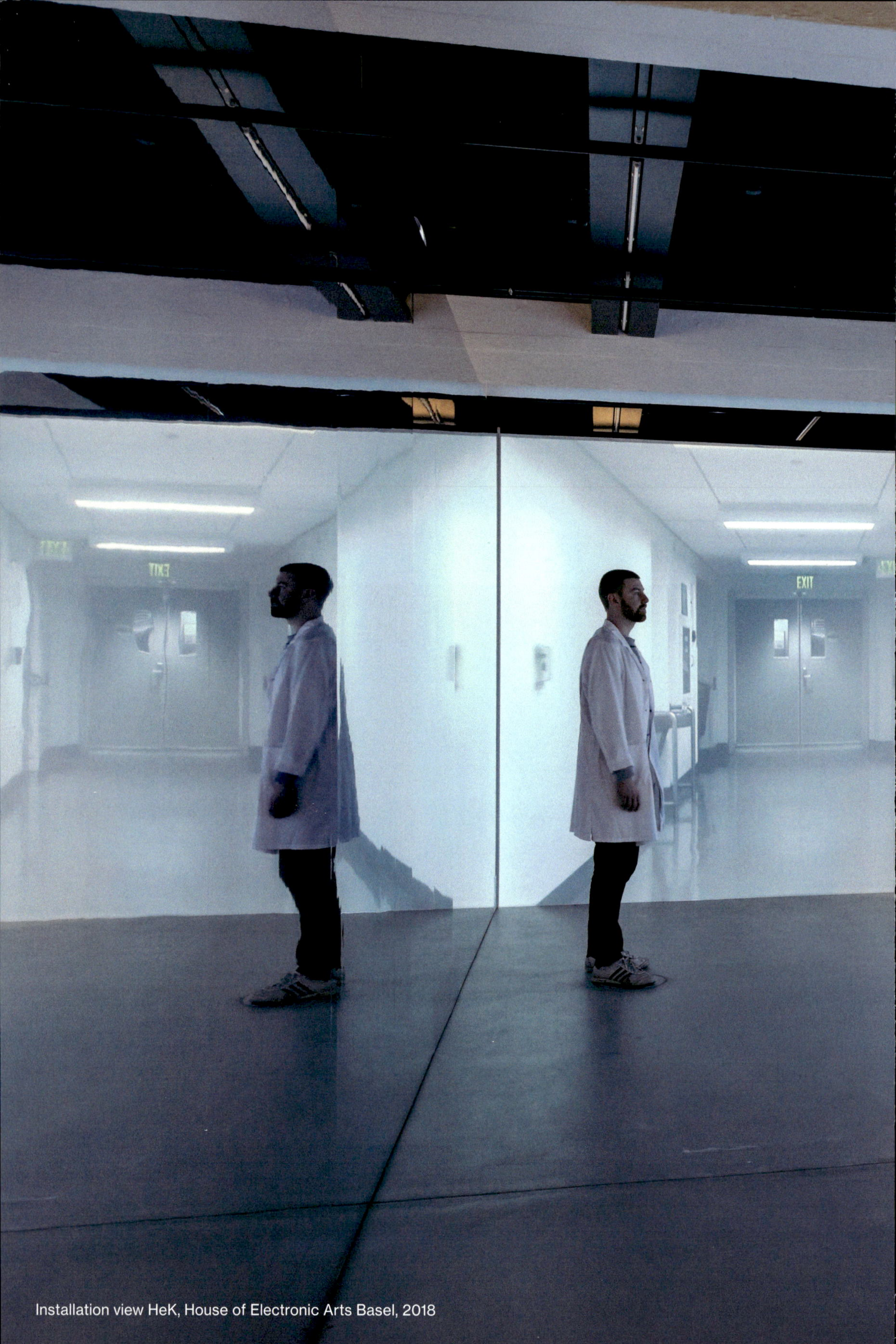


Installation view HeK, House of Electronic Arts Basel, 2018

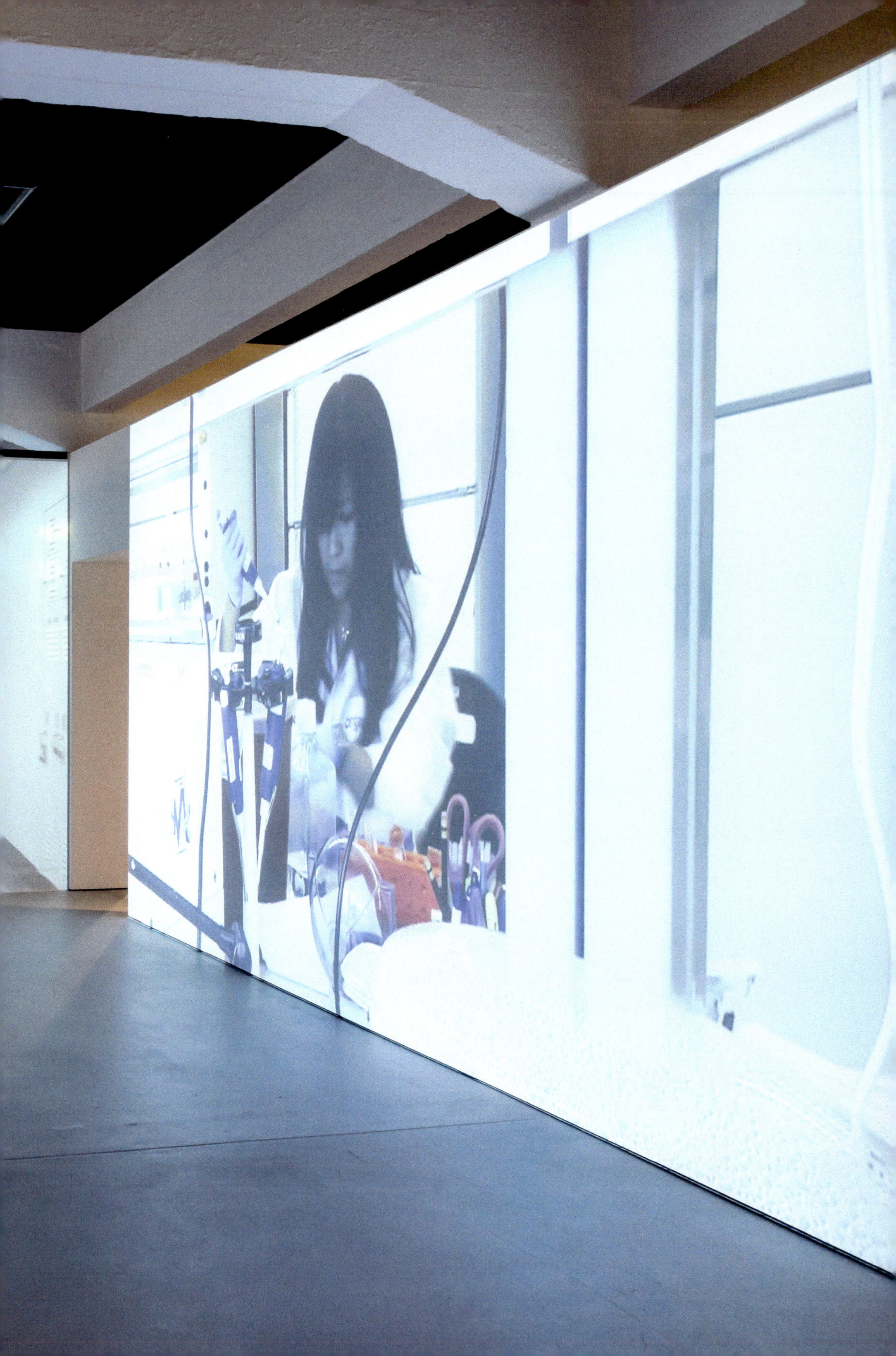

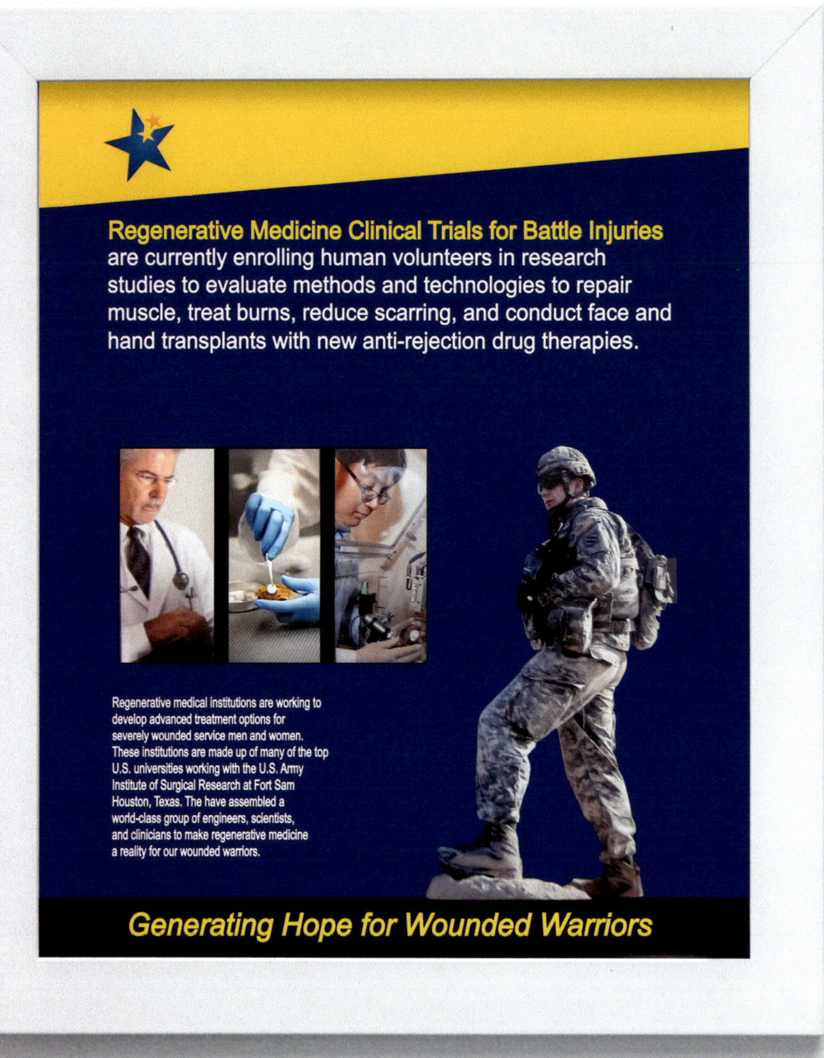


Wounded warrior poster from *The Infinity Engine,* 2014, reproduction of one found in genetics labs, archival digital print, 71.1 x 50.8 cm

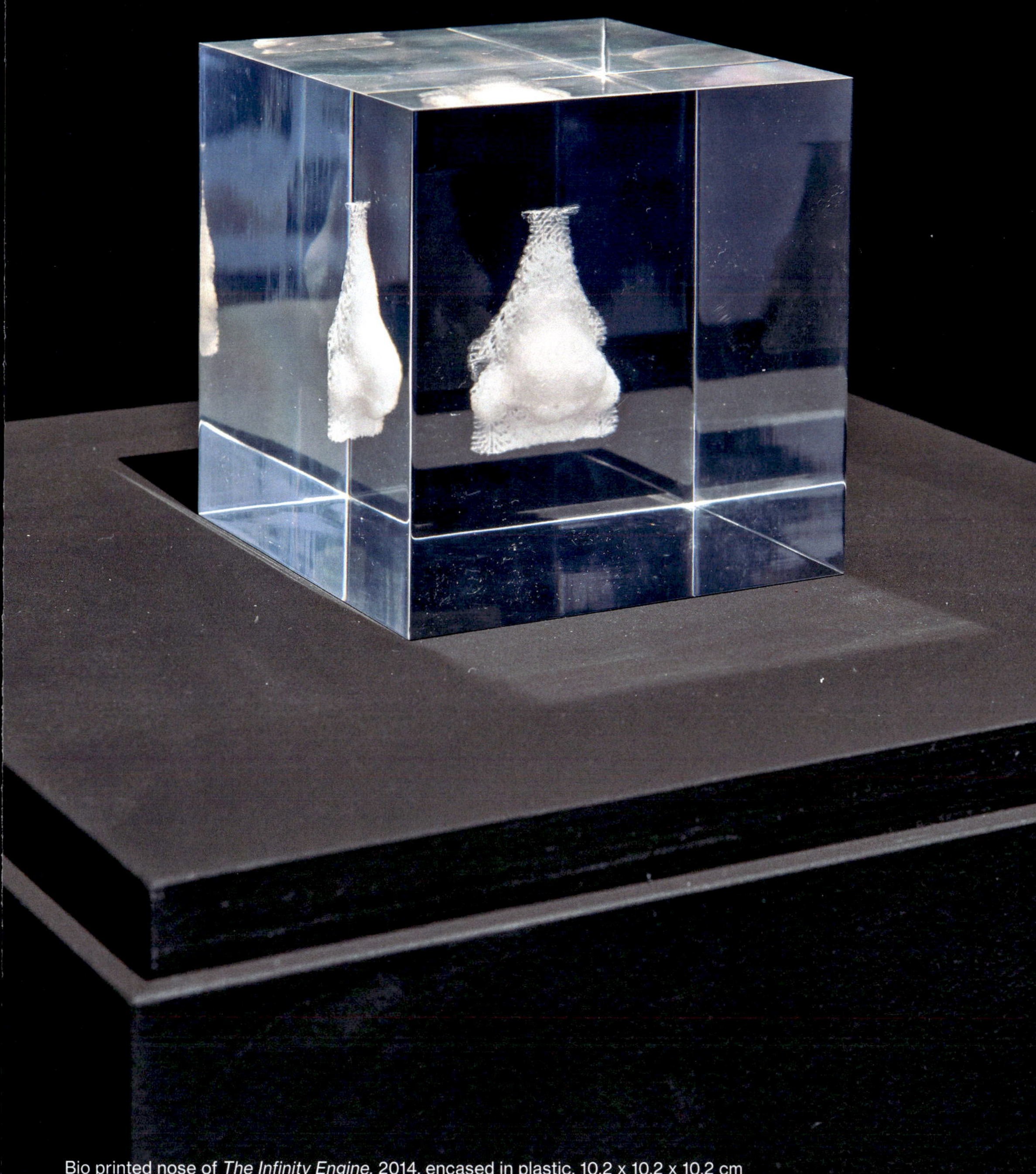

Bio printed nose of *The Infinity Engine*, 2014, encased in plastic, 10.2 x 10.2 x 10.2 cm
courtesy of Dr. Anthony Atala, Wake Forest School of Regenerative Medicine

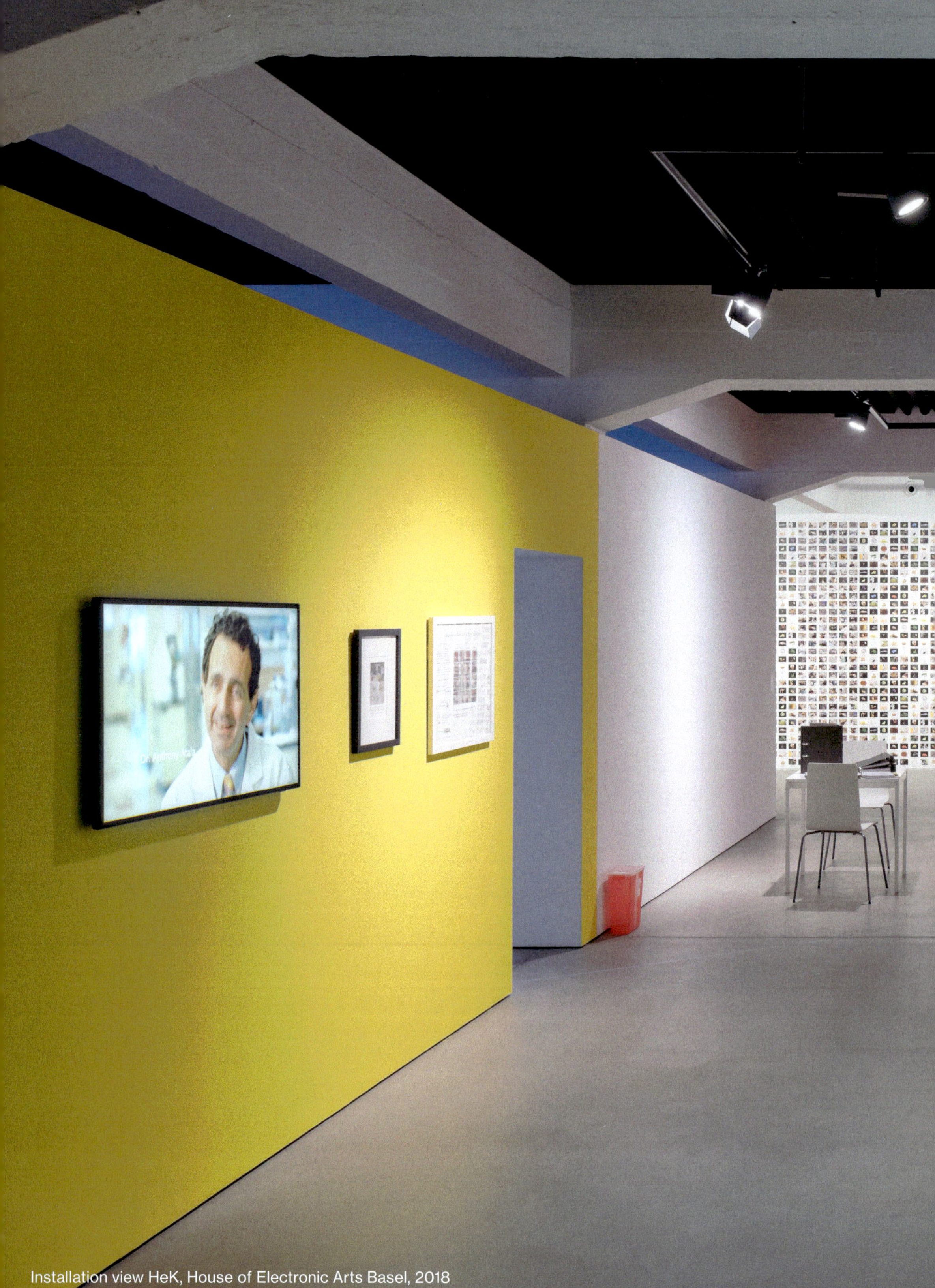

Installation view HeK, House of Electronic Arts Basel, 2018

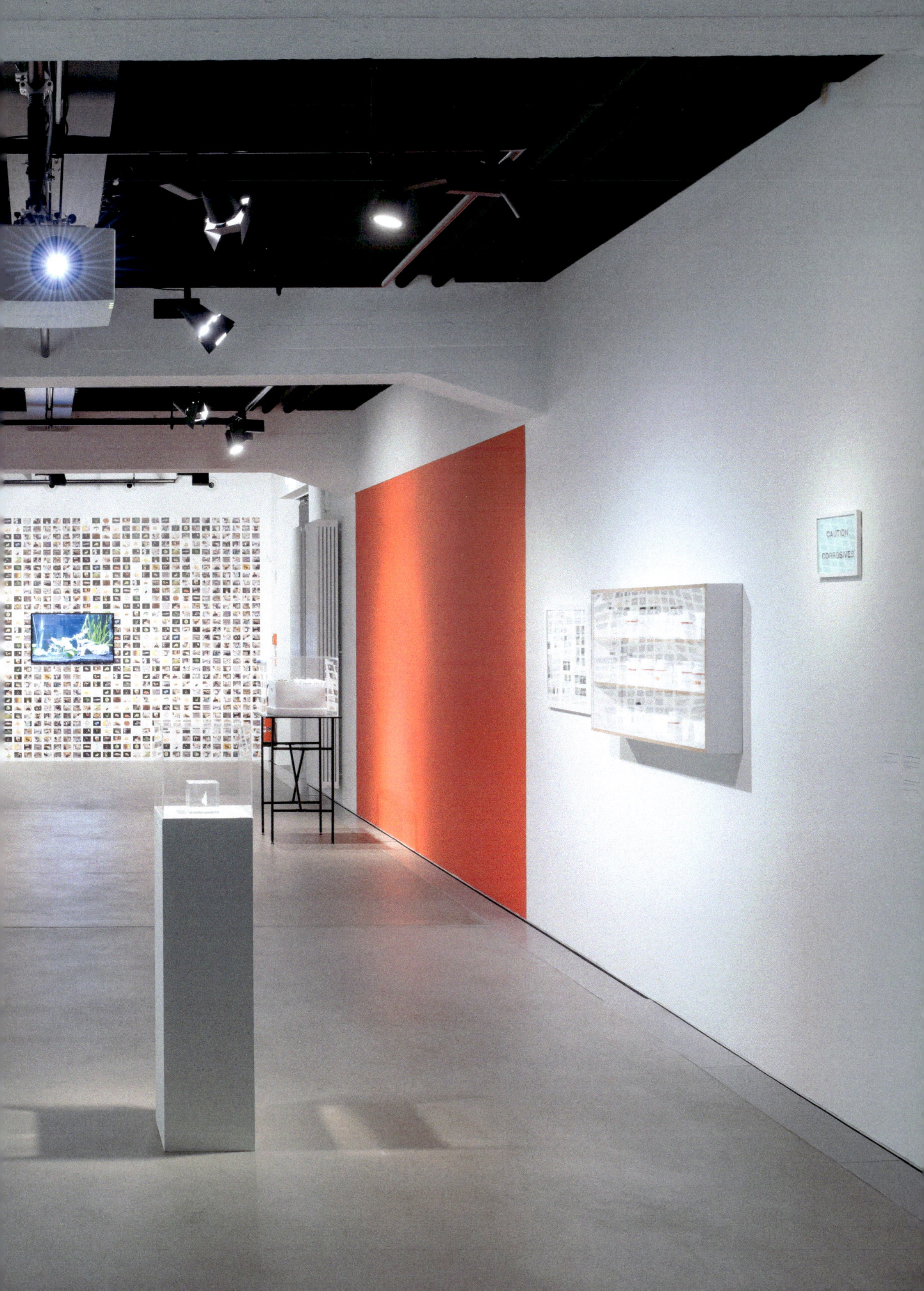
CAUTION
CORROSIVES

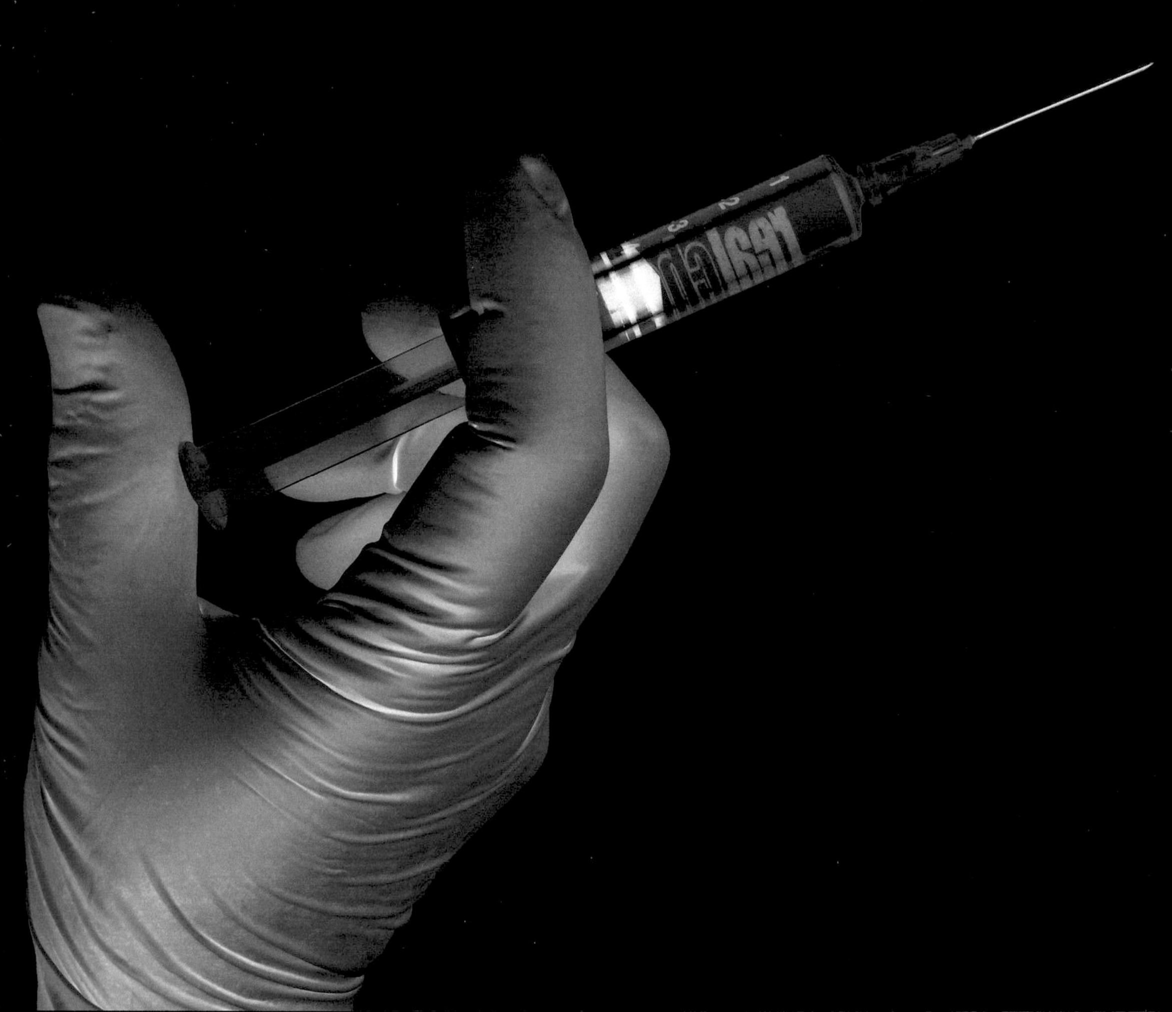

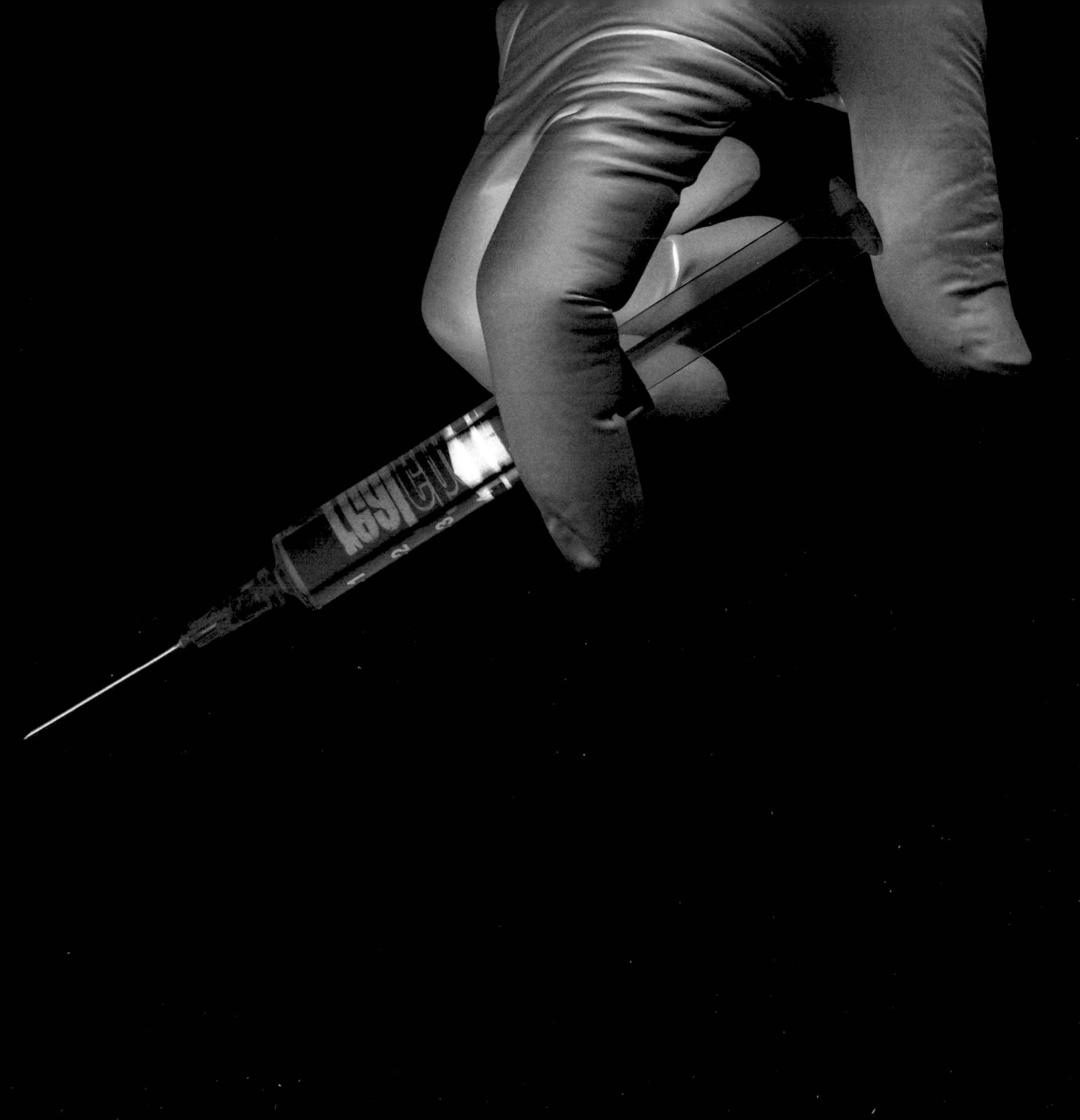

Double Syringe from *The Infinity Engine*, 2018

 The Infinity Engine
Room 3

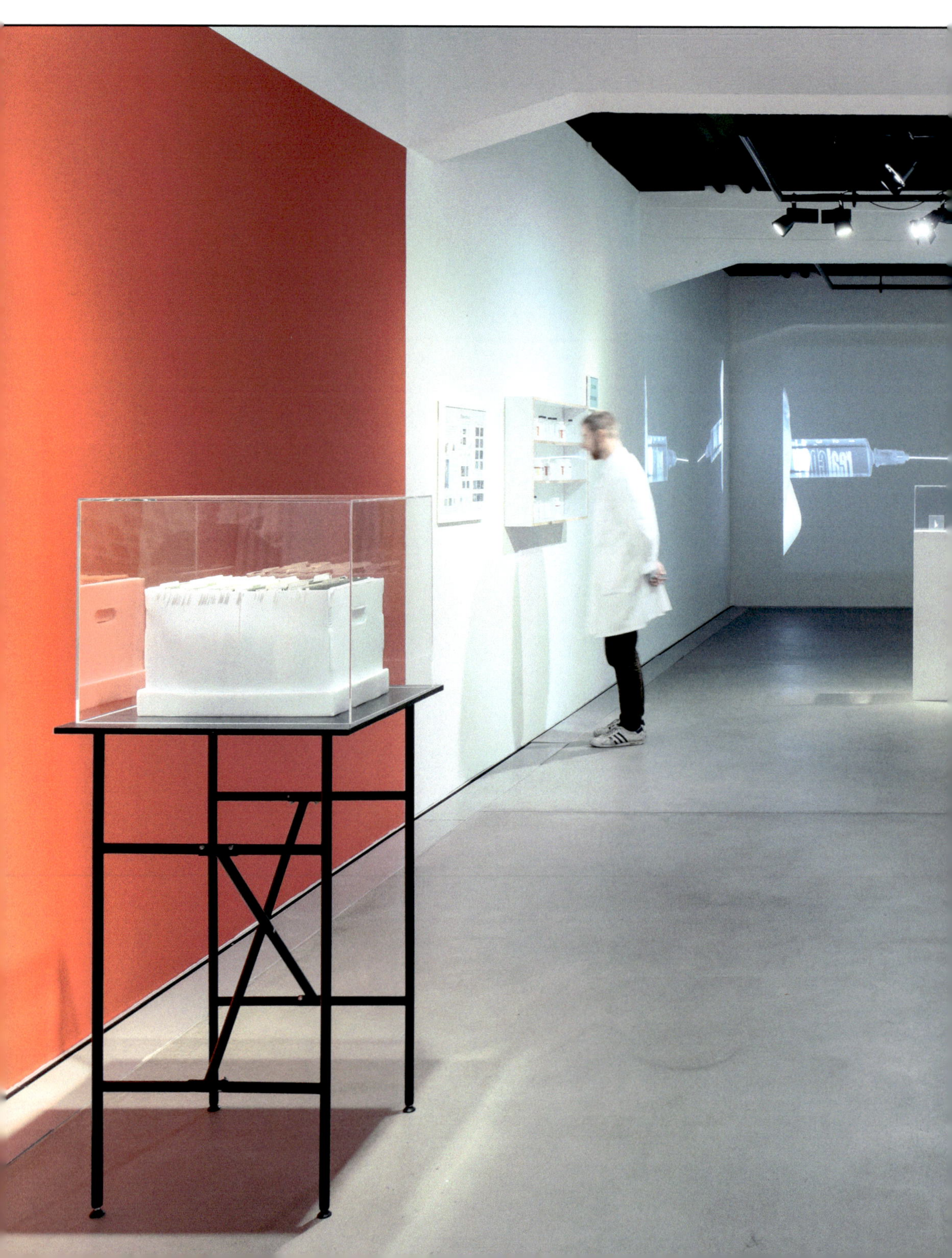

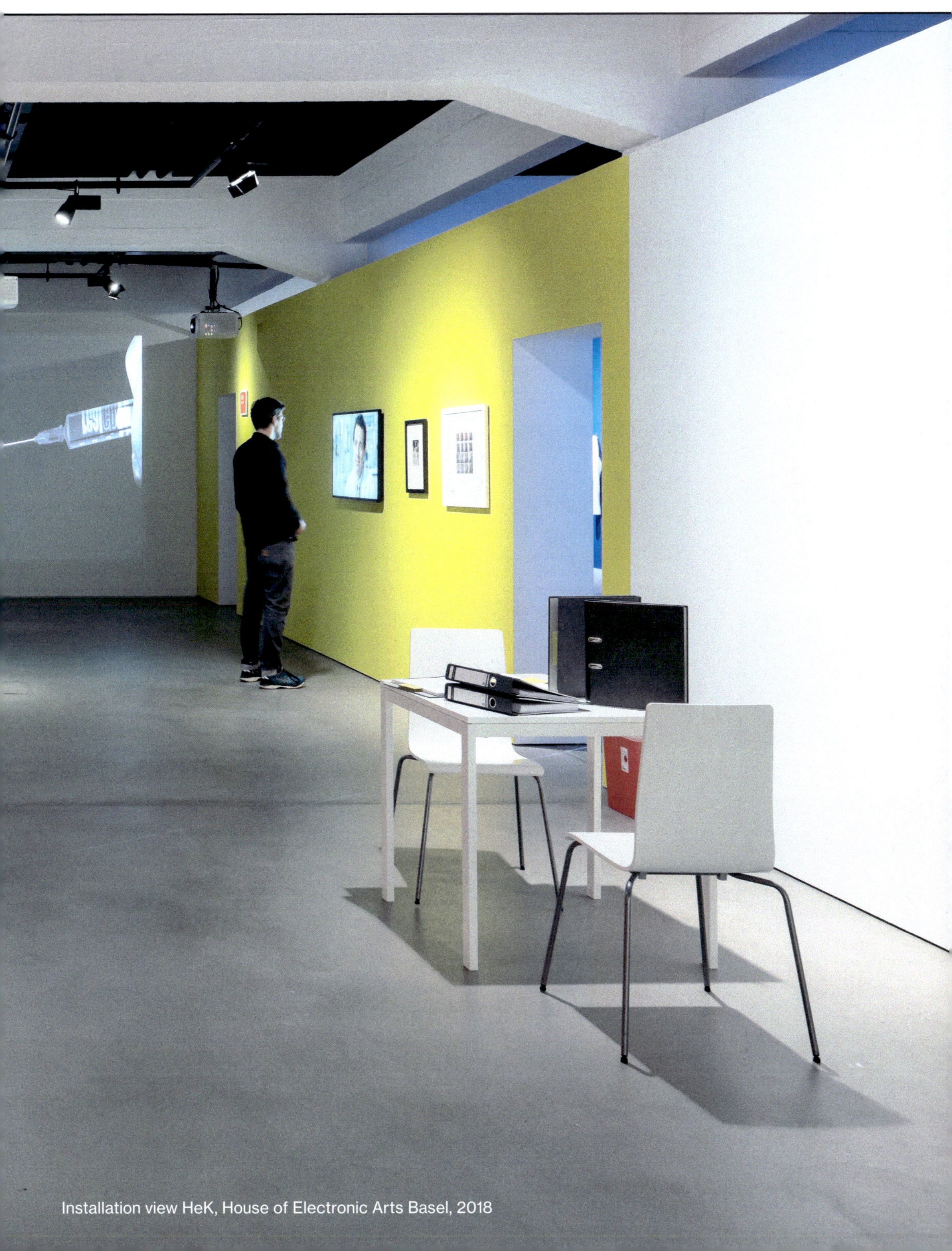

Installation view HeK, House of Electronic Arts Basel, 2018

# 22 The Infinity Engine Room 4

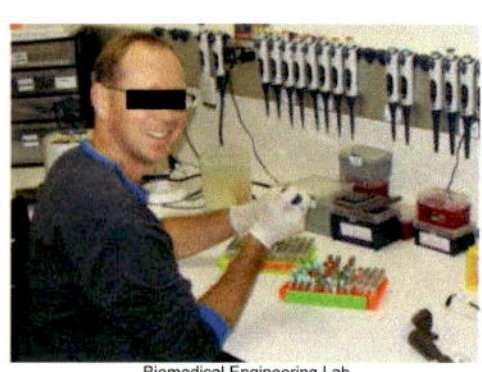
Biomedical Engineering Lab
Arizona State University
Tempe, Arizona, USA
Cellular & tissue engineering

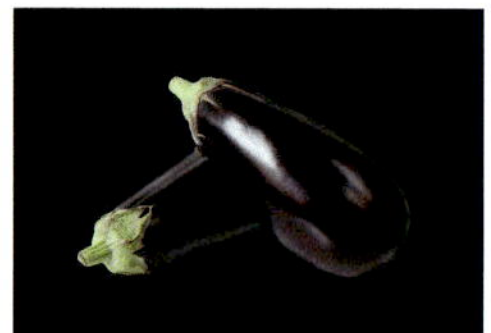
BT EGGPLANT
CREATED: 1996
Mahyco, an Indian seed company based in Jalna, Maharashtra
GENE MUTATION: Cry1Ac GENE+ EGGPLANT = BT BRINJAL
*Created to be resistant to the insects

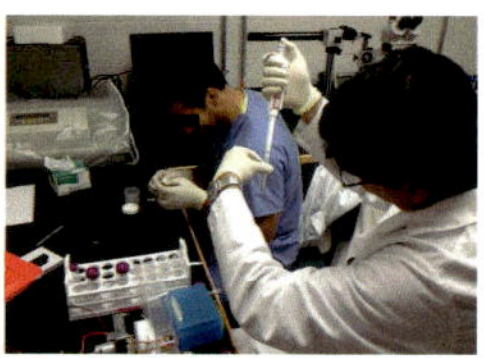
Biomedical Engineering Lab
Case Western Reserve University
Cleveland, Ohio, USA
Innovative approaches to biomedical technologies & devices

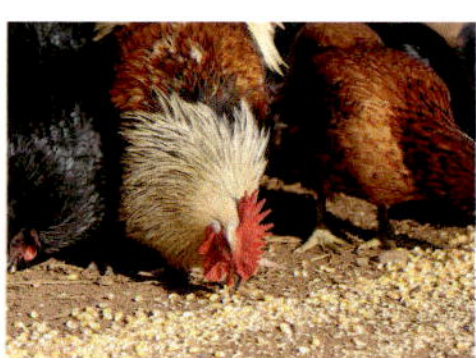
ANIMAL FEED
CREATED: LATE 1990's
BASF, World-wide
Gene Mutation: GM Soy, Corn, Flax, Canola oil & Vitamins
Motivation: Resistance to pesticides

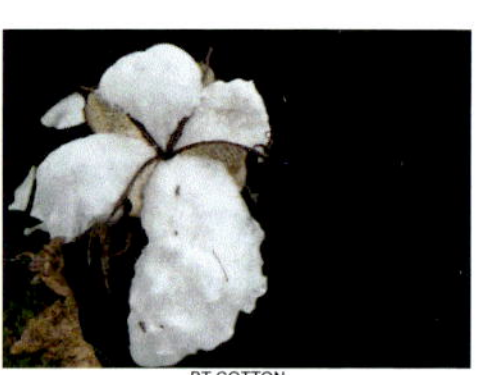
BT COTTON
CREATED: 2001
Dupont, Dow Agrosciences, Calgene, Syngenta, Bayer, Monsanto Canada & USA
Gene Mutation: Cotton + 5-enolpypruvyl shikimate-3-phosphate
Motivation: Resistance to pesticides

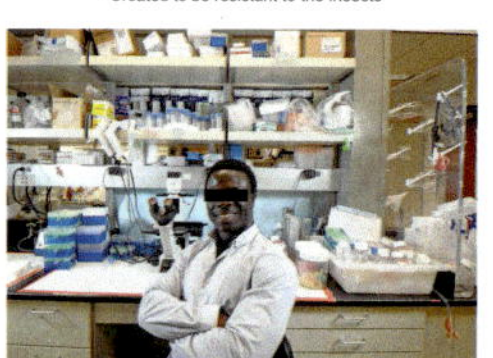
Biomedical Engineering Lab
University of California
San Diego, California, USA
Tissue engineering & regenerative medicine

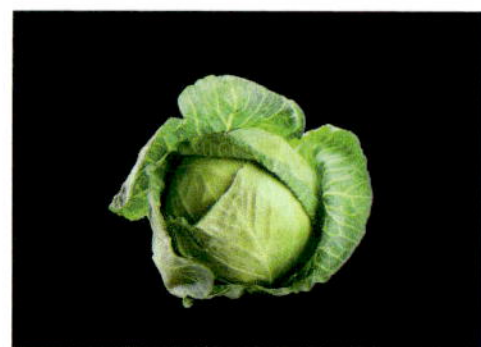
GENETICALLY MODIFIED CABBAGE
CREATED: 1986
Bigelow USA
Gene Mutation: Scorpion Poison + Cabbage
Motivation: Resistance to slugs

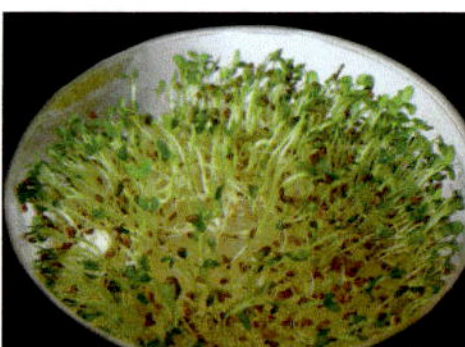
Roundup Ready Alfalfa
Created: 2005 Monsanto Company and Forage Genetics International
Gene Modification: Alfalfa & CP4 EPSPS
Motivation: Resistance to pesticides

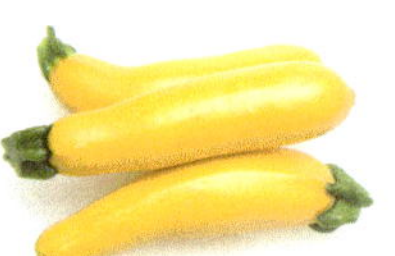
SUMMER SQUASH
CREATED: 1995
Gene Mutation: Viral Coat Protein Genes + Squash
Motivation: Resistance to disease

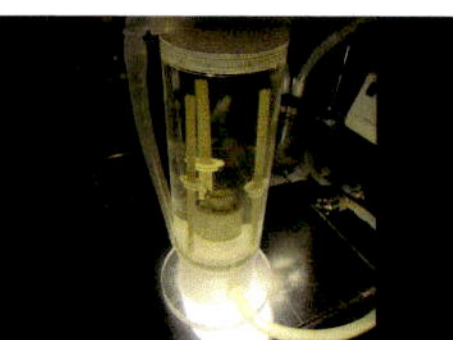
Biomedical Engineering Lab
Wake Forest Institute for Regenerative Medicine
North Carolina, USA
Cell, tissue & organ regeneration

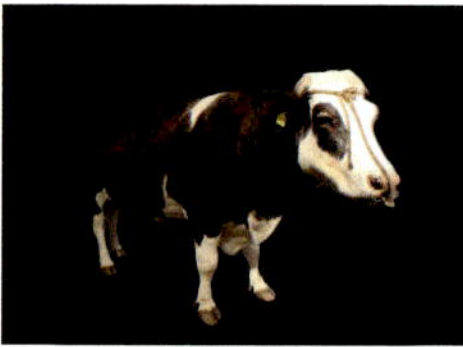
HERMAN THE BULL
CREATED: 1990 Gen Pharm International
Mountain View, California, USA
Gene Mutation: Bovine + Human Gene Coding First genetically modified/transgenic bovine in the world

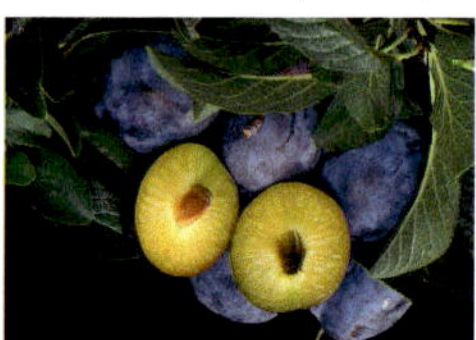
C5 PLUM
CREATED: 2009 U.S. Department of Agriculture
Gene Mutation: Plum Pox Virus & Tetracycline
Motivation: Resistance to the Plum Pox Virus

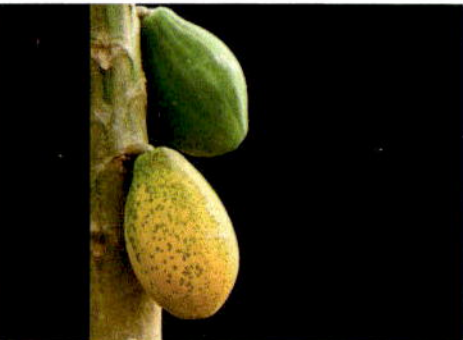
RAINBOW PAPAYA
CREATED: 1998
Dennis Gonsalves & Richard Manshardt, Hawaii
Gene Mutation: Ringspot Virus Gene + Papaya
Mutation: Immunity to the Virus

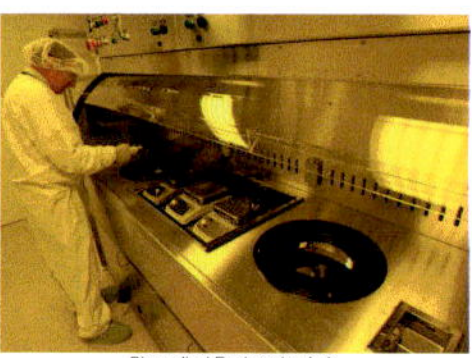
Biomedical Engineering Lab
University of Rochester
Rochester, New York, USA
Cell & tissue engineering, neuroengineering

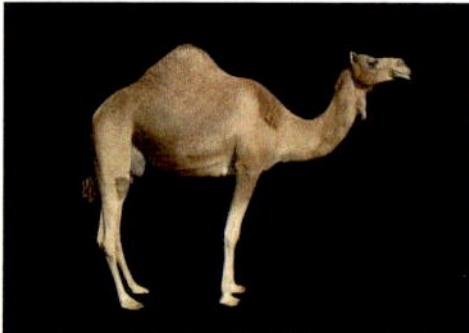
TRANSGENIC CAMEL
CREATED: Camel Reproduction Center, Dubai
Gene Mutation: Camel + Various Exogenous DNA
Motivation: Production of cheaper pharmaceutical proteins

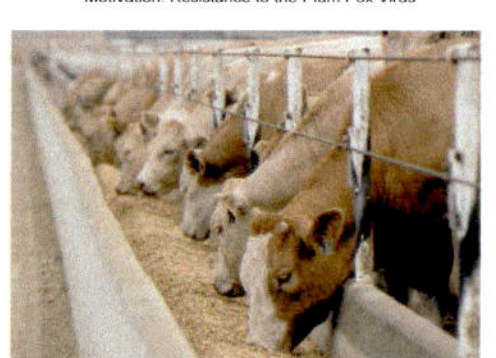
ANIMAL FEED
CREATED: LATE 1990's
BASF, World-wide
Gene Mutation: GM Soy, Corn, Flax, Canola oil & Vitamins
Motivation: Resistance to pesticides

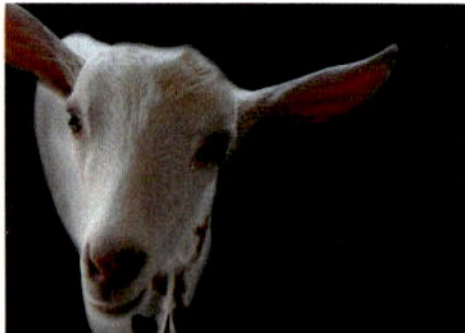
SPIDER GOAT
CREATED: 2002
Nexia Biotechnologies Inc. USA
Gene Mutation: Spider + Goat
Motivation: To create Biosteel

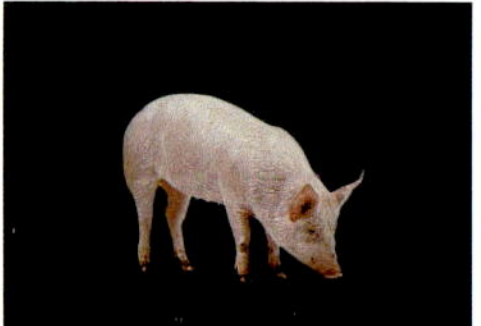
ENVIRO PIG
University of Guelph
Ontario, Canada
Gene Mutation: Escherichia Coli + Mouse + Yorkshire Pig
Motivation: More efficient digestion of plant phosphorus

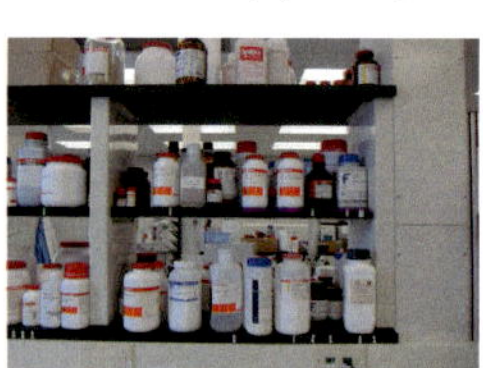
Biomedical Engineering Lab
Wake Forest Institute for Regenerative Medicine
North Carolina, USA
Cell, tissue & organ regeneration

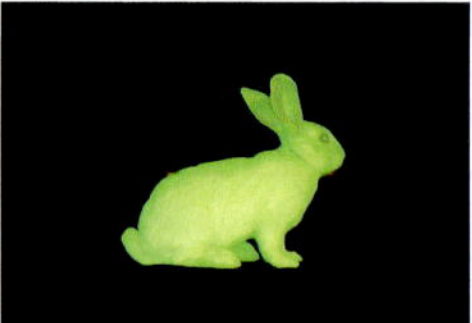
"ALBA" THE GLOWING RABBIT
CREATED: 2000, National Institute of Agronomic Research, France
Gene Mutation: Rabbit + Jellyfish
Motivation: Created for artist Eduardo Kac as "transgenic art"

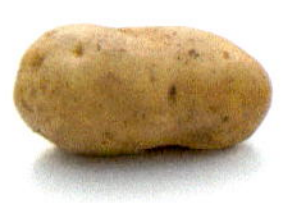
AMFLORA & NEWLEAF POTATOES
CREATED: 2010
BASF, Germany
Gene Mutation: Potato - amylose gene
Motivation: Resistance to disease, increased efficiency, & for use in animal feed

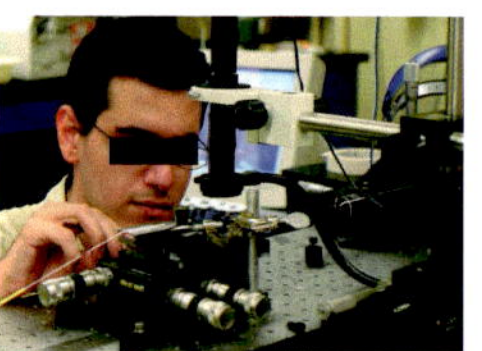
Biomedical Engineering Lab
Institute of Biomatrials & Biomedical Engineering
Toronto, Canada
Biomaterials research, tissue engineering & regenerative medicine

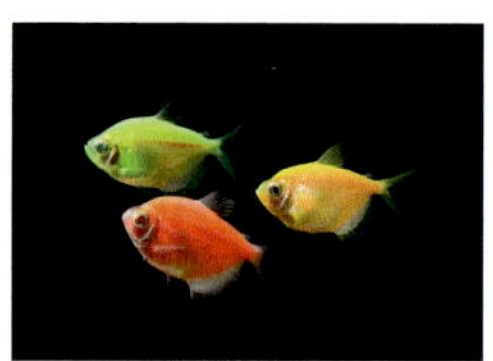
GLO FISH
CREATED: 1999
National University of Singapore
Gene Mutation: Jellyfish + Zebrafish
Motivation: First GM organism sold as a pet

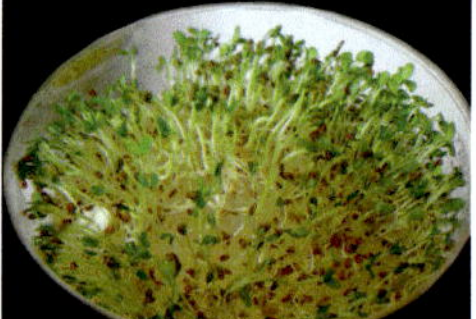
Roundup Ready Alfalfa
Created: 2005 Monsanto Company and Forage Genetics International
Gene Modification: Alfalfa & CP4 EPSPS
Motivation: Resistance to pesticides

Wallpaper from *The Infinity Engine*, 2014

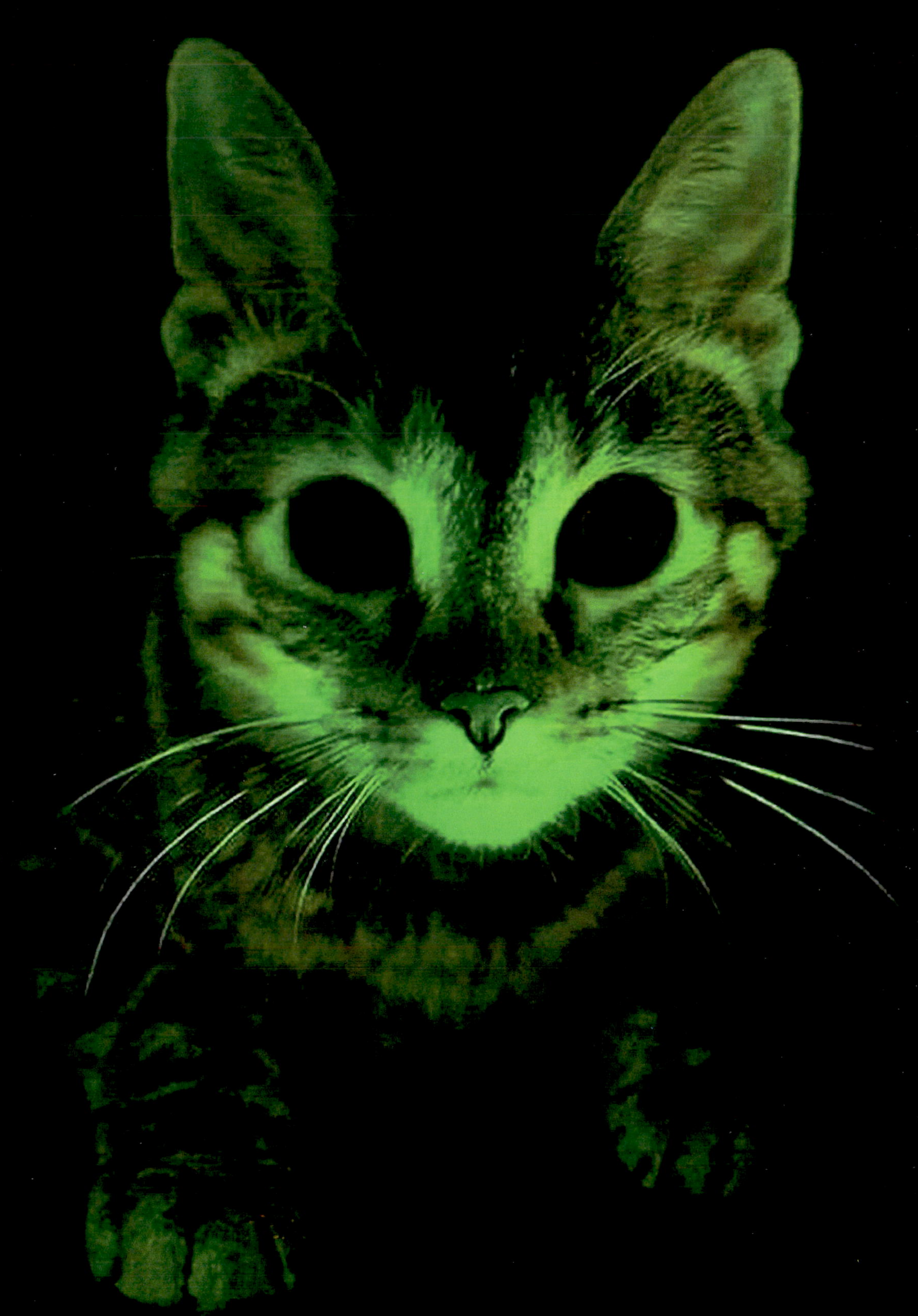

Genetically modified cat from *The Infinity Engine,* 2014, archival digital print, 101.6 x 76.2 cm

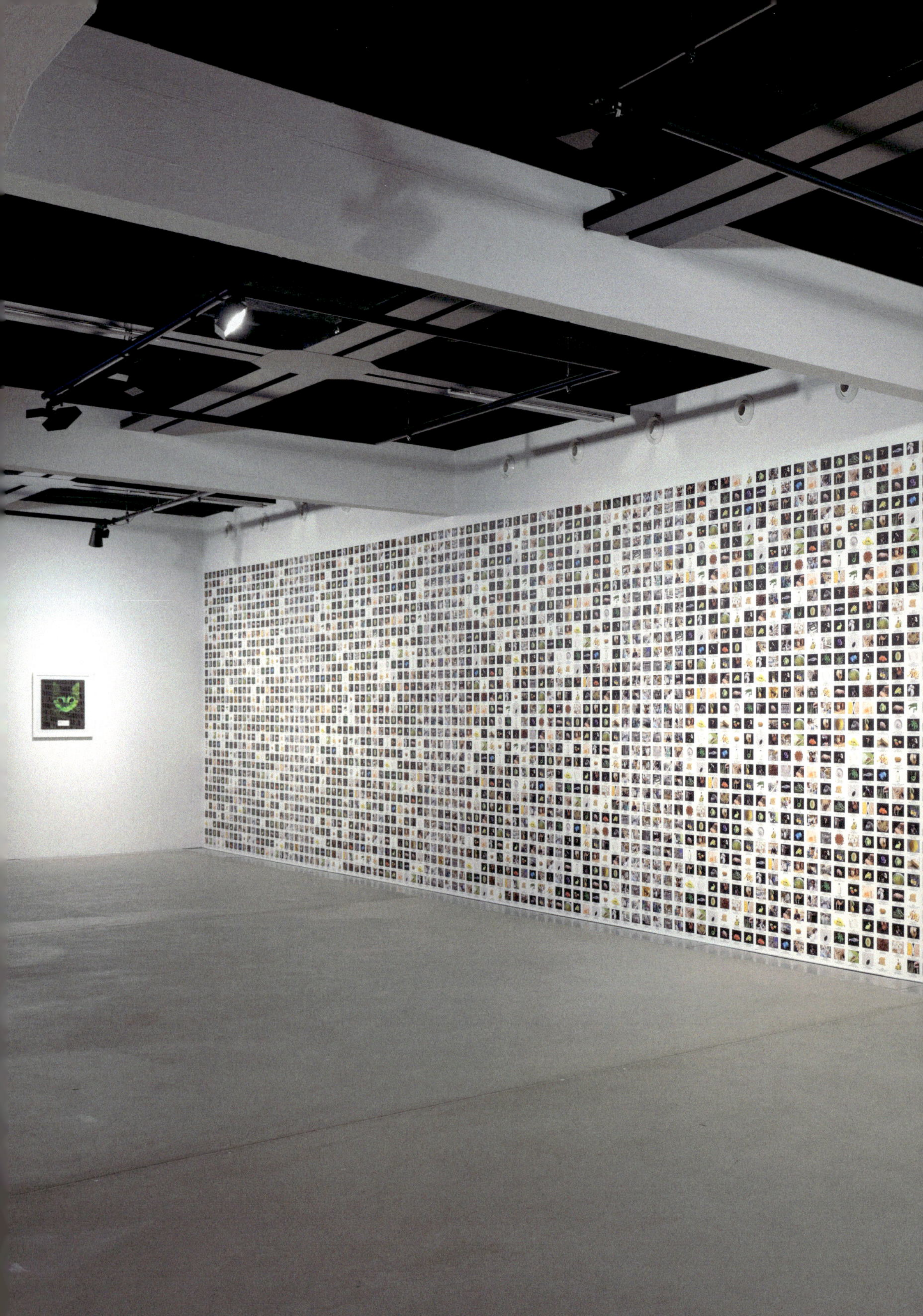

Installation view HeK, House of Electronic Arts Basel, 2018

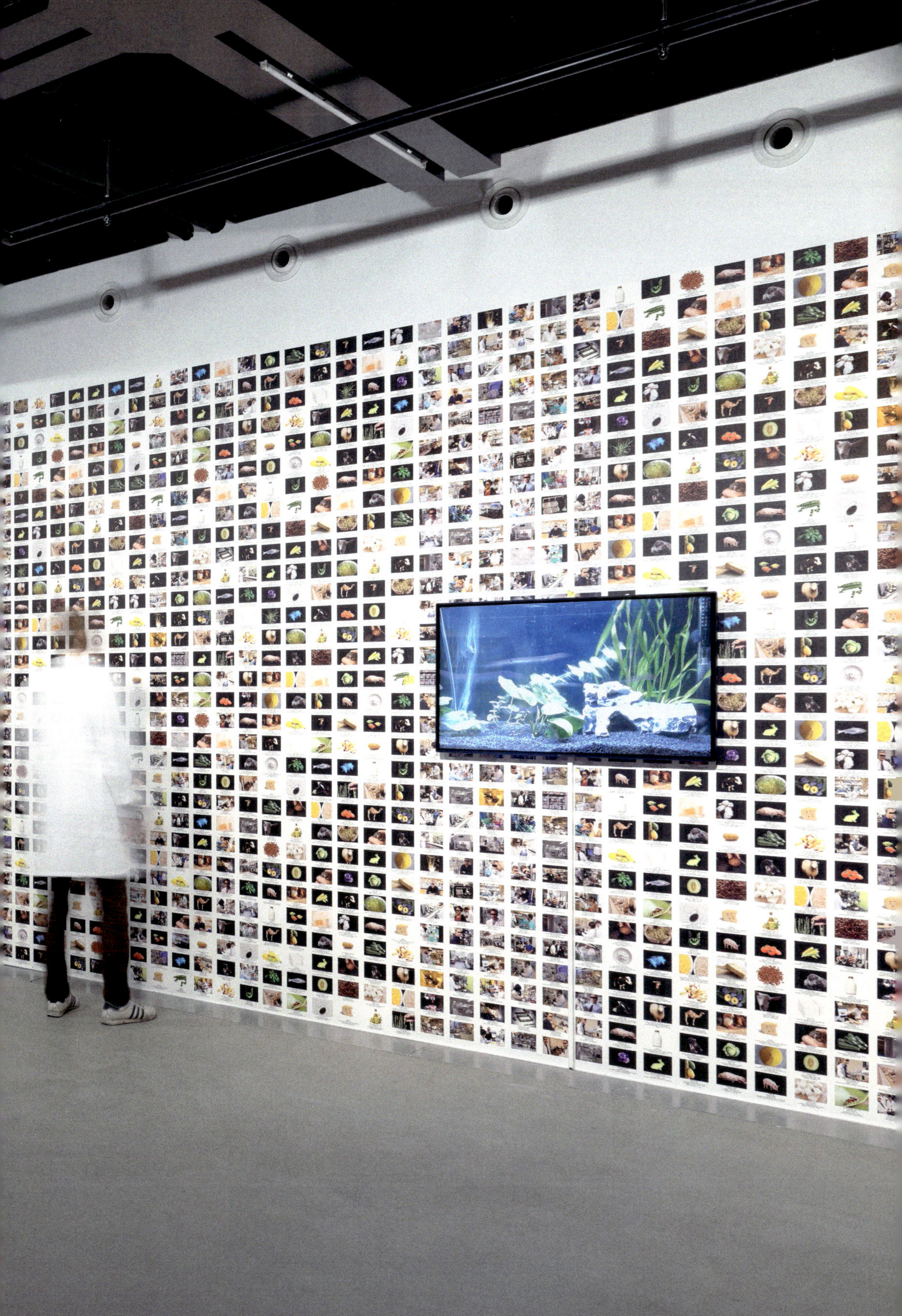

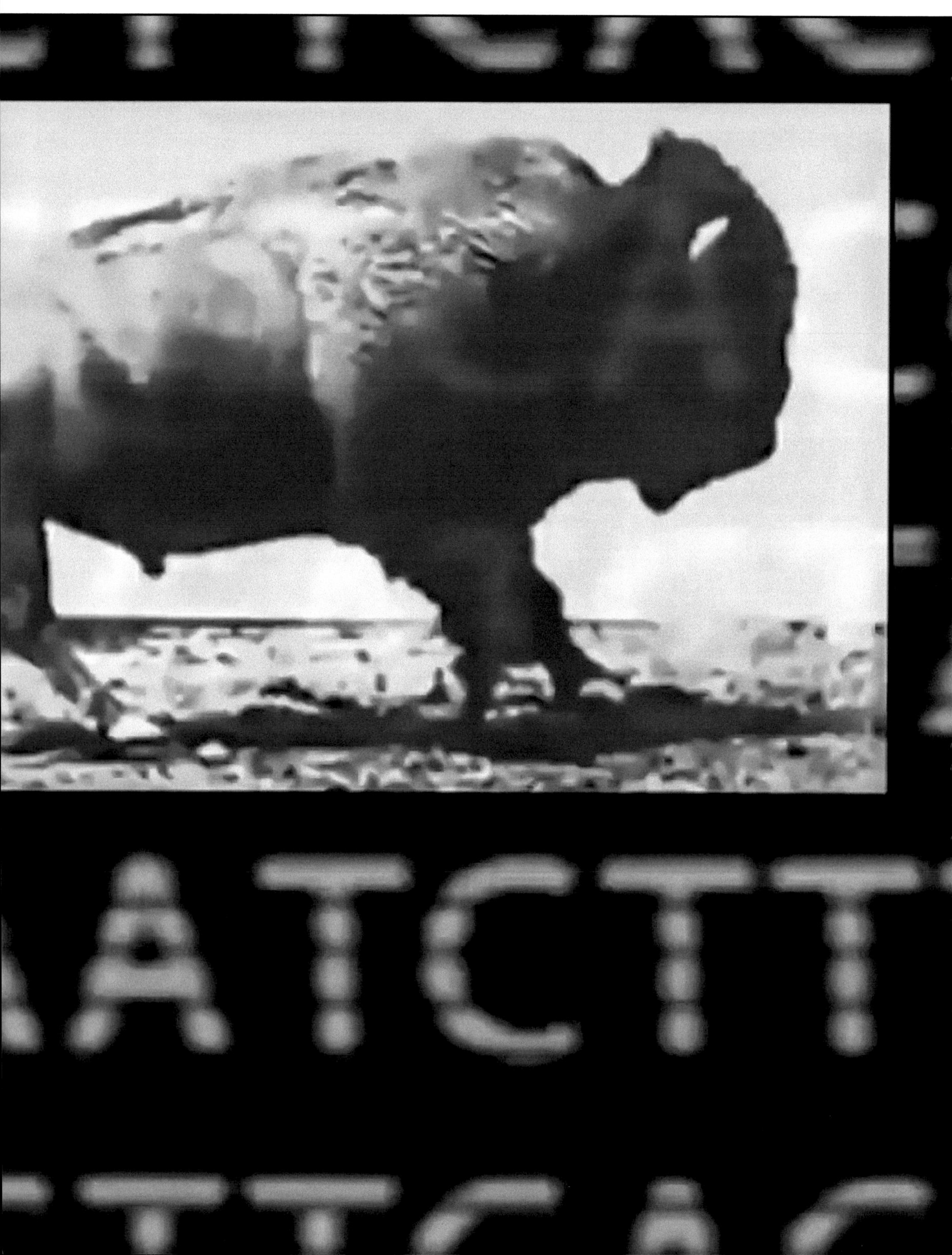
ATCTT

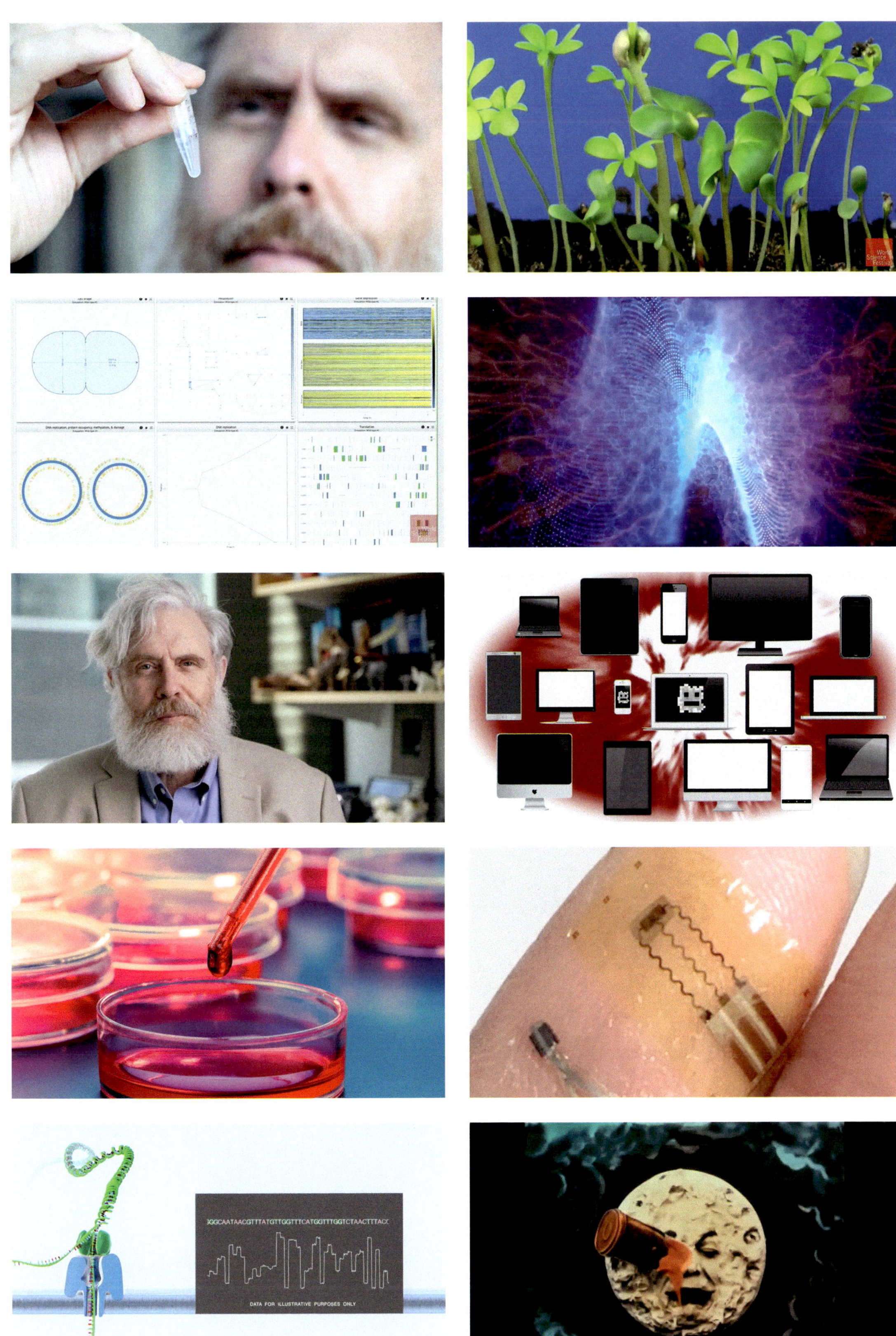


Videostills from *A Perfect Archive.* George Church interviewed by Lynn Hershman Leeson, 2017

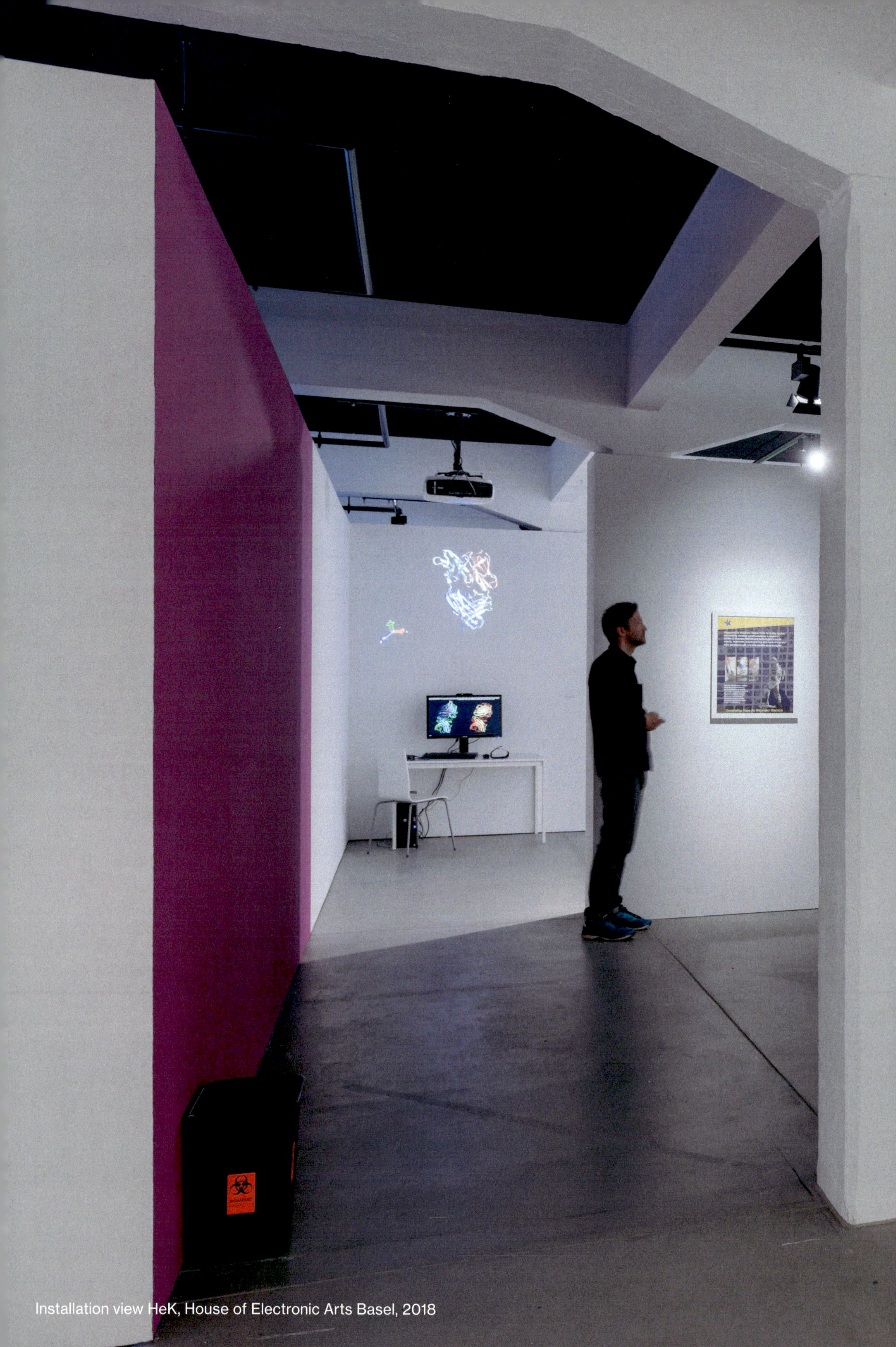

Installation view HeK, House of Electronic Arts Basel, 2018

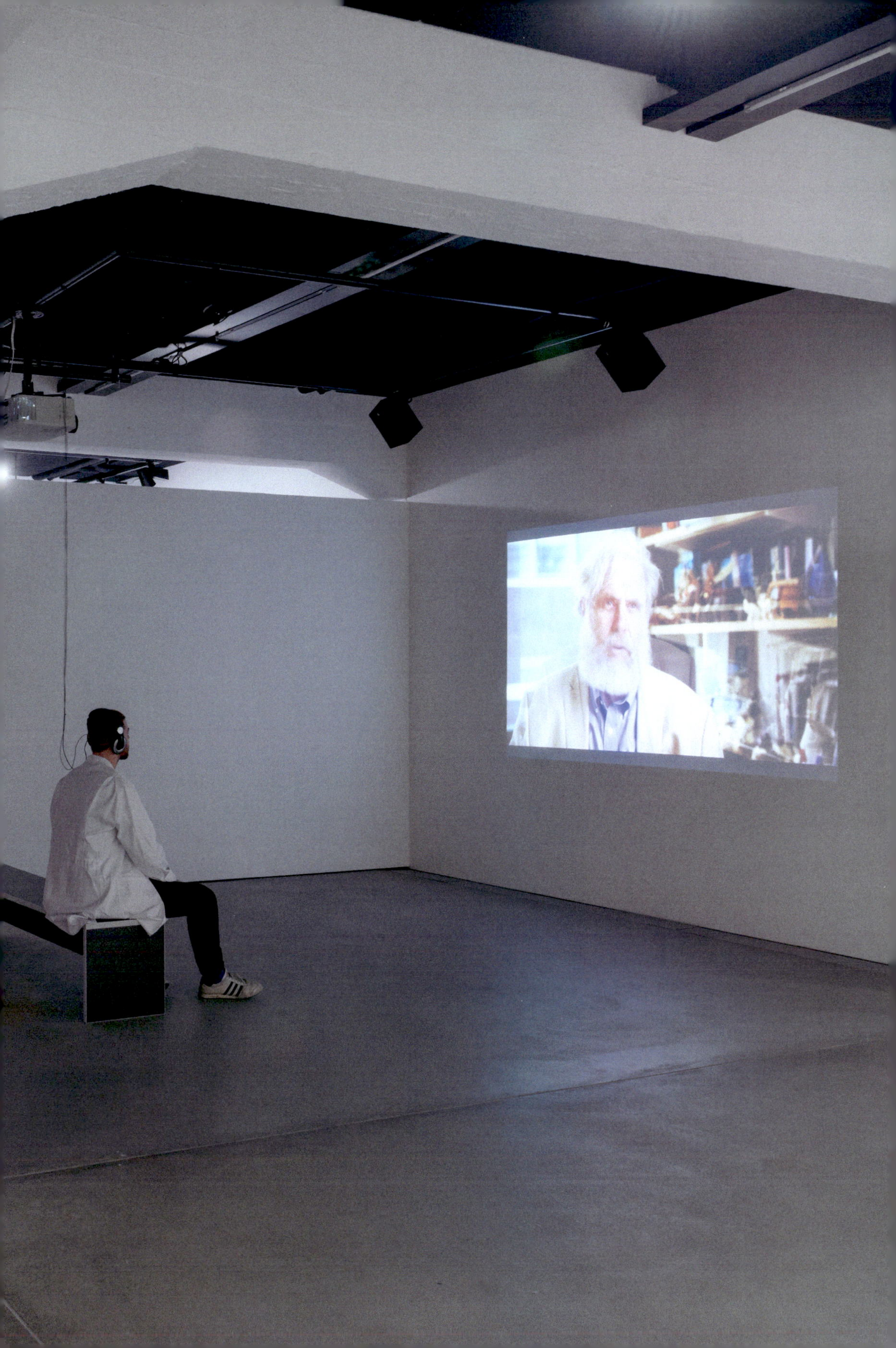

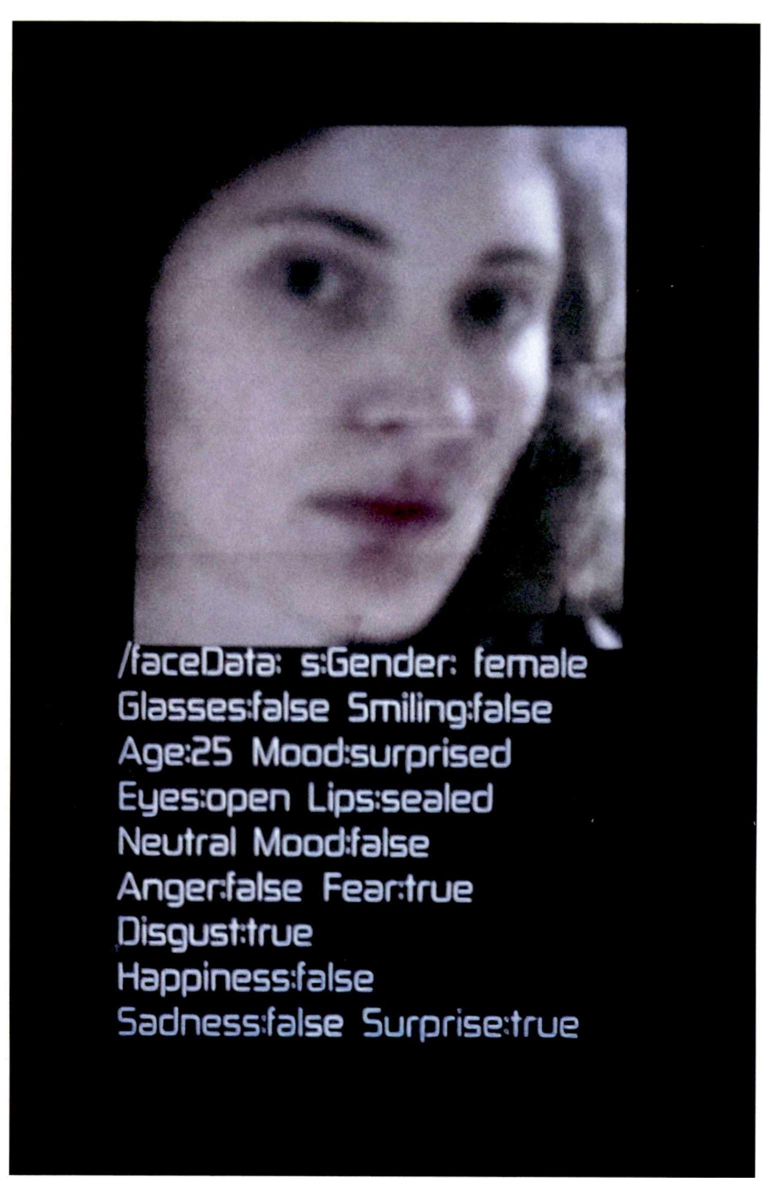


*Facial Recognition System*, 2018

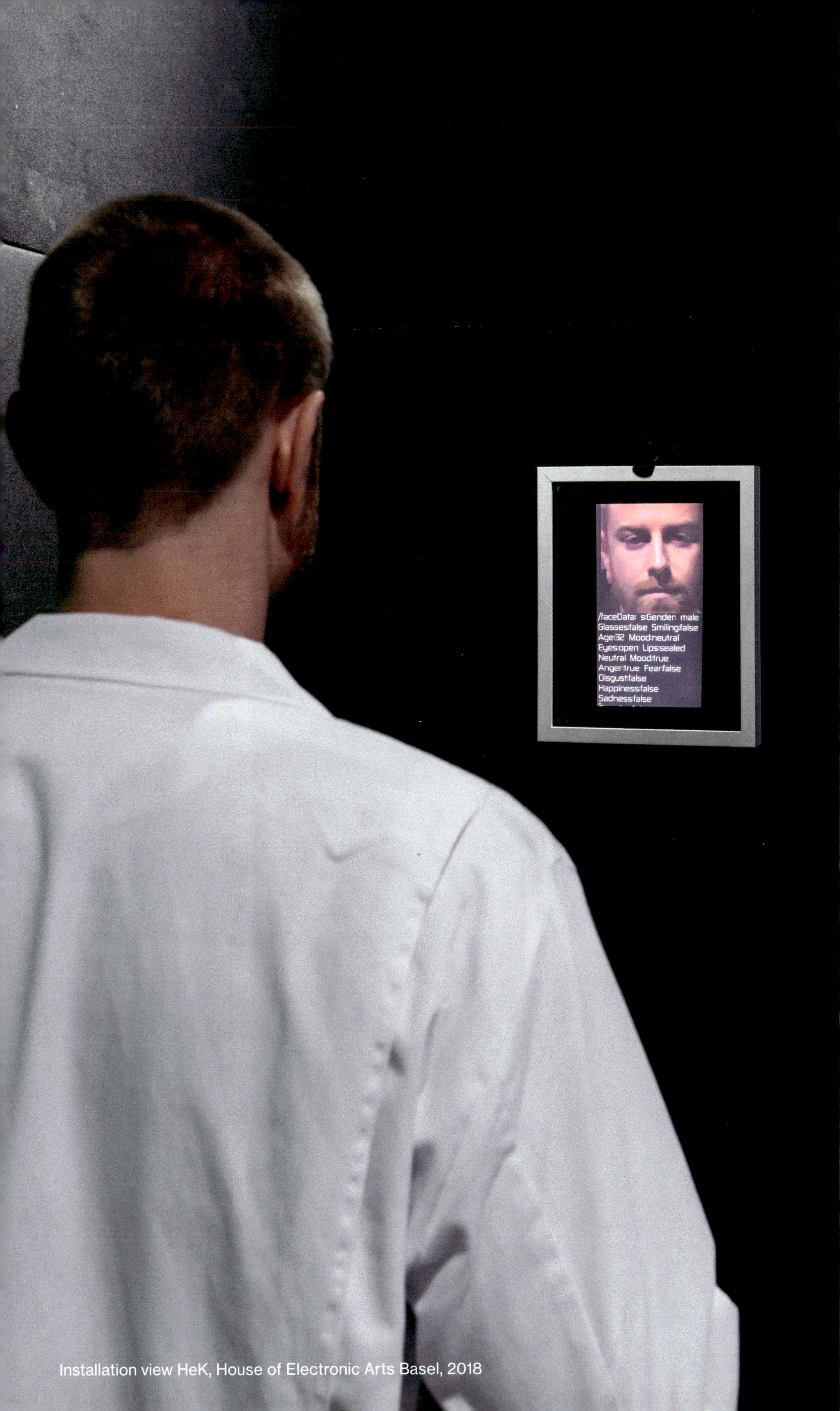


Installation view HeK, House of Electronic Arts Basel, 2018

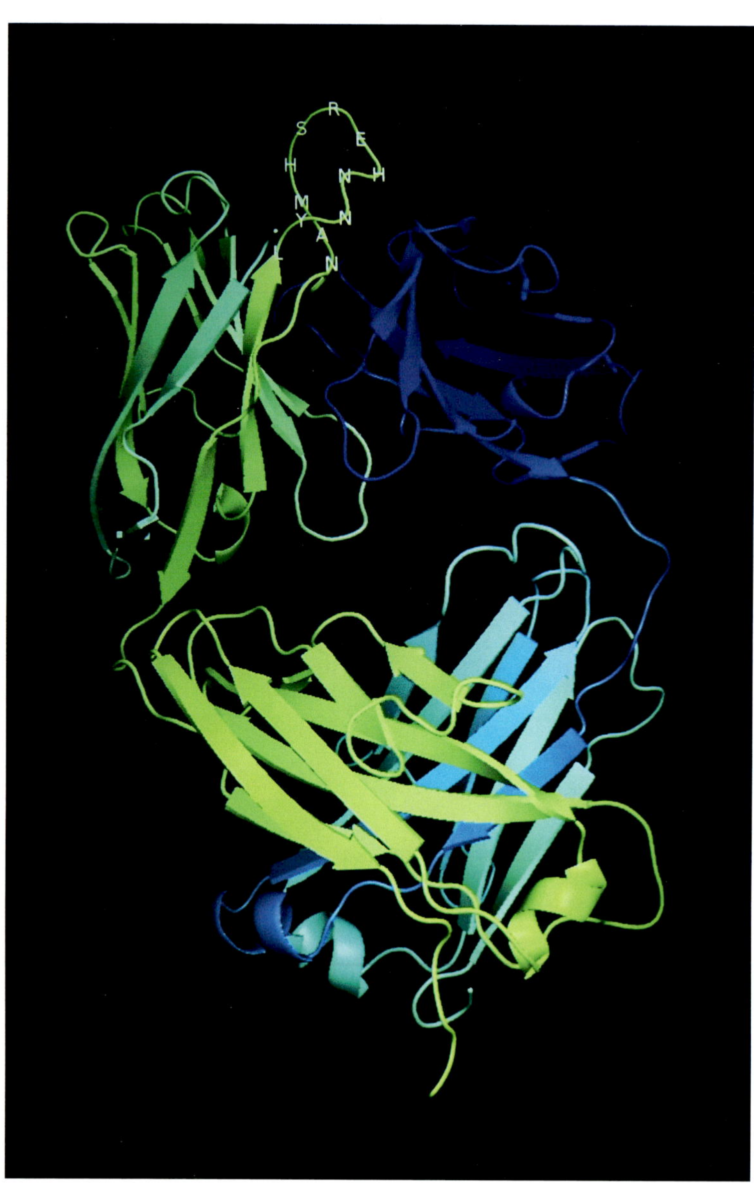


Antibody 3D visualisation by the team of Dr. Thomas Huber

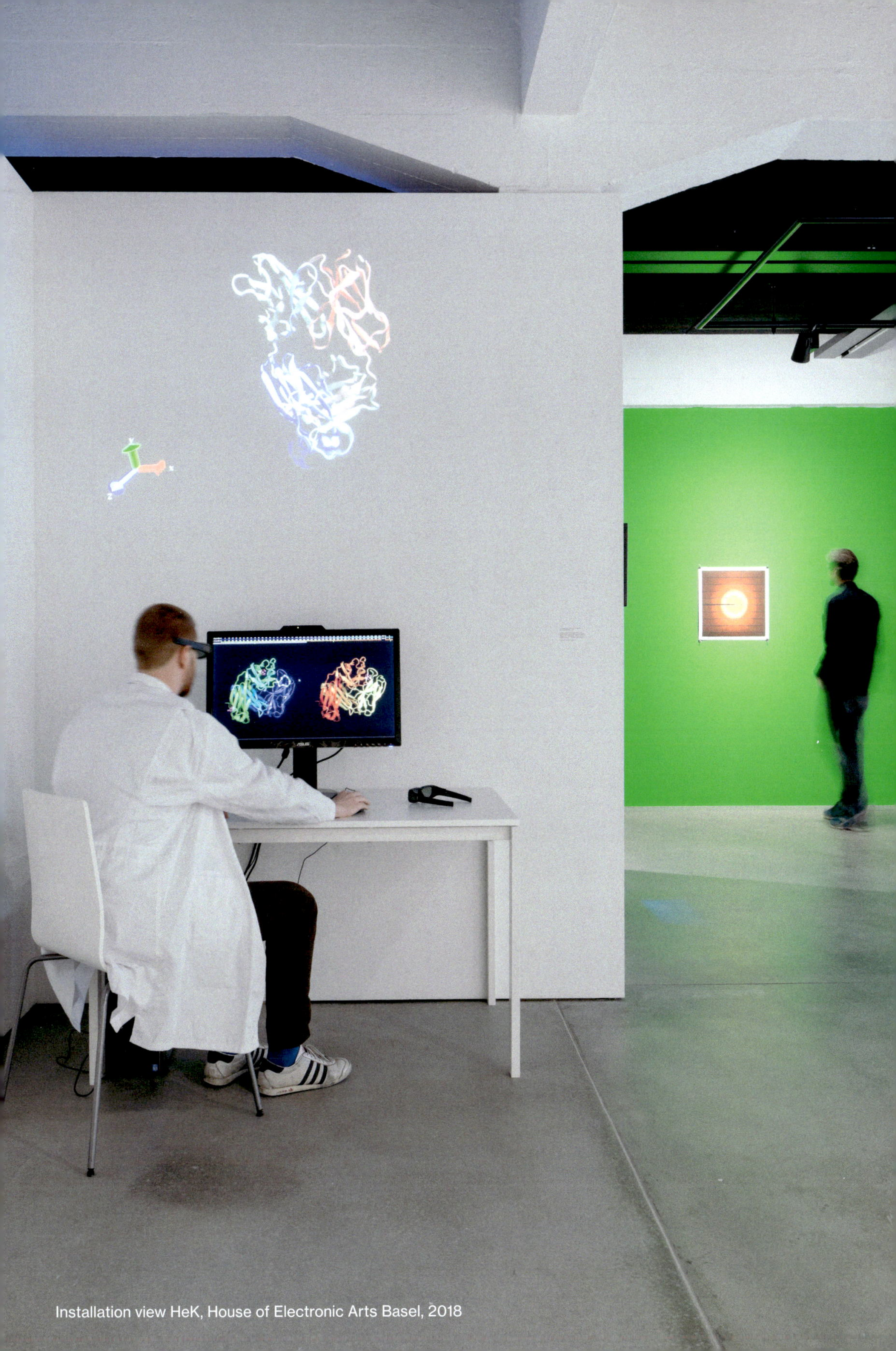

Installation view HeK, House of Electronic Arts Basel, 2018

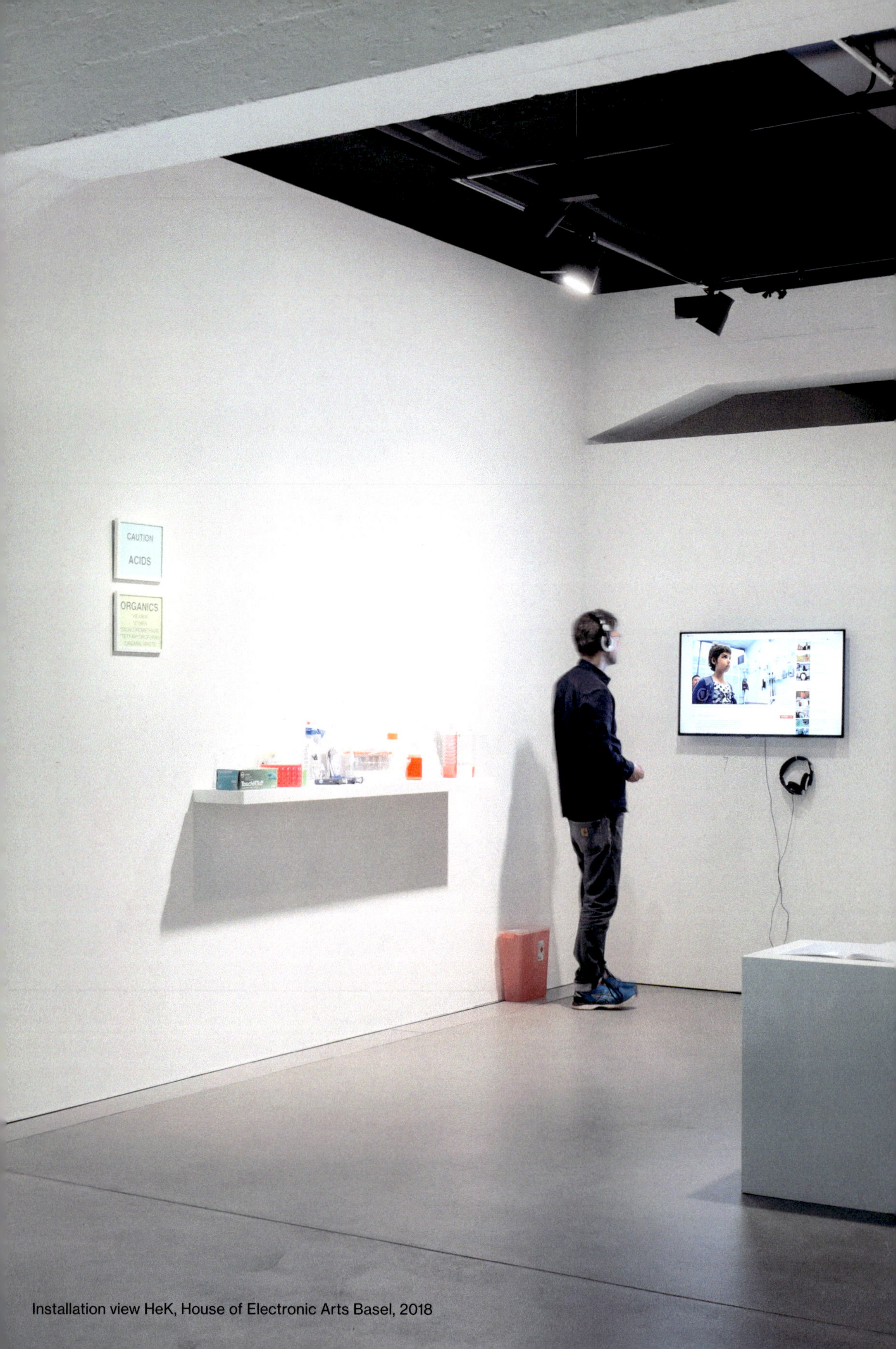


Installation view HeK, House of Electronic Arts Basel, 2018

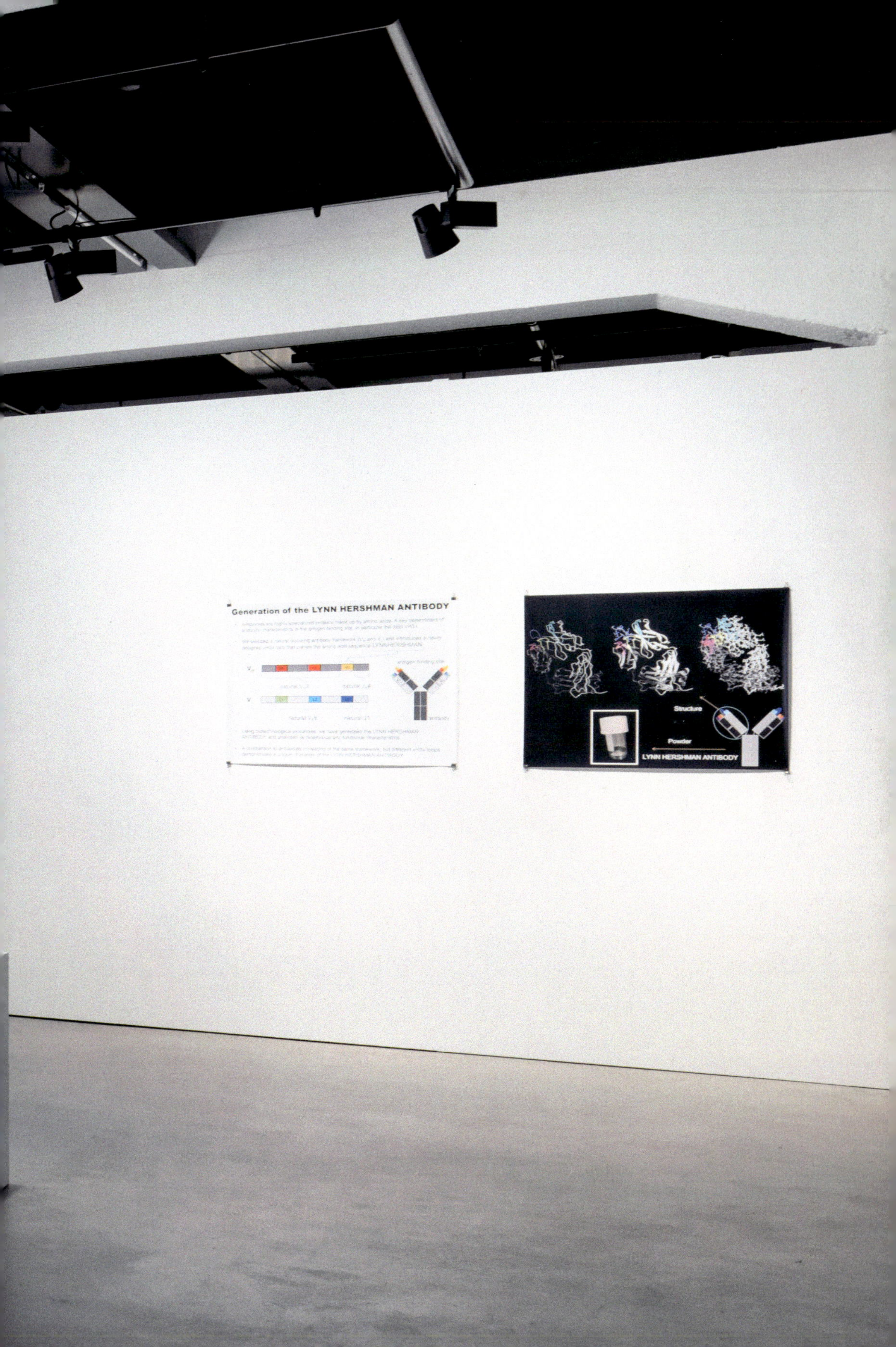
Generation of the LYNN HERSHMAN ANTIBODY
Structure
Powder
LYNN HERSHMAN ANTIBODY

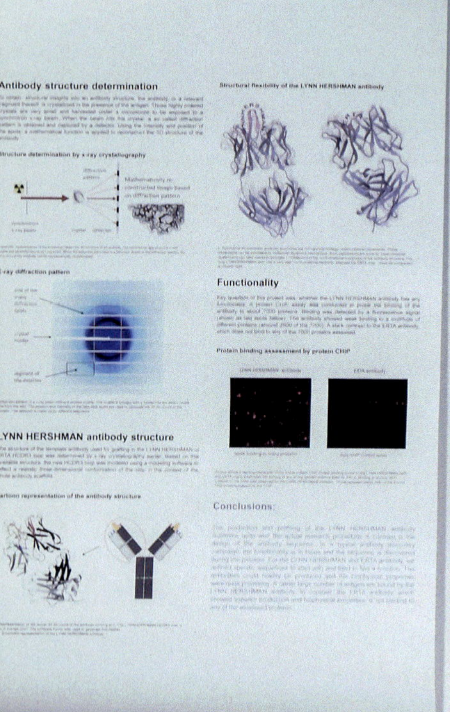


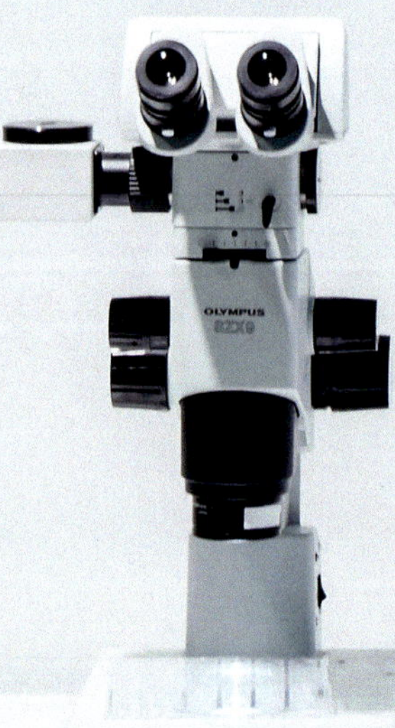


Installation view HeK,
House of Electronic Arts Basel, 2018

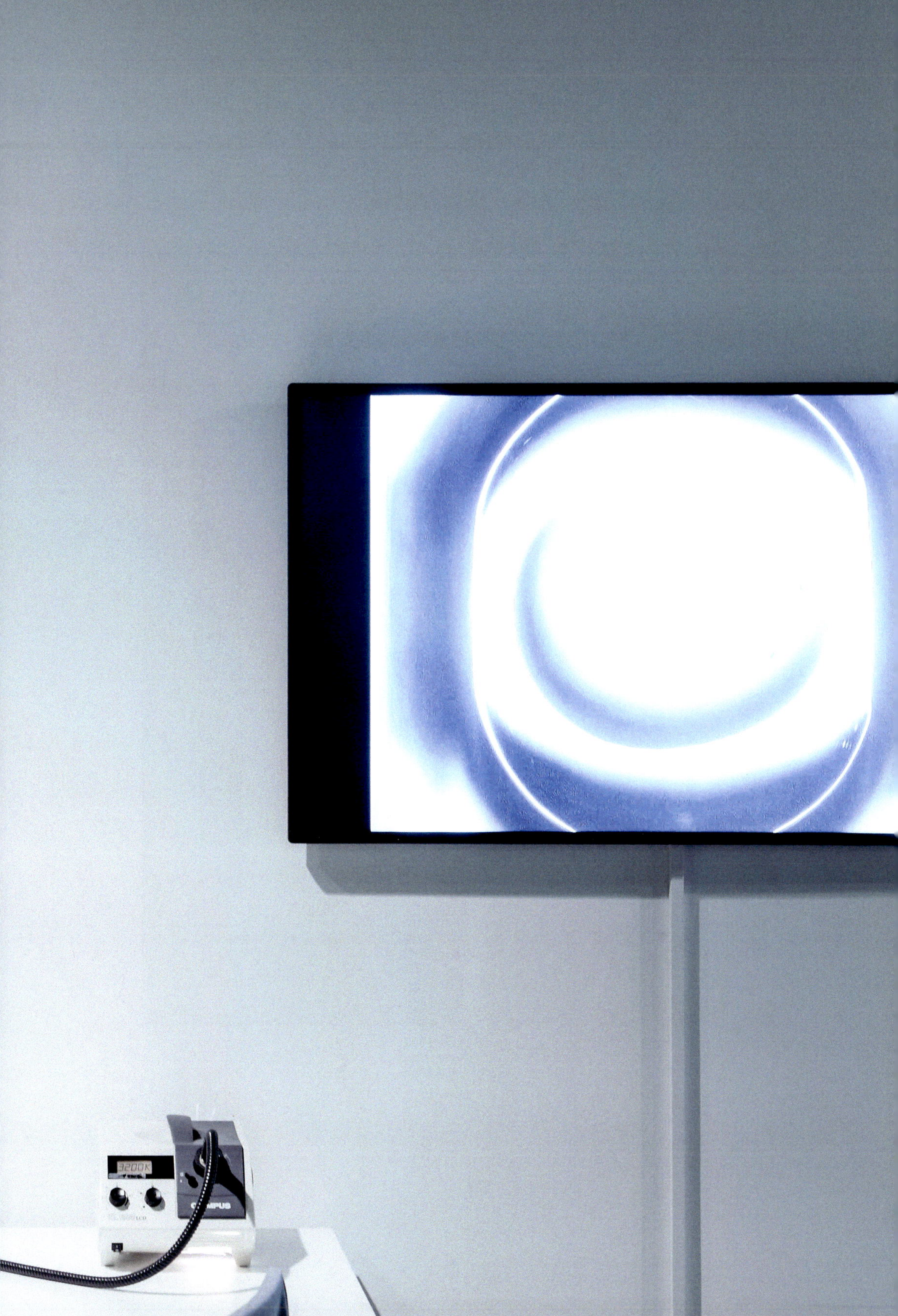
3200K

# 38 The Infinity Engine
Room 8

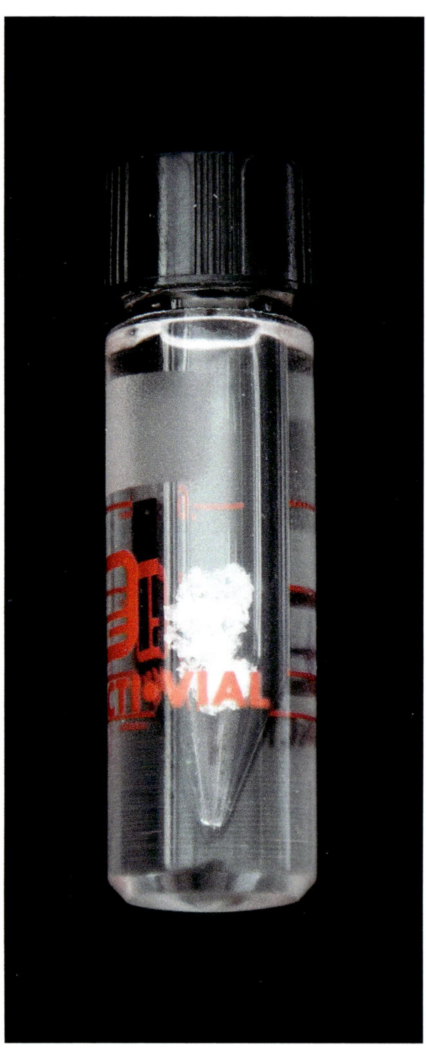


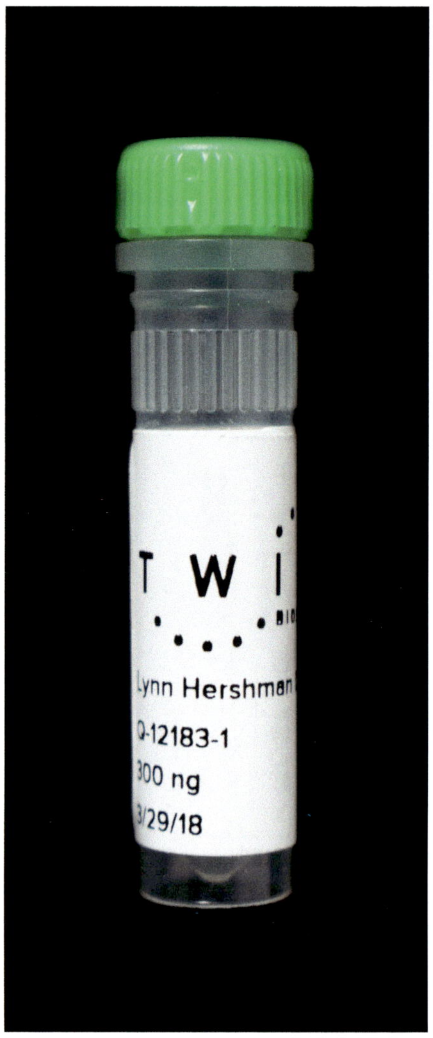


Vials of the antibody and DNA from *The Infinity Engine*, 2018

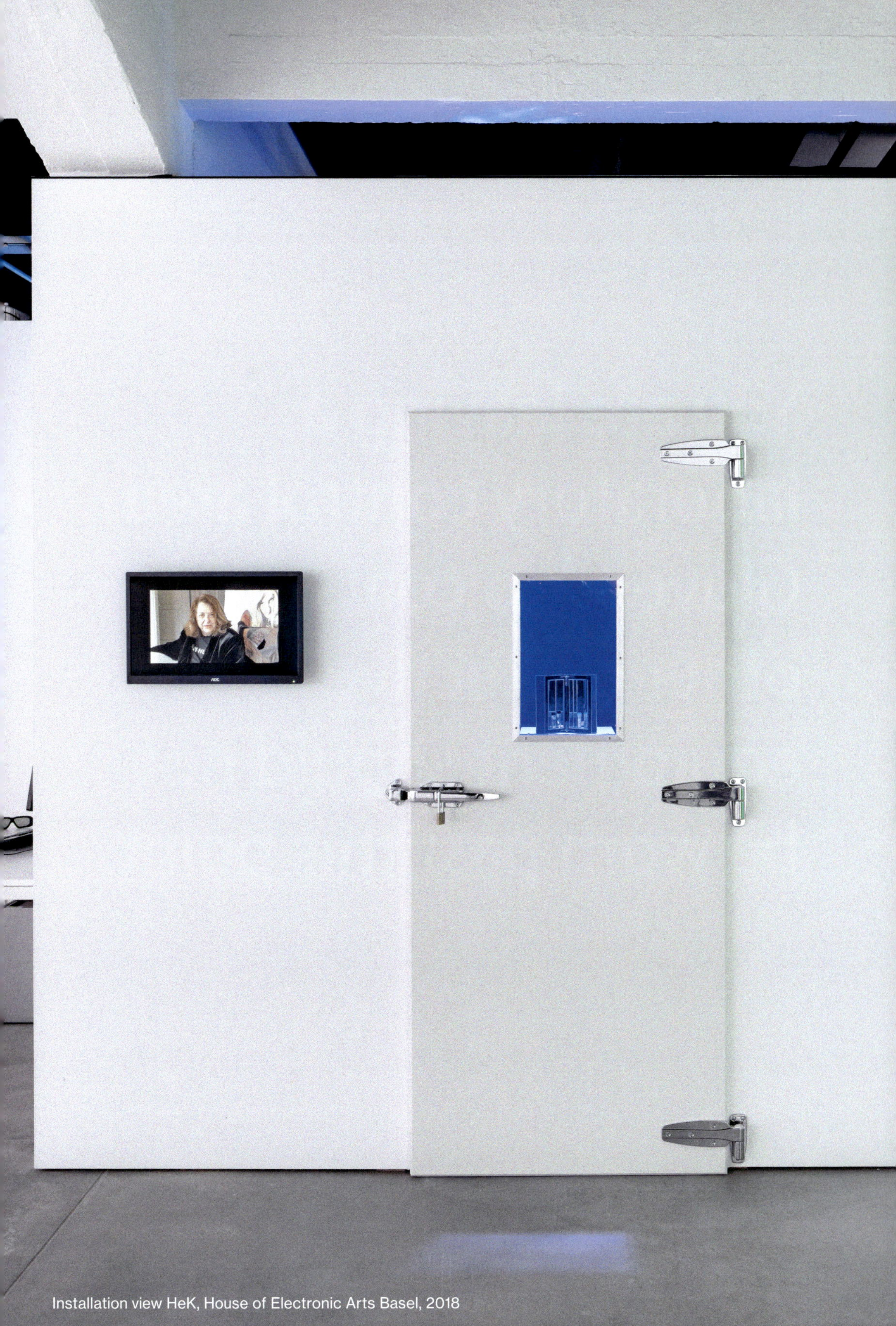

Installation view HeK, House of Electronic Arts Basel, 2018

You are leaving a laboratory control area. Gloves, lab coats, and other protective equipment should not be worn past this point.

Lab sign from *The Infinity Engine*, 2014

"I try to live in the present, because most people live in the past. If you live in the present, most people think you live in the future, because they don't know what happens in their own time."
Lynn Hershman Leeson[1]

The American artist and filmmaker Lynn Hershman Leeson is rightly described as the portraitist of the information age, a keen observer of the protocols and institutions that will shape our notions of identity and individuality.[2] Like a seismograph, she reacts through her art to societal developments, particularly to the impact of technological advances. At the start of her career, in the 1960s, she already was portraying humans as hermaphroditic amalgams of man and machine in her cyborg drawings and watercolors. Personal traumas and groundbreaking technological developments played an equal role in shaping her work, in her ongoing confrontation with notions of identity and individuality. The impacts of media technologies and the associated new possibilities for social interaction have surfaced in her works time and again. In her touch-screen installation *Deep Contact* (1984) the screen became a window into a virtual world that is now a permanent part of our landscape. In her works *Agent Ruby* (1996–2002) and *DiNA* (2004), she traces the increasing virtualization of the world as well as our fictional digital identities. These and other works also reflect the emergence of the World Wide Web and global connectivity. Time and again, Hershman Leeson has been a pioneer in art, experimenting with new technologies. For example, in 1984 she created *Lorna,* the first interactive videodisk installation, in which the observer can intervene and influence the protagonist's life story.

In recent years, Hershman Leeson has returned to grapple with the profound impact of technological progress on our lives. Groundbreaking developments in the life sciences have brought radical changes to our understanding of the self, as life has become designable. The opportunities, the possibilities, but also ethical boundaries of biological sciences are themes that Hershman Leeson explores in her art.
So it made sense, in planning the exhibition *Anti-Bodies* 2018 at HeK (House of Electronic Arts Basel), to focus on this new complex of works that encompass regenerative medicine, genetic research and antibody research in equal measure.[3]

As a jumping off and reference point for the exhibition at HeK, we chose the film *Strange Culture* (2007), which was based on a true event and triggered Hershman Leeson's intense interest in biotechnologies. This staged documentary was a plea for artistic freedom and a statement of support for a fellow artist: It was based on the story of the artist Steve Kurtz, a member of the *Critical Art Ensemble,* who was accused of bioterrorism after the unexpected heart failure and death of his wife, and the discovery of petri dishes and other scientific equipment used for biological research in his home. Hershman Leeson's film re-enacted the story using actors, and included interviews with those affected. Her film helped Kurtz in his court case and revealed how state paranoia prevailed in the handling of biotechnologies after the terror attacks of September 11, 2001 in the USA. Steve Kurtz's artistic work, which falls into the category of BioArt, aims at providing broad access to current methods and practices in biotechnology. Hershman Leeson, too, grappled for many years with the subject of this "Black Box" of biotechnological developments.

The focal point of the HeK exhibition was the complex multi-room installation *The Infinity Engine,* which dealt with genetic engineering, DNA manipulation, the production of transgenic organisms and regenerative medicine; it concluded with a reflection on central new scientific findings. The project began in 2014 in Hershman Leeson's comprehensive retrospective, *Civic Radar,* at the ZKM | Center for Arts and Media in Karlsruhe, where the installation's first four rooms were shown. In *The Infinity Engine,* Hershman Leeson shows how the boundaries between natural and artificial life are increasingly dissolving in the age of synthetic biology, and how life can be designed artificially. Or, as media theorist Peter Weibel puts it in the accompanying catalogue to the *Civic Radar* exhibition, "Hershman Leeson's work redefines the nature of human identity in the Information Age."[4]

Gottfried Wilhelm Leibniz already had described the living body as a "machine of nature."[5] Nature is an "Infinity Engine," a limitless machine that enables countless variations and developments and whose evolutionary process is carried out daily within our bodies. Today, modern biotechnologies allow us to actively shape our selves and evolutionary processes.

Today, Hershman Leeson's long-standing preoccupation with questions of identity and individuality find expression in her most recent work on biopolitics. In *The Infinity Engine* she imitates a functioning genetics laboratory and uses eight rooms to provide a critical look at developments in the biosciences – from regenerative medicine and the complex branches of genome experimentation to the use of DNA as a biological storage medium.[6] The number "8" refers to infinity and is reminiscent of the double helix, the twisted strands of DNA – the "software of life."[7] The following is a brief introduction to the eight rooms of *The Infinity Engine.*

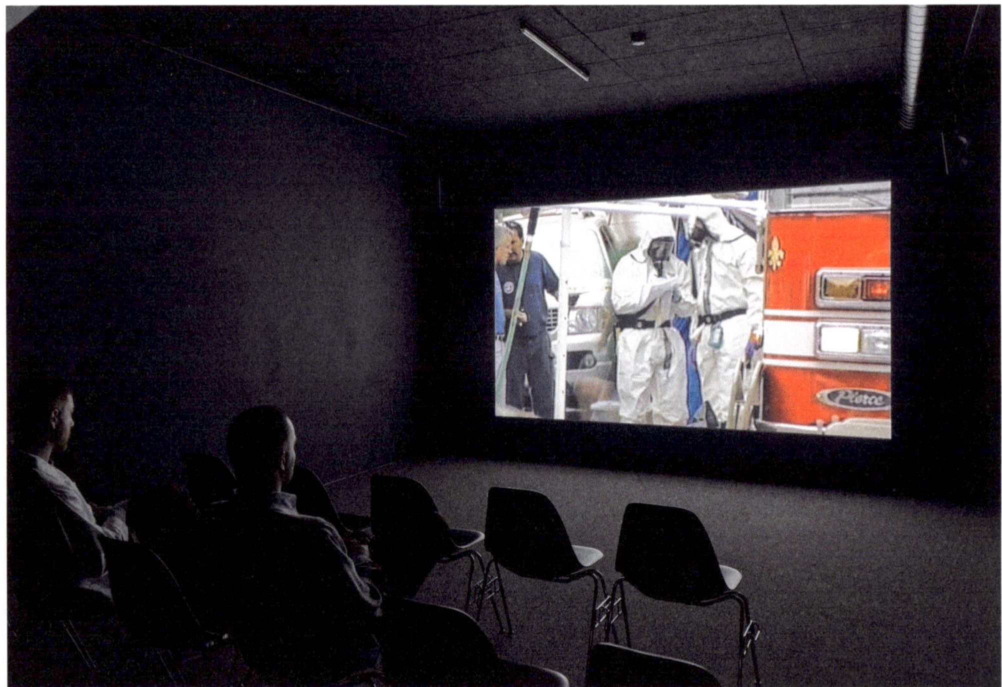

Lynn Hershman Leeson, *Strange Culture,* 2007, installation view HeK, House of Electronic Arts Basel, 2018

Room 1: Access to the lab

Upon entering the exhibition, visitors were asked to don a lab coat and slip into the role of a scientist who is permitted to open the heavy double door, entering a space that is off limits to most of us. In the foyer, immersive projections created the sense of being in a laboratory, with corridors and generic scientific production sites that could be anywhere and have no relation to a specific location, but that define the laboratory as the epistemological origin of modern life sciences and the location of today's knowledge production. Through this "change of location," which turns the museum into a scientific lab, Hershman Leeson demonstrates the importance of becoming familiar with new epistemologies and the logic of technical-scientific regimes, as cultural scientist Ingeborg Reichle writes in a text about the first four rooms of *The Infinity Engine.*[8]

Room 2: Bio printing

The first room within the "laboratory" was dedicated to techniques of regenerative medicine and the artificial production of human organs using 3D bioprinting. The room contained several devices used in regenerative medicine. One also could watch Hershman Leeson's taped interview with Dr. Anthony Atala, a researcher behind the development of 3D bioprinting. The video presents two case studies of people whose quality of life was dramatically improved through the bioprinting of organs. A central object was a three-dimensional tissue and cell structure in the shape of a human nose, which Hershman Leeson presented in a glass case like a valuable museum object.[9] Hershman Leeson staged the accomplishments of regenerative medicine in her unique aesthetic, appropriating existing scientific materials like "readymades" and transferring them into the art context.

The possibilities opened up by regenerative medicine triggered a development that leads to humans assuming the role of creator. Nature is not the only "infinity engine," or perpetual machine; now, the human being becomes the lord over creation, the "Homo Deus," as Israeli historian Yuval Noah Harari writes.[10] To illustrate this constructability of life, Hershman Leeson created her video installation *Infinity Engine (Syringe)* (2018), which includes an impressive image improvising on Michelangelo's famous Sistine Chapel fresco in which God's finger touches that of man, breathing life into him. But in Hershman Leeson's version, the hands are replaced by hypodermic needles.

Room 3: Genetic engineering / CRISPR mutations

Another room dealt with the current spectacular developments made possible by the manipulation of genetic material.[11] In 1953, American biologist James D. Watson and English physicist Francis Crick presented the structure of DNA as a double helix; they were awarded the Nobel Prize for their discovery, in 1962. Since 2003, the entire human genome has been considered decoded. Today, one can order genetic tests online for a small fee. Such developments contribute to an increasing tendency to attribute individual characteristics or identity to DNA, as writer Markus Jansen says in his book, *Digitale Herrschaft* (digital domination).[12]

With the relatively recent development of the so-called "gene scissor" CRISPR-Cas9, it has become quite simple to process and modify the genetic material of any organism. Hershman Leeson demonstrates the degree to which genetically manipulated organisms already populate our planet, by completely covering a wall with wallpaper – *Infinity Engine (Crops/Animals/Labs)* (2014) – that depicts a range of hybrid cultures and countless images of genetically manipulated animals and plants as well as the labs in which they are produced. It also lists the motivations behind the production – such as increased food production in cereals, or resistance to agricultural pests. A video of transgenic luminous zebra fish in an aquarium – *Infinity Engine (Aquarium Glowfish)* (2014) – or the image of a glowing cat –

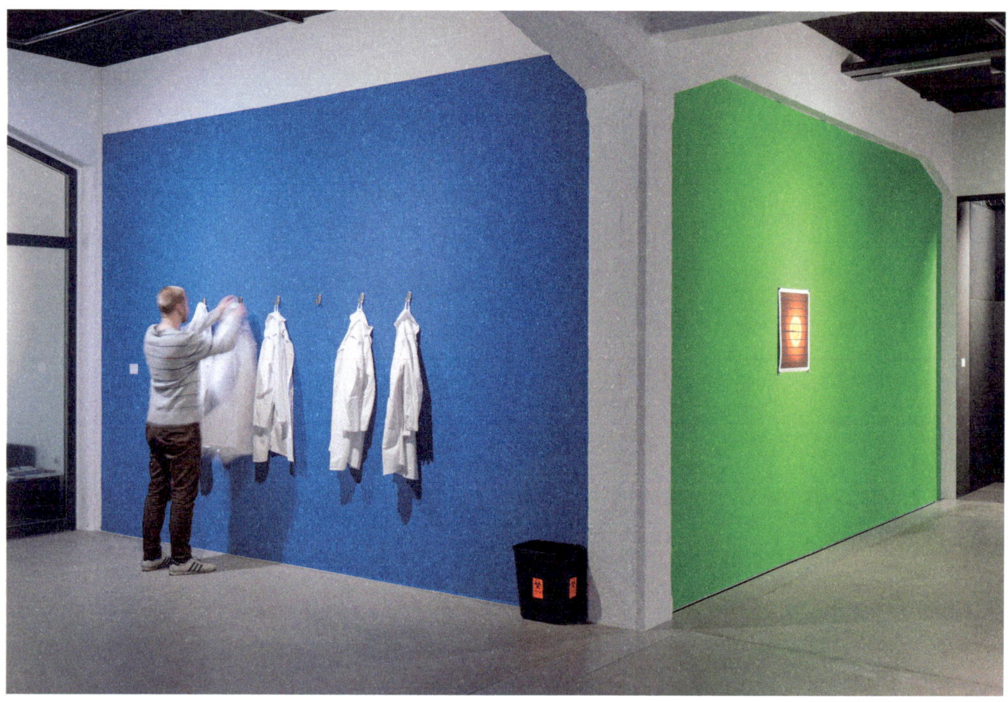

Installation view HeK, House of Electronic Arts Basel, 2018

*Infinity Engine (Jellyfish Feline)* (2014) – both of which came to be through added genes of jellyfish, made it clear how widespread the use of genetic engineering achievements has become. Today, organisms are nothing other than digital information consisting of a four-figure "software of life"[13] that can be rewritten and re-encoded. The transhumanist Ray Kurzweil also called DNA nature's "Nano-Computer."[14]

Room 4: Ethics

Because these new possibilities are accompanied by complex ethical questions, the next room was devoted to questions raised by genetics and biopolitics. Here, visitors could view Hershman Leeson's collection of legal documents and information on patents related to genetic engineering, which illustrate ethical dimensions. Thus the artist also addresses the moral dilemma that we face today when biotechnological developments represent new healing methods on one hand, but can be used for the manipulation and genetic surveillance of humans on the other. Hershman Leeson's staging is never judgmental, but rather affords us a deeper look behind the scenes of scientific production, boosting us toward a more profound understanding. And her personal view is always positive: "You have to be optimistic about the advantages of technology – I have a desire for utopia, and I hope that the technology is used in an inspired way. I may be naïve, but I think an awareness of both the dangers and the benefits can provide a method of survival in an enhanced and profound manner."[15]

Room 5: George Church

In her complex installation, Hershman Leeson repeatedly gives voice to scientists through interviews. For example, she speaks with George Church, professor for genetics at Harvard Medical School and a prominent representative of synthetic

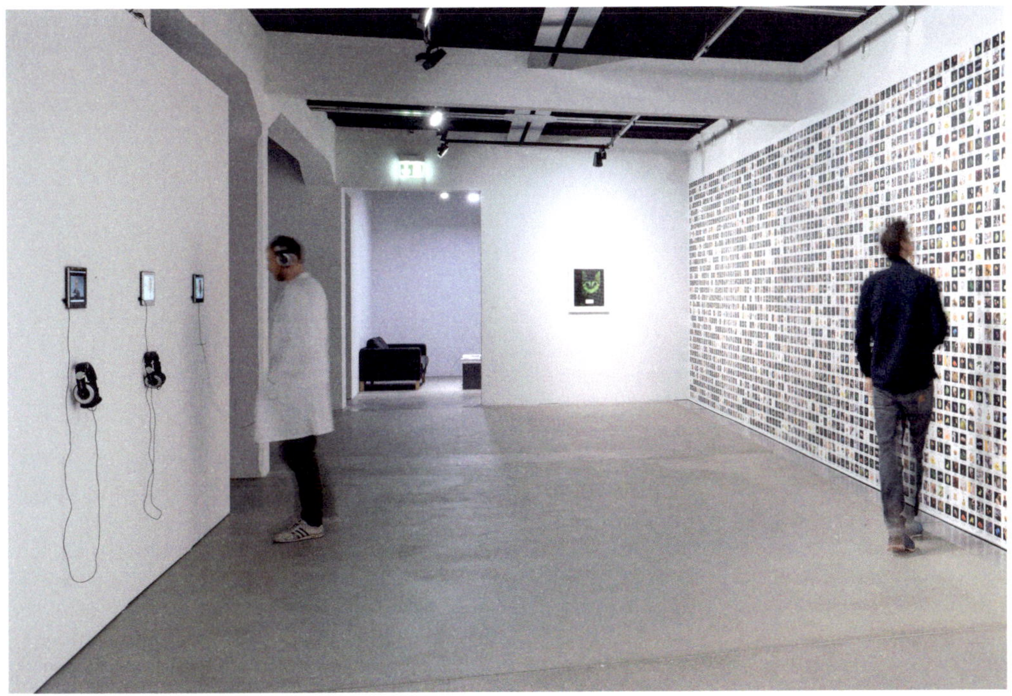

Installation view HeK, House of Electronic Arts Basel, 2018

biology, whose book, *Regenesis,* poses the provocative question about how synthetic biology will re-create nature and mankind and how we might develop into a new species.[16] In the video interview, *A Perfect Archive* (2018), Church tells Hershman Leeson about the possibilities of using DNA for biological storage of information, thanks to a revolutionary new technology: A binary digital code based on a sequence of zeros and ones is converted into a sequence of letters A, C, G and T, the bases of the biological code of DNA, using special software. The biological molecule thus created can be retranslated into digital code using a commercially available DNA sequencing machine. Up to 215 petabytes of data fit onto one gram of DNA, which is extremely durable as a biological storage medium. This new technology promises a solution for the long-term storage of digital data, the need for which is growing exponentially each day. Church and his team already have stored incunabula of film history – like George Méliès' *Le voyage dans la lune* (The Journey to the Moon) from 1902 – in DNA and converted it back into digital code. Hershman Leeson used this new technology to store her own works, which could be seen in the final room of *The Infinity Engine.*

Room 6: Forensic traces

While the previous rooms showed how one can manipulate and shape DNA – the building block of life – Room 6 showed how humans also can be monitored on the basis of their biological data. In the interactive video installation *Infinity Engine (Facial Recognition Software)* (2018), the faces of visitors were analyzed and interpreted by facial recognition software. The algorithms tried to identify each person's gender, age and – based on facial expressions – their emotions. Surveillance is a common theme and motif in Hershman Leeson's work. Today, surveillance can take place at the cellular level, as she herself writes.[17] From the fictional character *Roberta Breitmore* (1973–1978), whose life was based on fictitious data, to the machine-controlled gaze of *CybeRoberta* (1996), the artist's new works show how our bodies today are no longer monitored exclusively from the outside by cameras, but increasingly also from the inside, through our DNA.

Room 7: Antibodies

The next room, the heart and namesake of the *Anti-Bodies* exhibition, was dedicated to antibody research. Dr. Thomas Huber, Senior Investigator at NIBR Biologics Center at Novartis Pharma AG, and his team developed an antibody that reflects the name "Lynn Hershman" in its molecular structure.

Antibodies are special proteins that play an essential role in the natural immune system and are therefore developed for therapeutic purposes. They recognize foreign or changed body structures (or antigens) and mark them so that they can be easily recognized and eliminated by other components of the immune system responsible for defense. They are used specifically for the treatment of certain diseases, such as in cancer therapy. To that end, artificial antibodies can be produced in the laboratory using genetic engineering, and tailored to recognize specific structures.

Dr. Thomas Huber and his team of scientists researched and documented the properties and possible applications of the LYNNHERSHMAN Antibody. The entire working process was documented in the exhibition, using digital and microscopic images. In addition, the room contained various elements and equipment used to produce an antibody and showed how it could be applied towards personalized medicine.[18]

The LYNNHERSHMAN Antibody turned out to be extremely versatile in its structure. But the simultaneously produced antibody ERTA, whose amino acid structure refers to the alter ego of Lynn Hershman's fictitious figure "Roberta Breitmore,"[19] could barely make any connections to antigens. Hershman Leeson interpreted these surprising results as consistent analogues to her own artistic practice.[20] With the production of her antibody, Hershman Leeson took her exploration of identity and uniqueness to a new biological dimension.

Room 8: DNA

The eighth and final room of *The Infinity Engine* was not accessible; one could only view it through the narrow glass window of a locked laboratory door. The room was bathed in an intensive blue color. In the center was a pedestal upon which a mirror box with two glass vials were placed. They were reflected in it, to an almost infinite depth. One vial contained the powder of the LYNNHERSHMAN antibody; the other held 300 nanograms of DNA in which all the digital documentation of the exhibition were stored in low resolution: videos and pictorial material as well as the artist's video journal, *The Electronic Diaries* (1986–1994). The American laboratory Twist Biology stored the binary data packets in the biological code of the DNA. As Rudolf Frieling writes so wonderfully in his essay in this publication, Room 8 thus became the culmination of Hershman Leeson's entire oeuvre. The artist succeeded in making fragments of her work, her artistic legacy, permanently available to posterity in a biological repository.

It was in the early 1990s that Hershman Leeson coined the term "Anti-Body" for her research and work, which plumbed the depths of identity and individuality, and explored the possibilities of virtual identity in cyberspace, where one no longer needs a physical body to assume a fictitious identity in the global network.[21] In the *Anti-Bodies* exhibition, this search was no longer focused on the biological entity and its virtual representations, but on our biological essence: "While the search for antibodies exists in all of my works, identifying the antibody moves inwards with this project and becomes an inverted biological gesture that has as its goal healing from the inside out, a cyborgian dream of infiltrating the body itself and thereby attempts to create a radical and curative recovery of individual culture."[22] On one hand, *Anti-Bodies* brought Hershman Leeson's long-standing examination of current developments in the biosciences to a preliminary conclusion; on the other hand, it generated an essence of the exhibition itself, to which she added central aspects of her life with her video diaries – preserved for posterity in the biological memory of DNA.

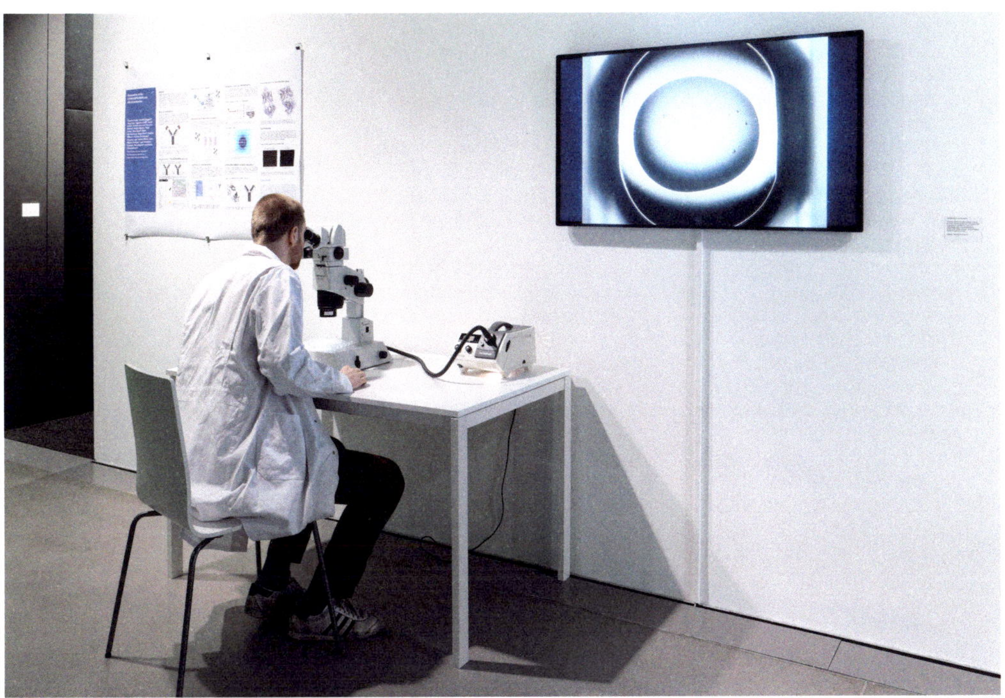

Installation view HeK, House of Electronic Arts Basel, 2018

1 Lynn Hershman Leeson in an interview in *die tageszeitung,* 2014.
2 Dr. Pamela Lee on Lynn Hershman Leeson's website: http://www.lynnhershman.com/current/ (accessed on April 7, 2019).
3 The exhibition *Lynn Hershman Leeson: Anti-Bodies* was shown from May 3 to Aug. 5, 2018 at HeK, House of Electronic Arts Basel.
4 Peter Weibel, "The Work of Lynn Hershman Leeson: A Panoply of Identities," in *Lynn Hershman Leeson: Civic Radar,* pub. by Peter Weibel, exh. cat., ZKM | Zentrum für Kunst und Medien, Ostfildern 2015, p. 55.
5 Gottfried Wilhelm Leibniz, *Monadologie und andere metaphysische Schriften* (1714), published and translated by Ulrich Johannes Schneider, Hamburg 2002, cited in Markus Jansen, *Digitale Herrschaft. Über das Zeitalter der globalen Kontrolle und wie Transhumanismus und Synthetische Biologie das Leben neu definieren,* Stuttgart 2015, p. 197.
6 For each individual room, we worked with color codes oriented to the usual shades representing the double helix building blocks of DNA.
7 Craig Venter, *Life at the Speed of Light. From the Double Helix to the Dawn of Digital Life,* London 2013, p. 7.
8 Ingeborg Reichle, "The Infinity Engine," in *Lynn Hershman Leeson: Civic Radar,* pub. by Peter Weibel, exh. cat., ZKM | Zentrum für Kunst und Medien, Ostfildern 2015, p. 335.
9 The object is a gift to the artist from the American scientist Dr. Anthony Atala of the Wake Forest School of Regenerative Medicine.
10 Yuval Noah Harari, *Homo Deus. Eine Geschichte von Morgen,* Munich 2018.
11 The room also includes several interviews with scientists who go into greater depth on the developments and offer additional information.
12 Jansen 2015 (see note 5), p. 127.
13 Venter 2013 (see note 7), p. 7.
14 Ray Kurzweil, *The Singularity Is Near. When Humans Transcend Biology,* New York 2006, p. 117.
15 Lynn Hershman Leeson interviewed by Hou Hanru, in *Lynn Hershman Leeson: Civic Radar,* pub. by Peter Weibel, exh. cat., ZKM | Zentrum für Kunst und Medien, Ostfildern 2015, p. 177.
16 George M. Church and Ed Regis, *Regenesis. How Synthetic Biology Will Reinvent Nature and Ourselves,* New York 2012.
17 See the interview with Lynn Hershman Leeson in this publication.
18 The story of Emily Whitehead was also shown in a video. Emily Whitehead, a seven-year-old American girl, suffered from acute lymphoblastic leukemia and had little hope of surviving. In 2012, she was the first child to be treated with an experimental method called CAR-T, which hit the headlines and was tested by Novartis. Emily Whitehead has been cancer-free since her treatment.
19 See also the text by Rudolf Frieling in this publication.
20 See the text *Antibody Reveal* by Lynn Hershman Leeson in this publication.
21 Lynn Hershman Leeson (ed.), *Clicking In: Hot Links to a Digital Culture,* Seattle 1996, pp. 325–337.
22 Lynn Hershman Leeson in an e-mail to this author.

# Rudolf Frieling
# What is LYNNHERSHMAN? A question out of the blue

"Hi, my name is Lynn Hershman. Come and see me at the Chelsea hotel."[1]

To dive deeper into Lynn Hershman's work, a good place to start is the TV-commercial quoted above where the same sentence is spoken by five different people with only the first one being the "real" Lynn Hershman.[2] Clearly, a name is just a name that can be appropriated by others or attributed to others. But the disturbing link between five faces and one's own name hides, as the artist expressed, the fact that one's own name is above all "the archival, bureaucratic and thus political marker of identity."[3] A name is thus a record and the multiplication of the artist's identity in this "drama" deliberately and critically points to the need to be mindful of these processes of identification, to cover one's tracks, cast doubt, and playfully avoid a notion of identity that would be prescriptive and limiting. At the same time, in art and public life, a name is also the perception of a continuous and identifiable body of work that can be called an artist's signature. In this sense, Lynn Hershman has made herself a "name" that stands for the critical examination of shifting identities while constantly challenging herself, in ways often tied to the exploration of new technologies. The question of what's in a name will, however, resonate with us differently once we look at her most recent work – *Room #8* (2018) – which posits quite literally the name of the artist as the physical core of her work. This text will thus follow a line of inquiry that will address the most radical turn in her work: the physiological conjunction of her name with a body or rather the building blocks of antibodies, so that I will be able to recast the question of "Who is Lynn Hershman?" as "What is LYNNHERSHMAN?"

Let me start with the easier question: What has she done that justifies this particular perspective via the name? Looking more closely at a career of milestones from the early responsive machines – a series of masks of the 1960s that incorporated the visitor's presence to trigger sound – to the first interactive narrative in *Lorna* (1983) or the early dive into Artificial Intelligence in *Agent Ruby* (1999–2002) and *DiNA* (2004), I was intrigued by questions that surfaced in my recent conversation with the artist regarding her *Room #8* and its specific component of the "antibodies." I began to wonder if this recent work could indeed be the culmination of her whole career. Her short answer was that there is not much to which one can reconnect it and that this new work is rather unique, but I left her studio in San Francisco with two sentiments, which require me to search for a different and somewhat longer answer. The first sentiment was the uncanny observation that Lynn Hershman is already thinking about her legacy, about what remains of her work. She is thus facing the question of mortality not only as a human being, as we all must, but also as an "artist" or a "persona." The second sentiment was my surprise when she characterized the installation of the "antibodies" of *Room #8* – which she also translates into *Room ∞* or the mathematical symbol for infinity in her much larger exhibition of *The Infinity Engine* – as a "haiku" of the exhibition. Struck by this reference, I was wondering if the politics of her work, her pioneering use of performance and technology, had often overshadowed her poetics. Could one use her earlier work to highlight a poetic transformation and abstraction of the "self" that is essential to her most recent work? What follows is thus an attempt to pursue the ramifications of these two sentiments throughout her whole career, from creating a name and identity to the contemporary concern of constructing or engineering the biological essences of our existence as a species.

If one name stands out in all of Hershman's work of identity constructions, it is Roberta Breitmore, her legendary performance as a simulated character in the 1970s that ended in 1978 in an act of "exorcism" in the crypt of Lucrezia Borgia in Rome. Her name is a loose reference to one of the practitioners of alchemy: "The name Roberta referred to the founder of alchemy [the artist is probably alluding here to Robert Fludd, who is regarded as one of the great Western alchemists] and, indeed, her life has an alchemical quality. She was about process, change, and transformation, and the androgynous double."[4] Linking the series of Roberta Breitmore manifestations to the notion of alchemy is not far-fetched, it was prompted by some early commentary of the artist and Arturo Schwartz on the occasion of the first public mention of the name in the exhibition "Roberta Breitmore: An Alchemical Portrait Begun in 1975." Art historian Arturo Schwartz was, according to the artist, her teacher in these matters reflecting with her on an "Alchemical Opus."[5] Unlike the variability of Cindy Sherman's self-portraits as another person, all tightly controlled evocations of mediated pictures, mostly historical or genre references, in Hershman's work the framing of identity, its material manifestation, is an open-ended process intended to be generative rather than representative. The Roberta Breitmore series, as it spilled out into real life, blurred all distinctions. After five years of living with another "I" and even multiplying Breitmore's persona across multiple bodies, hiring three "clones" to represent her in public, Hershman put an end to it as the project had run its course and that she had learned enough about "the edges of her life" – moving on in the hopes that an exorcism might have therapeutic effects in the artist's own life.

At a very literal level, the ending in a crypt where a body is enshrined is more than a symbolic gesture. In Hershman's development as an artist, it actually reverses the previous shift from works that displayed masks in vitrines to site-specific interventions with masks in public spaces like hotels (*Dante Hotel,* 1972, and *Forming of a Sculpture Drama in Manhattan,* 1974) to the privacy of a locked room where a photographic record in which another record – namely one of Roberta Breitmore's *Construction Charts* – was burned to ashes. Having burned traces of her own work, Lynn Hershman walked out of the crypt with a vase of ashes which, however, was ultimately lost in the folds of her career. What remains today are photographs, archival records and documents, the name, and the iconic dress which, upon the occasion of the artist's retrospective exhibition *Civic Radar* at Yerba Buena Center for the Arts in San Francisco in 2016, miraculously reappeared on multiple bodies – a contemporary re-enactment or re-performance. Roberta Breitmore was resurrected from the dead via an homage of friends and collaborators.

With all of Roberta Breitmore's ephemera spread out in vitrines and frames, Hershman's retrospective accomplished the task of identifying the "Who" and the "What" of the artist and her work, providing a detailed and comprehensive answer to our question "Who is Lynn Hershman?" Going beyond curatorial decisions on how to make public what legacy is left of both the artist and her simulated character, Hershman tried to resurrect both her name and Roberta's legacy in her new body of work under the rubric of "antibodies" at the Haus der elektronischen Künste in Basel (2018) where she premiered *Room #8.* Prior to the opening, she sent me a picture of herself, out of focus, holding out her hand with a vial on which the camera was to focus on. The subject line functioned as a caption and said, "This is Lynn" without any further explanation. If "Lynn" is the powder in this vial with a label, i.e. name and archival record, I'm tempted to ask then: What is "Lynn" apart from being her first name? Is the inconspicuous powder like the alchemist's mythical gold, the result of an ultimate transformation, here morphed into a granular form and contained by a lab's standard vial? Is this for real? Can we verify what is in the vial and how "Lynn" got into it? Or should we simply allocate the physicality of the vial and its content to the framework of conceptual art where the proof is not in the pudding but in the idea – "Lynn" would then be a mind game and the vial could contain anything we want it to be or she claims it to be.

While this line of thought is certainly not out of the question, it is an unlikely interpretation. Lynn Hershman's career manifests a continuous investigation of our contemporary and real life, a conversation with alternate identities that are nevertheless grounded in very real experiences. She is as much a conceptual thinker and performer as she is a materialist looking for real embodiments. The beginning of her career provides a valuable clue. The material most closely associated with her earliest significant work is wax, a malleable substance subject to transformations when heat is applied. *Conversation* (1966), for instance, connects two facial fragments made of wax via a knot of colored wires inside three chambers in a Plexiglas vitrine. A related work, *Genealogy* (1968), shows eight life-size mouth fragments side by side. Both works are evidence that the most reliable facts in her artistic practice have been traces – or parts – of the artist's body. In a deliberate attempt to blur any biographical trace, she combined the imprint of her real body with the masking of her face – see another responsive machine such as *Self-Portrait as Another Person* (1965) in which the face is black and, as she often preferred, half hidden under a wig. The wearing of a mask has all kinds of psychological, social, and cultural traditions and connotations but here I'm simply interested in the fact that these malleable forms of body parts were a result of the real traumatic experience of being immobilized in a hospital under an oxygen tent where drawing was not an option but the body was always within reach. Some of these early masks are called "Breathing Machines." They have sensors and come to life when appropriate, meaning when another person approaches them. They are automata and yet also authentic replicas of the artist's face. They come to life in the presence of other life. Life, if you will, comes only through a co-presence. But the fascinating effect of these works on today's visitors is their dramatic enclosure. They are talkative

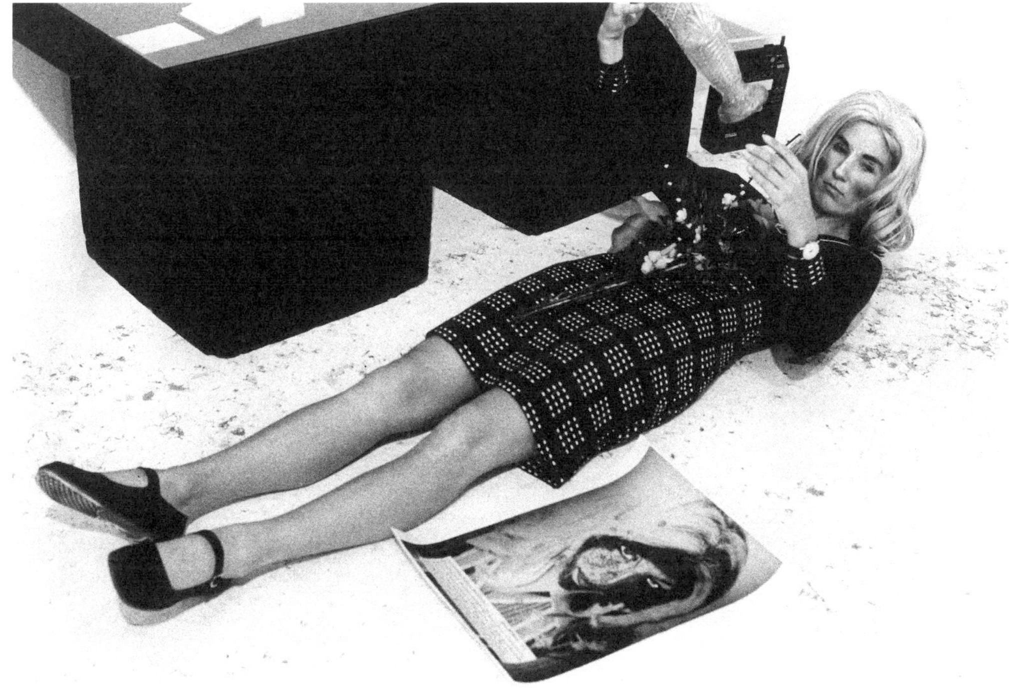

Lynn Hershman Leeson, Photograph of exorcism of Roberta Breitmore, 1978

but exclude dialogue. Some masks simply breathe, others have something to say, but none of them generates a feedback. On or off is their only option. They are tightly framed, covered under hair, and "live" in a transparent cube. This tension, I want to argue, runs deep through Hershman's entire career, where each work's specific embodiment and entanglement with the material reality is proof of a struggle not only for a name but for a human bond – as Agent Ruby says much later in her "e-dream portal" from 2002: "Let's connect." In fact, what had fascinated me in the past were the often elaborate and surprising ways that Hershman chose to sustain discursive bonds through conversations in various media, from an AI bot to real life and back, or addressing the viewer directly in her video series *Electronic Diaries (1984–1994).* With this long track record of engaging with the "real," it seems far-fetched to evoke the epiphany of a poetic phrase or a visual evocation of a haiku as the artist had expressed in our conversation. Lynn Hershman, it had always seemed to me, was too invested in the philosophical but also political implications of her works to seek a formalist reduction and poetic compression. And yet, when describing her installation of *Room #8,* Hershman speaks of a haiku and an art historical current that runs deep in her artistic DNA.

To address this disjunction, I take my first clue from a trusted resource, Merriam Webster's dictionary: "A haiku is an unrhymed verse form of Japanese origin having three lines containing usually five, seven, and five syllables respectively."[6] A haiku expresses much and suggests more in the fewest possible words. A scene, generated by a minimalist code, evokes for each reader differently a larger world and context from a single description of an event in a natural setting. If we were to associate color to a haiku, we would probably say it should be either monochromatic or maybe a careful juxtaposition of only two colors. *Room #8* operates with that logic. It is an enclosed space in blue light, connoting the color of infinity or eternity – see Yves Klein's blue or an abstraction of the cool design in Stanley Kubrick's science fiction classic *2001: A Space Odyssey* (1968) with its black monolith, or even a James Turrell immaterial, immersive environment. Yet this blue space is inaccessibly exhibited behind a closed lab door with a small window and a sturdy lock mechanism. Visitors peek through this window to see an object exhibited on a plinth, a mirrored box with two vials. They see the aura of a precious object in a deep blue void.

Yves Klein looms large – just think of his famous blue pigment or his photographic "haiku" of the leap into the void as well

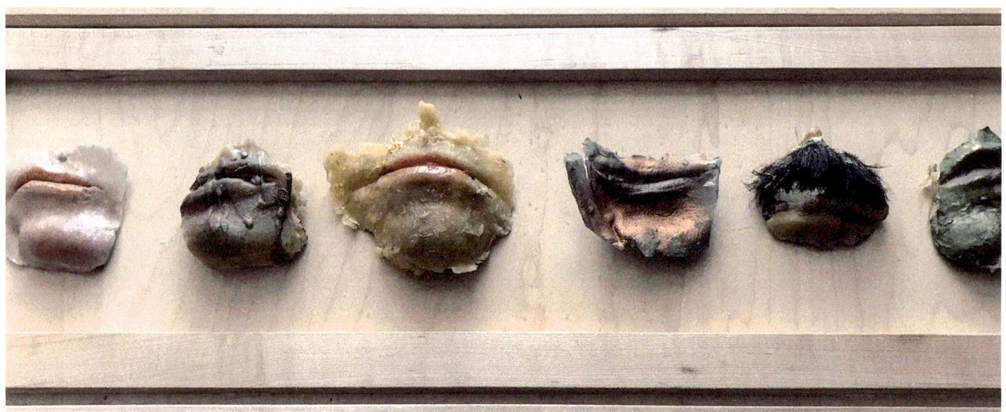

Lynn Hershman Leeson, *Genealogy,* 1968

as his 1958 exhibition *La spécialisation de la sensibilité à l'état matière première en sensibilité picturale stabilisée: Le Vide* (The Specialization of Sensibility in the Raw Material State into Stabilized Pictorial Sensibility: The Void). These works provide important marks of art historical references for Hershman. She also readily acknowledges Marcel Duchamp's influence on her thinking, specifically the famous installation of *Etant donnés: 1° la chute d'eau, 2° le gaz d'éclairage* (Given: 1. The Waterfall, 2. The Illuminating Gas) at the Philadelphia Museum of Art (1946–1966) [7] which is connected to *Room #8* via its use of a closed environment with a door and peepholes to control the gaze upon the exhibited object or room. The body in Duchamp's installation, provokingly sexualized in its display of a female nude, is obviously absent in Hershman's installation, replaced by the two unassuming ready-mades, scientific vials out of reach and thus made either more mysterious or more desirable depending on the viewer's disposition. Again, following the Duchampian analogy here, most importantly his works the "Boîte en valise (Box in a suitcase)" and the "Boîte alerte (Emergency box)" (1959), which contained a paperbound catalogue, ephemera, postcards, notes, envelopes, portfolio of artists' prints, a printed nylon stocking, and a 45rpm record, we recognize the mechanisms of display of something unattainable and removed, yet in close proximity. What *Etant donnés* adds to this strategy is the display of a sexualized body, possibly desirable but definitely locked away as if in a mausoleum. And yet, with the act of our looking through peepholes, the very essence of seduction comes into play. [8] Duchamp would have inserted the photograph of the exorcism of Roberta Breitmore, showing her stretched out next to a coffin in the crypt of Lucrezia Borgia, into a "boîte," a box of memories and blueprints for replicas and copies. Hershman's comment on the experience of seeing this famous artwork: "You had to speculate about it, there was [...] nothing you could walk around, nothing that was in your command, it automatically

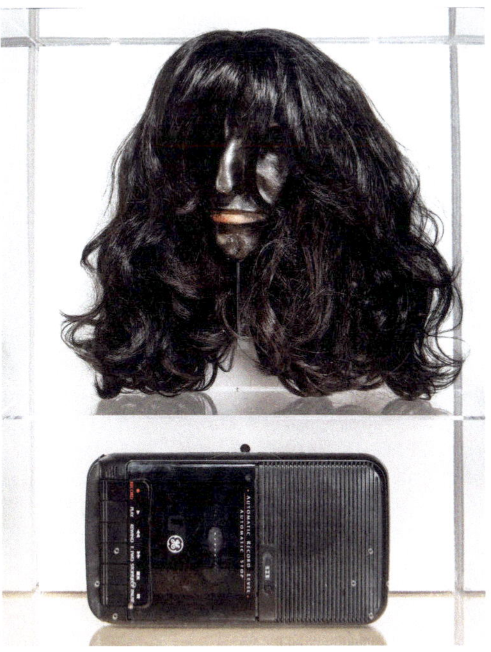

Lynn Hershman Leeson, *Self-portrait as Another Person,* 1965

said no, a non-entrance, which is what death is, not interactive." For her, the display of ephemera or the symbolic representation of a body is only secondary. The primary objective is to make a work productive, generative, and active. So how did she accomplish that in *Room #8*?

The medium description of *Room #8* contains these components: Lab door with hardware, Infinity Mirror Box, vial of LYNNHERSHMAN Antibody (produced by Novartis), vial of DNA (produced by Twist Biology), as well as additional contextual information that may or may not be added to an exhibition of Room #8. [9] The mirrored box attracts the gaze of the viewer. The glossy and endlessly reflective container for two vials is the essence of this room: one vial with the archive of *The Complete Electronic Diaries* stored as DNA, and a second vial with the white powder essence of an actual antibody based on the letters of the name LYNNHERSHMAN. [10] The closed lab door removes the object from the viewer and acts like a safe for the striking reflective luminosity of the mirrored box, enhanced by the deep blue light of the surrounding room. Vaguely reminiscent of mythological or fairytale connotations – see e.g. the imagery of a glass coffin and a seemingly frozen moment in time, not unlike a dream of infinite beauty and youth – provides a visual language that promises eternal life with a future action – to shatter the glass coffin. Hershman's striving for a human touch through media is now coupled with a setting in which a future life and a future action might emerge out of deep storage, the life of an artist's work stored in a vial of DNA and the life of real antibodies waiting to be used as catalysts or agents of immunization in the future. What strikes me is the romantic imagery that couples transparency with inaccessibility – a coffin with an inbuilt hope of rebirth and transformation.

Hershman's *Room #8,* however, cannot be reduced to a romantic image or an art historical response to Duchamp's mise en scène of the spectacle of the gaze. Her room is equally distant from her own wax sculptures of the 1960s, which partake in the rituals of death and museology as e.g. in Madame Tussaud's cabinet of celebrities. *Room #8* stands out in that it joins two rather disparate influences: It is clearly indebted to Yves Klein's aesthetic of non-representation but borrows its architectural parameters from the reality of a generic scientific lab with its functional techno-aesthetic. The neutral exterior look of a lab, an aesthetic of the anti-spectacle, is the frame for an interior that pays not only homage to Klein's blue and act of essential reduction. For Hershman, the *Room #8* haiku is "the very essence of a thought. And this is both a physical, spiritual, and intellectual essence of the research of genetic manipulation." It gradually dawns on the viewers who have read the description of the project's genesis that they are looking at the aesthetic of a treasure multiplied endlessly in a cabinet of mirrors. In other words, the vials are documents of a form of translation – film into DNA and letters into antibody – and the vials' content starts to unfold in their imagination. How can one re-translate film from DNA and what will the antibodies "do" in the future? The luxurious look of blue around this miniature hall of mirrors, a fitting display architecture for the artist's own work and name stored for eternity, speaks to a sense of drama as much as it is a tongue-in-cheek gesture towards the futility of eternal preservation.

So what is LYNNHERSHMAN then? LYNNHERSHMAN is the literal blueprint for the molecular code with which a real antibody was assembled. It is the chemical structure of amino acids and their symbols that exactly correspond to the artist's name.[11] This antibody LYNNHERSHMAN, we are told by Thomas Huber, the scientist from Novartis, is responsive and active while the conceptual counterpart, a second antibody experiment called ERTA, short for Roberta [Breitmore] because the letter O does not correspond to an amino acid symbol, is in fact "dead" or at least inactive so far. The "artist" is alive while the exorcised simulated character is still dead. And the artist interprets this unforeseen and unprecedented experiment half-jokingly with a biographical parallel: "Roberta was a manifestation of trauma. And the creation of Roberta allowed her creator to become healed. And that's what antibodies do. In a sense, they can heal a trauma. [...] The Hershman antibody is not really used because it bonds with everything. The Roberta antibody bonds with nothing and they [Novartis] aren't using that. The Hershman antibody likes everything. They never had one that liked everything. It can adapt to any condition, and Roberta is the opposite. She can't bond with anything which is sort of interesting. Roberta's relationship and bonding was limited to meetings with people so that she wouldn't bond. And I like too much, I do too much." And while we are equally unsure about the effects of art on the real world, after all these are hard to measure, the artist known as Lynn Hershman takes pride in the fact that the LYNNHERSHMAN Antibody is responsive, even if it is not the

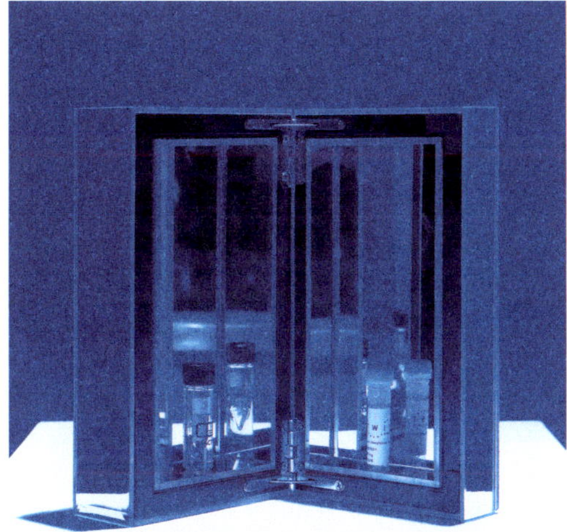

*Lynn Hershman Antibody,* 2018

medical alchemical gold or cancer cure she had hoped it might be. In her interpretation, "bonding" is a key term – it promises a process of healing while the artist claims to suffer from too much bonding? I am hesitant to speak of healing or curing in response to the future use of the LYNNHERSHMAN Antibody, but we cannot deny that it is responsive, it has agency and is thus metaphorically a promising artwork in real life.

And ERTA, the unresponsive antibody? ERTA is the final nail in the coffin of fictitious names used as playful detours to massage their environment as well as critically reflect it: From Juris Prudence, Herbert Goode, Gay Abandon – Lynn Hershman's first playful pseudonyms as art critics who nevertheless helped her built an artist's reputation – to the fictional identical characters of Ruby, Olive, and Marine in *Teknolust,* replicas of DNA and personifications of the three colors red, green, and blue of the electronic image spectrum, three virtual "leprechauns intent on self-realization beyond their creator's agenda."[12] These simulated characters all pale in comparison to the real molecular existence of LYNNHERSHMAN. Technically, this scientifically produced antibody was not created by the artist Lynn Hershman, but by the lab of the Swiss chemical giant Novartis, who collaborated on this experiment of creating a "medicine" without knowing what it might heal. The solution is looking for a problem to solve, not unlike an artist who produces a work without knowing whether it will have any meaning for or effect on the public at all. This is what Lynn Hershman likes about LYNNHERSHMAN. The name is active in real life.

We future citizens or scientists may be able to decode *Room #8* and its ingredients into yet unknown embodiments. The archived DNA and molecular substances are thus essential. They exist in real life and are not artistic gestures. The *Infinity Engine DNA* is the most advanced contemporary form of information storage and preservation for the future while the *Antibodies* are a generative program of yet unknown future connective processes, active agents with unknown effects. These two components of bioengineering assure the artist that she will have an active afterlife. Antibodies and Hershman's early responsive sound sculptures from the 1960s "only come to life when appropriate. They lay in a state of inertia until activated. They are not active all the time. They need the right conditions." Provided the two antibodies will be properly guarded and preserved in a safe scientific or museological environment, the responsive LYNNHERSHMAN Antibody will continue to be a catalyst for environmental, social, and political concerns that will emanate from the deep blue of *Room #8.* And with some probability, LYNNHERSHMAN will act like Ruby, Olive, and Marine in *Teknolust* intent on self-realization beyond her creator's agenda. The active bonding may turn out to be a blessing – maybe not for the artist but for future caretakers of the vial.

Conscious of an ultimately romantic desire in this utopian mise en scène,[13] I am reminded of the central scene in Andrey Tarkovsky's film *Stalker* (1979) in which the three protagonists have reached the center of the "zone," unable to take a further step into the vastness of sand dunes inside a building. There is nothing but sand in this vaulted endless space, but it is an epiphany of the end of the journey. It remains unclear how the three protagonists rejoin "real life" after this journey and it may remain unclear how the blue *Room #8* and the future application of the LYNNHERSHMAN Antibody may be useful, but both are poetic renderings of a journey towards consciousness and healing. Considering that she referred to herself as a witness to the events that were triggered by Roberta Breitmore – "One often survives trauma by making oneself a witness to it as it is happening, as a survival tactic"[14] – Hershman's career culminates in a celebration of active involvement, agency, and connectivity. A conscious loss of control, a central feature both in Roberta Breitmore as in the LYNNHERSHMAN Antibody, remains a key element of her aesthetic practice.

*Room #8* is not a crypt despite the fact that visitors can only look inside and only few people (members of a family for their crypt, and in a museum the conservator for the installation) have the key to unlock the interior. In a graveyard, impressive monuments and facades of crypts often suggest that their doors have never been opened once they were closed after the funeral. The dead bodies are locked away for good. The stone floor of a crypt does what it is supposed to do, and that is to keep the dead from coming back. *Room #8* is also not a mausoleum where an embalmed dead body is preserved for the public – there is, after all, no body, only an antibody. Lynn Hershman has this to say about her installation behind a locked door: "*Room #8* [is] a room you can't enter. We're always looking as artists towards that entrance/exit matrix. [...] It could be considered a performance over time because the encapsulated antibodies could be revived in 20 years. It's a preservative with the option of coming back. There is the possibility of making another entrance." We, the future scientists or conservators, would then interact with her and thus allow her to stay alive.

Linking this line of thought to art, the artist has made another logical conclusion: "I think art is an optimistic process, a process of belief."[15] The aesthetic morphology of Lynn Hershman – a term she had identified early on for her methodology – is in essence the art of producing systems of immunity against future toxins.[16] In *Room #8*, we learn, the cure might come for us but also for the artist. Preserving her own name, providing for a future comeback – this artwork is equally projection and for real: the condensation of a whole career of artistic experimentation into the real thing mesmerizing like the truthfulness of the evoked imagery in a haiku. The poetic image materializes in a vial made out of glass, a liquid material that manages to contain the dry granular powder of a name. The entire *Room #8* is thus a haiku about the ultimate alchemical transformation, where a vial is opened and life rises like Phoenix from the ashes. *Room #8* delivers on this utopian as well as spiritual transformation from death to rebirth as a real agent thanks to agent LYNNHERSHMAN. It is the artist laying the groundwork for her own future comeback, possibly in vain but too good to not believe in. In this perspective, "What is LYNNHERSHMAN?" is a question about not only but also *what* will have agency in the future. Conquering death in that way is not the worst outcome.

1 TV commercial for her site-specific installation *Forming a Sculpture Drama in Manhattan* (1974). All quotes by Lynn Hershman, unless cited with a footnote, are taken from an unpublished interview recording by the author in her studio in San Francisco on February 22, 2019.

2 I chose to refer to the artist, who changed her name to Lynn Hershman Leeson in 1992, by her original name to emphasize the continuity with her most recent artistic work *LYNNHERSHMAN Antibody* (2018).

3 LYNN HERSHMAN Antibody and ERTA Antibody Reveal, April 24, 2018.

4 Lynn Hershman (1992) quoted in *Lynn Hershman: Civic Radar,* ed. by Peter Weibel, exh. cat. ZKM | Zentrum für Kunst und Medien Karlsruhe, Ostfildern 2016, p. 110.

5 See also *Roberta Breitmore, An Alchemical Portrait Started in 1975, a cartoon* commissioned from Spain Rodrigues, 1978, and her dinner for Arturo Schwartz *The Alchemical Machination, or The Bird Striped Bare with Herb Batchlors, Even* [sic], an also orthographic parody of Marcel Duchamp's famous work *The Bride Stripped Bare by Her Bachelors, Even.*

6 See "haiku," *Merriam Webster's dictionary,* https://www.merriam-webster.com/dictionary/haiku (accessed April 11, 2019).

7 See the detailed medium description provided by the museum: "Mixed media assemblage: (exterior) wooden door, iron nails, bricks, and stucco; (interior) bricks, velvet, wood, parchment over an armature of lead, steel, brass, synthetic putties and adhesives, aluminum sheet, welded steel-wire screen, and wood; Peg-Board, hair, oil paint, plastic, steel binder clips, plastic clothespins, twigs, leaves, glass, plywood, brass piano hinge, nails, screws, cotton, collotype prints, acrylic varnish, chalk, graphite, paper, cardboard, tape, pen ink, electric light fixtures, gas lamp (Bec Auer type), foam rubber, cork, electric motor, cookie tin, and linoleum." *Philadelphia Museum of Art,* https://www.philamuseum.org/collections/permanent/65633.html?mulR=884479142|5 (accessed April 11, 2019).

8 See the photographic collage *Seduction* (1988) and a video titled *Seduction of a Cyborg* (1994), a poetic allegory about technology's invasion of the body and the destruction of the immune system.

8 These are a two-minute videotape, the file of the "Antibody Wallpaper," six archival digital photographs to be selected by the curator.

10 "I collapsed all the pertinent information of *The Infinity Engine* [and] my 'archive' which is *The Electronic Diary,* but put them into extreme low res to be able to afford it. In *The Infinity Engine* information, each jpg and text is on a single frame of the time line. Normal costs for doing this now are $20,000 per second, so I had to count on generous people and low res to do it and make it conceptually sound. [...] I insisted it be both conceptually sound as well as going through the transformation and conversion process which took 4 months." Lynn Hershman in an e-mail to the author, March 25, 2019.

11 The 20 natural amino acids that form the grammar of antibodies or immunoglobulins are commonly abbreviated by letters so that the LYNN-HERSHMAN Antibody corresponds to the following string of amino acids, the building blocks of protein: L (Leucine) – Y (tyrosine) – N (asparagine) – N (asparagine) – H (histidine) – E (glutamic acid) – R (arginine) – S (serine) – H (histidine) – M (methionine) – A (alanine) – N (asparagine).

12 *Ruby Rich* in *Civic Radar* 2016 (see note 4), p. 259.

13 Lynn Hershman wrote an essay, "Romancing the Antibody: Lust and Longing in (Cyber)space," first printed in *Cameraworks Magazine,* 1994, which looked at the digital construction of bodies.

14 *Civic Radar* 2016 (see note 4), p. 175.

15 *Civic Radar* 2016 (see note 4), p. 177.

16 See e.g. the *Alchemist Wand for the 21st Century (2011) - a wooden broom whose brushes have been dipped in 24-karat gold and modified to detect invisible toxins in local environments; readings are transmitted to a nearby screen allowing users to remedy the invisible toxicity of their location.*

## Defending Our Body

Our immune system protects us from foreign pathogens and helps recognise and fight malignancies, such as cancer, that originate from altered body cells. Antibodies are an essential component of the immune system enabling our body to identify potential threats as yet unknown. This is truly extraordinary. We are born with the ability to generate an incredibly large number of new and different antibodies on a daily basis. The immune system promotes antibodies that are able to neutralise foreign pathogens and eliminate non-functional or harmful antibodies. A complex process, that can be compared to the "Theory of Evolution by Natural Selection" by Charles Darwin and Alfred Russel Wallace – and this is happening every day in our body. Most of the time we don't notice it at all. Malfunctions of this process will have severe consequences – autoimmune diseases or cancer are two examples.

## Let Us Take a Closer Look at the Antibody Features

Antibodies are proteins and built up by chains of amino acids. There are 20 different natural amino acids, each one is typically abbreviated by a single letter. "L" for example, stands for Leucine (refer to Figure 1 for a full list of abbreviations). Four chains of around 1330 amino acids in total make up one antibody. These chains have a complex structure, but are often simply depicted with the symbol "Y". Most parts are identical amongst different antibodies. A tiny but crucial region at the tip of the "Y" is highly variable and different in every antibody. This tiny part, also referred to as "HCDR3" loop, is involved in the binding to the pathogen and highlighted in Figure 2. Nature is picking a particular amino acid string for each antibody. This process is not entirely random and some amino acids can be observed more often than others. The natural frequency of amino acids in the "HCDR3" loop correlates with the letter size in Figure 3. The amino acid sequence in this loop gives each antibody its individual functionality. Let us call it personality.

| Amino Acid | Letter | Amino Acid | Letter |
|---|---|---|---|
| Alanine | A | Methionine | M |
| Cysteine | C | Asparagine | N |
| Aspartate | D | Proline | P |
| Glutamate | E | Glutamine | Q |
| Phenylalanine | F | Arginine | R |
| Glycine | G | Serine | S |
| Histidine | H | Threonine | T |
| Isoleucine | I | Valine | V |
| Lysine | K | Tryptophane | W |
| Leucine | L | Tyrosine | Y |

Fig. 1: One letter abbreviation of the 20 natural amino acids

## The LYNNHERSHMAN Antibody Idea

While discussing natural antibody generation and antibody personalities during Lynn's visit at Novartis Institutes for BioMedical Research (NIBR), we came up with the idea of generating a truly personalised antibody. Defining the amino acid sequence of the key "HCDR3" loop to imprint LYNN HERSHMAN in the molecular structure, provides us with the "LYNNHERSHMAN-antibody". Theoretically, there is a chance – though a very tiny one – that one of us, or even Lynn herself, once generated this antibody sequence naturally in the body. Would it have had any function and increased our life quality?

Lynn's name offers the advantage that each letter can be linked to the abbreviation of one of the 20 natural amino acids. Scrabble players will notice that six letters of the alphabet, namely B-J-O-Q-U-X-Z, are not used as abbreviation of a natural amino acid, hence there is no amino acid string for ROBERTA BREITMORE or THOMAS HUBER or SABINE HIMMELSBACH. Why not work with nicknames instead? We came up with the ERTA representing Roberta. This leads us to the second design: the "ERTA-antibody".

## Making of the Antibody

Our immune system is clever and stores the blueprint of each useful antibody. This accelerates the immune response to pathogens attacking us a second time. We are likely not to get sick, we became "immune" to this particular pathogen.

DNA is the blueprint of antibodies. Specialized B- or plasma cells in our body are able to generate substantial amounts of antibodies according to those blueprints. Technological advancements make it feasible to synthesise a blueprint chemically. Immortalized cell lines, such as Chinese Hamster Ovary (CHO) cells or human embryonic kidney (HEK) cells, are used to produce recombinant antibodies outside the body, known as *in vitro.*

This procedure, shown in Figure 4, was applied for the LYNNHERSHMAN- and ERTA-antibody. In a cell culture flask, we cultivated 1-litre of HEK cells that produced sixty quadrillion (60'000'000'000'000'000) antibody molecules within about seven days. Due to the tiny weight of only 0.000'000'000'000'000'000'25 grams, this unbelievably large number of molecules manifests in only about 0.015 grams of purified antibody.

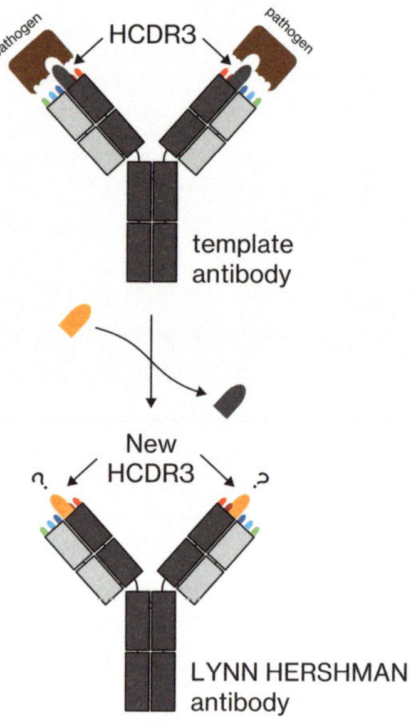


Fig. 2: Antibody cartoon in typical Y shape. Symmetrical molecule made up by 2 shorter (light grey) and two longer peptide chains (dark grey). Key loop (HCDR3) at the tips of the Y mediating antigen binding are colored in orange.
The DNA (antibody blueprint) encoding HCDR3 amino acid sequence of the template antibody (grey) was replaced with DNA encoding the amino acid sequence LYNNHERSHMAN (orange). In the same way, we generated an antibody containing the amino acid sequence ERTA as HCDR3.

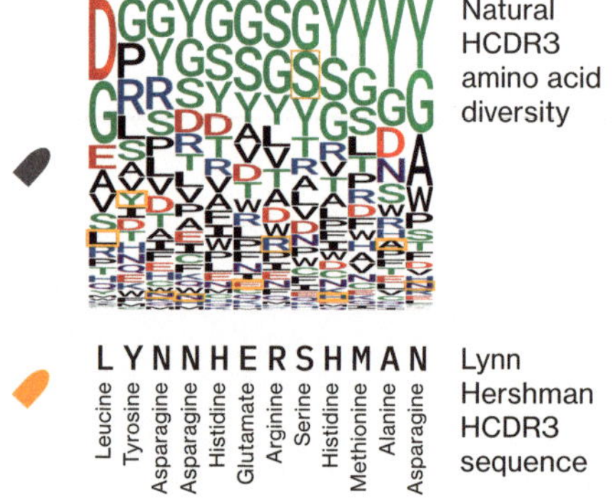


Fig. 3, upper panel: Occurrence of natural amino acid in the HCDR3-loop in single letter code. The size of the letter reflects the likelihood of the amino acid to be found at this position. Lower panel: Lynn Hershman amino acid string for HCDR3.

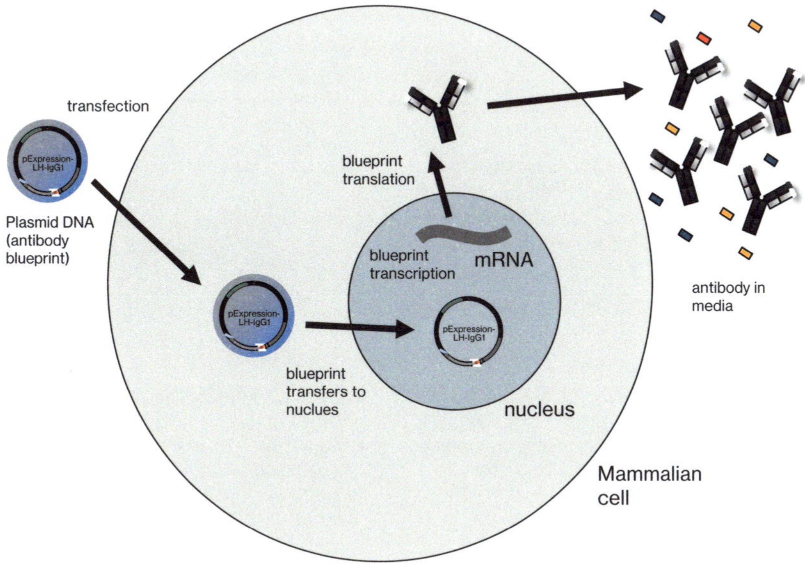


Fig. 4: Mammalian cell producing antibodies. Expression plasmid DNA (antibody blueprint) is transferred into a mammalian cell nucleus. Using the cell's own machinery antibodies are produced and secreted into the culture media.

## Antibody Structure

Antibodies can neither be seen by the eye, nor with the help of a microscope. One molecule is less than 0.000'005 mm. Sophisticated technologies, such as x-ray crystallography, are needed to visualise the structure. With some efforts, we were able to generate crystals of the scaffold antibody used as basis for the LYNNHERSHMAN and ERTA-antibodies and exposed them to an x-ray beam. We were able to reconstitute the structure of the antibody from the x-ray diffraction pattern by a mathematical procedure. The "HCDR" loop encoding the LYNNHERSHMAN or ERTA sequence was modeled into the structure using a modeling software to reflect a realistic three-dimensional conformation of the loop in the context of the whole antibody scaffold (Figure 5–8).

## The Experiment

The two loops, LYNNHERSHMAN and ERTA, differ significantly in size. What personalities will they provide, what function? Will they be different at all, considering the tiny portion of the antibody we changed? The answer has to be found by an experiment. Binding is the key function of an antibody. It has to bind and neutralise pathogens. We put around 7000 different proteins on a small CHIP and tested which one of them is bound by the antibodies. Therapeutic antibodies used to treat diseases bind exactly one antigen. Such antibodies are screened by their function. The amino acid sequence is initially unknown and is literally "discovered" during the process. The design of the LYNNHERSHMAN antibody reflects the inverse process so to speak. But it would be even more exciting, if the design also showed a particular function.

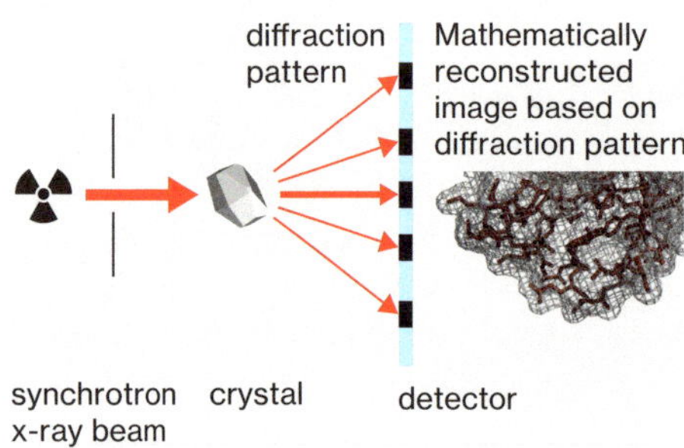


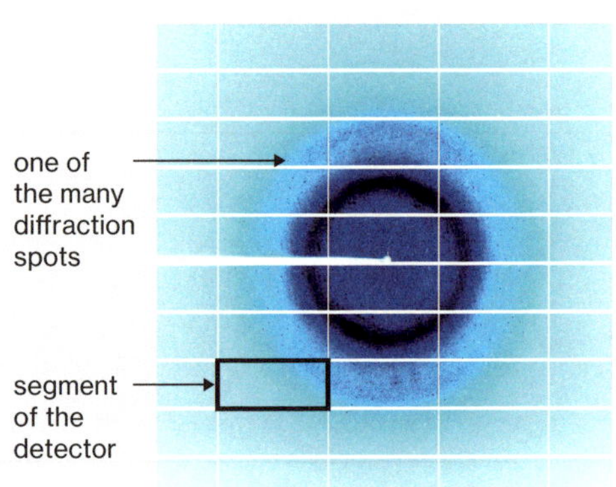


Fig. 5: Schematic representation of the process to obtain the 3D structure of an antibody. The synchrotron light source is a very stable and powerful source of x-ray beam. When the beam hits the crystal it is difracted. Based on the diffraction pattern, the structure of the antibody can be mathematically reconstructed.

Fig. 6: Diffraction pattern of a x-ray beam hitting a protein crystal. The crystal is brought with a holder into the beam (white line from the left). The position and intensity of the little dark spots are used to calculate the 3D structure of the protein. The detector is made up by different segments.

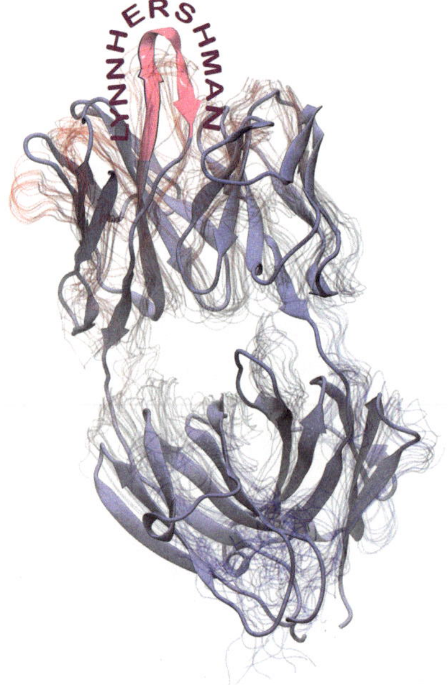


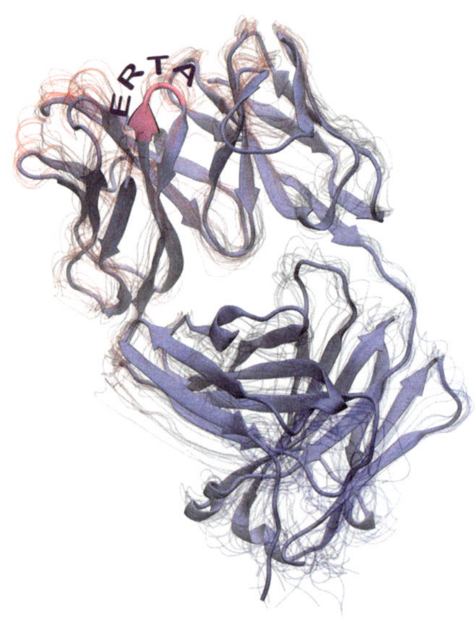


Fig. 7/8: In their native environment, antibody structures are not rigid but undergo conformational movements. Those movements can be simulated by molecular dynamics calculations. Such calculations are done by supercomputer clusters and can take weeks to simulate 1 millisecond of the conformational movement of the antibody structure. The long LYNNHERSHMAN loop has a very high conformational flexibility, whereas the ERTA loop, made as comparator, is virtually rigid. (by Ting Zhou)

## The Result

The two personalities could not be more different. The LYNNHERSHMAN-antibody binds the multitude, namely 2500 out of the 7000 proteins tested, whereas the ERTA-antibody does not even bind a single one. On the protein-CHIP in Figure 9 only the positive controls show up for ERTA. This is truly extraordinary, as it is not straightforward to design an antibody that has no function at all – and therefore conclusive proof becomes a rather philosophical task. Just think about it, while finding happiness seems difficult, it is easy to know what make us unhappy. Anyhow, despite this interesting observation, both antibodies will not be of any therapeutic use. The ERTA-antibody can possibly serve as a negative control in experiments during therapeutic antibody discovery.

The generation of LYNNHERSHMAN- and ERTA-antibodies still illustrated the overall process and the personality difference a little loop can make. To Lynn's question whether an antibody is intelligent or not, our answer is yes. Not only the evolutionary process to protect us from new diseases is, but also the antibody architecture itself is clever. Variation of just a few amino acid loops provides the lifesaving diversity of antibody personalities in a highly resource efficient way.

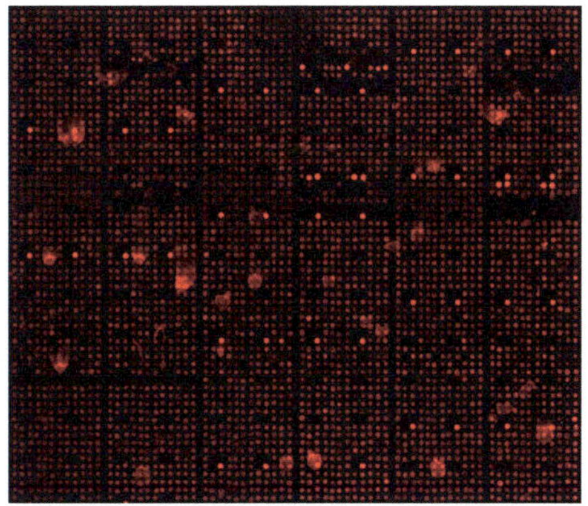

LYNN HERSHMAN antibody:
weak binding to many proteins

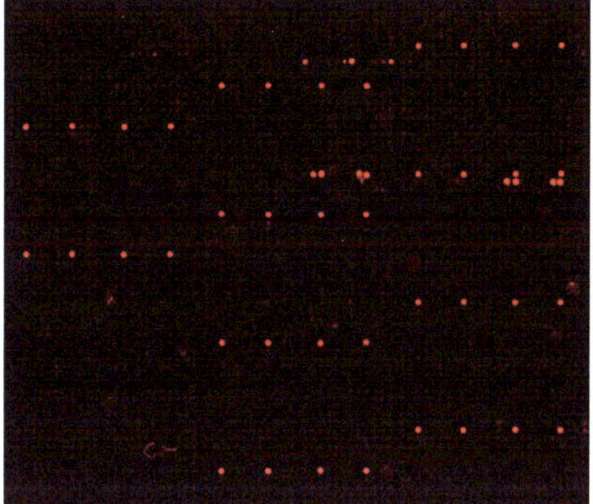

ERTA antibody:
only CHIP control spots

Fig. 9: Protein binding assessment by protein CHIP. Picture shows a representative part of the whole protein CHIP. Protein binding profile of the LYNN HERSHMAN (top) and ERTA (bottom) antibodies. No binding to any of the spotted proteins seen for ERTA. Binding to around 2600 proteins on the CHIP was observed for the LYNN HERSHMAN antibody. Those represent about 35% of the around 7000 proteins present on the CHIP.

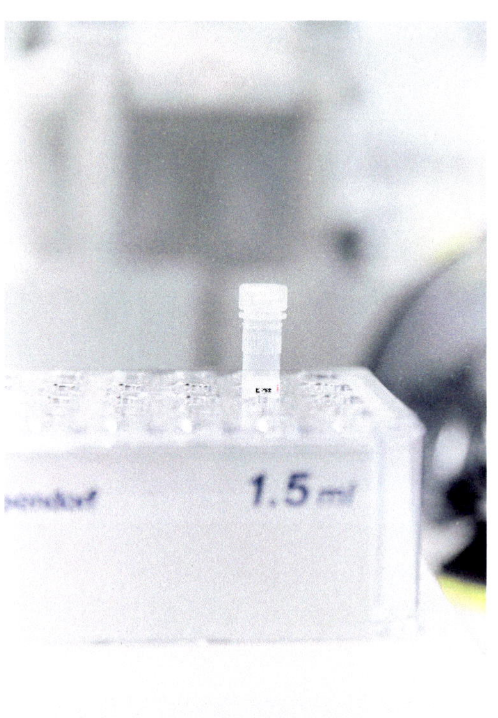


Fig. 10: Tube containing the blueprint of the Lynn Hershman antibody.

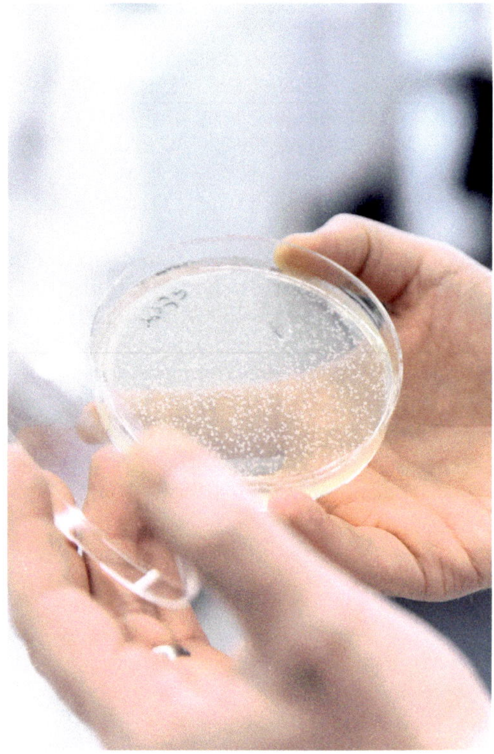

Fig. 11: E.coli bacteria colonies. Amplification of the blueprint.

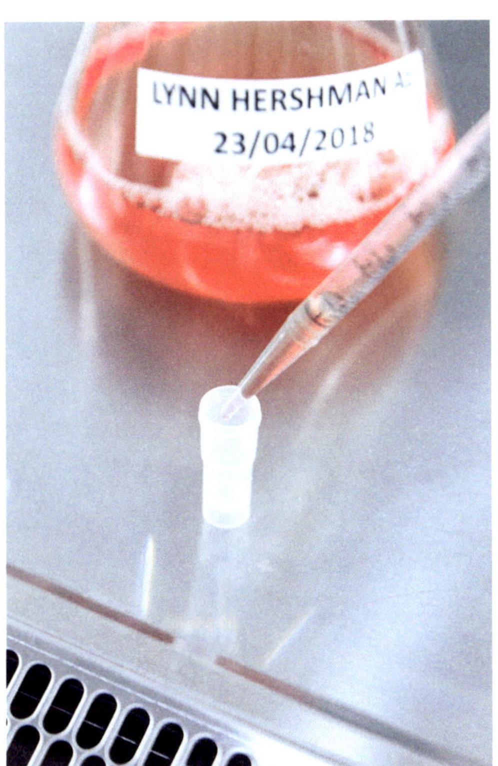


Fig. 12: Mammalian cells were transfected with the blueprint.

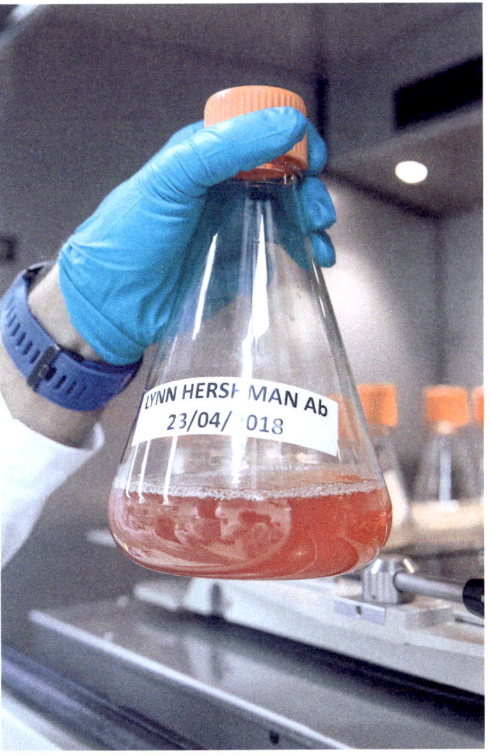


Fig. 13: Cultivation of transfected mammalian cells producing Lynn Hershman antibodies. Antibodies can be purified from the culture media.

The LYNNHERSHMAN-antibody project required a multitude of specialists and I would like to thank you all for your contribution:
Sandra Schlüchter[1], Lionello Ruggeri[1], Ting Zhou[1], Agostino Cirillo[1], Xavier Leber[1], Barbara Brannetti[1], Brendan Kerins[1], Brigitte Menary[1], Regis Cebe[1], Remi Boeuf[1], Meike Scharenberg[1], Mauro Zurini[1], Frederic Villard[1], Christian Schleberger[1], Claude Logel[1], Adriano Marra[1], Jean-Michel Rondeau[1]
Lynn Hershman Leeson[2], Boris Magrini[3] and Sabine Himmelsbach[3]

1 Novartis Pharma AG, Basel, Switzerland
2 LYNNHERSHMAN.com, San Francisco
3 HeK, House of Electronic Arts Basel, hek.ch

# George Church interviewed by the artist

The interview with George Church (GC), professor of genetics at Harvard Medical School and professor of health sciences and technology at Harvard and the Massachusetts Institute of Technology (MIT), was conducted by Lynn Hershman Leeson (LHL) on March 23, 2017 at Harvard Medical School in Boston, Massachusetts. The discussion centered on regeneration and the archiving of materials onto DNA.

LHL What is it that you do?

GC For most of my career, we've been developing exponentially improving technologies to read and write DNA. [And finding a way to] put those together into a system for archival storage of digital and analogue information seemed like a natural thing to do in 2012. We can store the information either in biological systems or in completely non-biological systems. When stored that way, in the best possible way, the information is probably stable for a million years. Nothing changes in a desiccated form. If information is stored in biological systems, it's usually intended for much shorter-term storage, meant to interface with complex systems like the brain or medical systems, like a black box recording. In that case, we don't really care how stable they are as long as they accurately reflect the physiological state as a function of time.

LHL Is it true that you are archiving film now by converting it into DNA?

GC Yes. My lab, Microsoft, and Technicolor have stored a number of videos in DNA. In fact we've encoded a 1902 film into digital format first. and then digital zeroes and ones and put those into As, Cs, Gs and Ts, because zeros and ones are essentially very easily mappable onto As, Cs, Gs and Ts; but we can also go directly from analogue data into DNA.

LHL And what about projecting it or reconverting it?

GC Showing it is the same as showing a digital film. So, in a digital film there are no photons inside your disc drive. The DNA is reconverted so that it can be read off the disc drive and then projected onto a screen or displayed on a monitor.

LHL What films have you restored this way?

GC We have converted this 1902 movie, *Trip to the Moon,* to digital zeros and ones and then to DNA, and then back to zeros and ones, and then back to a displayable movie and you can't tell the difference. It's exactly the same colors, and sound, and so on.

LHL Why that film?

GC It was chosen by Technicolor... It was possibly their most precious film, in that the director and producer [Georges Méliès] became disillusioned towards the end of his life and tried to destroy all of his films. Everyone thought he had destroyed this classic, which was the first colorized film. Each frame was hand colored with transparent paints. They eventually found a copy that wasn't in great shape, and so they restored it manually, and with great labor. Then they made digital backups, but they're in the business of archiving. This is something that they wanted to archive in a way that would be as permanent as possible. And so as long as we're a DNA-based life form, it's likely we'll be able to read DNA. That's the idea.

LHL Doing this kind of work is utopian. Do you see yourself as an optimist?

GC Yes, there's an optimistic side and a pessimistic side. The idea of having to store something in a form that would persist for a million years presupposes that we're going to lose our current technology or maybe our civilization and then have to recover it. So that's the negative scenario. The same thing goes for extraterrestrial surgery: It might be premised with the fact that we need to get off the planet because we're sitting ducks for asteroids and super volcanoes if we keep all of our eggs in this one planetary basket. Nevertheless, on the positive side, this work has opened opportunities because if we leave the planet, we might leave with a small enough number of people, well enough funded, that it would be feasible to eliminate all pathogenic microorganisms or possibly all microorganisms. It might also be necessary and possible to reduce radiation and gravitational sensitivity, and maybe even pain sensitivity, at least for a short period of time. You can turn pain on and off in a way that doesn't make you dopey, as typical anesthesia and opiates do, because there's a known genetic mechanism whereby people are born insensitive to pain. It's a risk factor if you're always insensitive to pain, but when it comes to a surgery, you could in principle, do something without anesthesia, without antibiotics, without sterilization, and you could just walk in in your street clothes and be cut open, or even cut yourself open. These are all interesting possibilities you start thinking about when you consider the necessity of us getting off the planet. What are the opportunities for changing ourselves and meeting new needs in the future?

LHL Do you think it will be essential to move to an unpolluted planet, one that is sustainable?

GC I think the motivation for getting off the planet is not necessarily to avoid pollution. I mean pollution is a characteristic of life, not just of human life. If you look far enough back, the atmosphere had essentially zero oxygen originally. Photosynthetic organisms polluted the atmosphere till it was 21% oxygen, which is toxic to many, many life forms. That was big time pollution in the dawn of life. Humans will almost certainly pollute subsequent planets because our population grows. If our population grows, then at a minimum, we're polluting the planet with human beings, even if we don't pollute it with hydrocarbons and toxic atmosphere, and so forth. That's not why I think we should leave the planet. The reason we should leave the planet is that the planet will be destroyed by an asteroid or a super volcano, eliminating all the work that we've put into our intelligence and civilization. So we need to have colonies all over the place. The further away the better.

LHL What are some of the other dangers for this planet?

GC We've already had several volcanoes, and asteroids that have hit the planet, destroying many species by obscuring all light from coming to the planet. You cut off photosynthesis, you cut off most of the resources of food. It would, at a minimum, endanger civilization and it could cause biological extermination if the impact is big enough.

LHL So you anticipate a possible unknown entity that could cause a massive extermination or urgent need to migrate away from Earth?

GC Unknown – that's the point. It could be thousands of years from now, or it could be tomorrow. We just had a fairly close encounter with an unexpected asteroid. It was undetected until alarmingly late. It was small and it was far away, but still alarming. How fast could we get off the planet? Well, I think we've got priorities. If we focus on diseases of developing nations, and poverty, and raise up everybody's standard of living, then we'll have more wealth to spend on this rather than having it be the competing situation we have right now. But I wouldn't be surprised if we get off the planet within the next century in terms of viable, sustainable colonies where people don't expect to come back. Could be sooner.

LHL Do you think human nature causes many of the devastations, particularly climate disasters and pollution, that we are experiencing now?

GC Human nature has changed. For the most part not genetically. I don't draw a sharp line between genetic and non-genetic inheritance. We inherit things like our ability to travel on jets, and travel into space, and use computers, and so forth. That's as surely inherited as our eye color. In fact, in some cases, probably a little better inherited. Inheritance is more penetrant. We will continue to change; the fastest and most impactful evolution today is cultural evolution, and culture now includes technology. Technology now includes genetics. Our genetics might catch up to the speed and impact of culture because it is now part of culture. For the first time in history, if we have a good idea, it can spread through the Internet in a day. If it involves manufacturing, it spreads via the Internet and other resources in a year. DNA can't spread that fast [through procreation]. You know it takes twenty years for every cycle of innovation.

LHL What do you see as our options?

GC It's important to accompany each new technology with a lot of education and dialogue. It's not a one-way street. It requires listening as well as communicating, letting people know that this technology is available. The technology can be brought down radically in price. We've seen that already with cell phones, computers, Internet searches, DNA reading and writing. All of these things come down to the point where they're almost free. They come along with advertisements or similar products. People need to know the benefits and the risks involved.

LHL How are these choices made? Who controls them?

GC Decisions are made in the usual collection of less than ideal, higgledy-piggledy decision making that includes politics, economics. It's mostly influenced by market forces. If some clever entrepreneur can think of a reason why seven billion people should have access to cell phones, there will be seven billion cell phones. The same thing for DNA. If they can find a reason why seven billion people could benefit, whether or not they can afford it, somebody in the system will figure out how to get it to them if there's a financial benefit. I think that's how the decisions are made de facto; whether or not the particular locality or nation or United Nations makes a decision is probably less predictable than the people speaking their economic needs and demands.

LHL How do we contain and archive culture?

GC I think it's very important that we keep track of history in an archival sense, in a living sense. That may not be the top priority, but it's one of the reasons for de-extinction, one of the reasons for frozen zoos. It's better if we can keep it as an intact ecosystem, because we don't know enough about ecosystems to recreate them from frozen storage and we may not have the will to do so. But to the extent that we can keep historical versions and living versions of everything, cultures, languages, we really have to preserve our technological progress, refuges, archives.

LHL Optimists look at risks and find solutions to potential dangers, right?

GC Well, I worry about everything, but I wouldn't classify myself as an optimist particularly. I mean if I were a complete optimist, then there's no reason to do technology, because we're all set, you know! There's no problem with having nine billion people on the planet. So, we don't need to do anything. There's no problem with emerging diseases. There's no problem with diseases of civilization. So, I'm a pessimist on all those, and I think that's why doing nothing is not a great option.

LHL Exactly what an optimist would say.

GC Not only do I worry about everything; I try to encourage everybody else to worry about it, too. It's one way of engaging the public, and even if it weren't a particularly good way, it's important that they know about it. And as technologists, we have a better view of it. Some scientists don't consider that it's necessary to convey that view. But I do. I think it is important to do it as soon as possible. So, if we over-anticipate problems, that's much better than under-anticipating them. So, for example, it was predicted that it would take six decades before we could read the human genome for hundreds of dollars, and instead it took six years. I think that there may be many other things like that that threaten us. I worry about natural problems like super volcanoes. I worry about unnatural problems that aren't particularly technological at this point, like the size of our population. It has origins in technology; the green revolution allowed us to double our previous population limits. And I worry about enabling technologies that allow the average citizen or very small numbers of citizens to have powers that only nations would have in the past, or maybe nobody had them. It used to be that one person couldn't do that much damage, but now with nuclear, biological and chemical weapons, one person can have an impact. In particular, this applies to biological weapons, because they can be spread from a single cell, or a single virus, and one person can invent something that's of global significance. I think that, again, to do nothing is not an option. You have to be proactive. You have to come up with technologies that are good at surveillance, that are good at removing some of the psychological and social motivation for abusing existing technologies.

LHL And how do you see that manifesting?

GC Certainly diagnostics is a kind of surveillance, but the surveillance I'm talking about in the pessimistic view of the future is surveillance on the environment for emerging diseases. We want to do surveillance on all researchers, official or unofficial, as to what they're doing, whether or not they want you to know what they're doing. No one has the right to do whatever they want with synthetic biology. They all should be under surveillance. But there are many positive aspects of surveillance. I think we're going to get better and better at having distributed surveillance throughout our bodies that will anticipate and help us to practice preventative medicine.

LHL I totally agree with this: It is an internal biological surveillance system that reads information that is not normally seen. Is this done through cells or sensors?

GC In particular, sensors that read out new infectious agents can help us stop epidemics at patient zero. We don't have to wait until there are a million people flying around in airplanes spreading their contagion. We can stop it as soon as we see it.

LHL That would be a remarkable advancement.

GC We are getting a little bit better at diagnostics. I think it's one of those paradoxical things where we have the technology to do a lot better diagnostics than we currently do; but in standard medical practices, if you have a respiratory infection, you are treated but, typically not diagnosed. And that has to do with the perceived realities of the relative costs of diagnostics and treatments.

LHL How would you envision this?

GC Some of the current sensors can take a little saliva and run it through a DNA sequencer and you can get a readout of all the viruses and bacteria in your mouth, or any other part of your body, or in the air. That tends to be slow, but we're getting faster. You could actually sense this readout as you walk into a room: you can see whether you're allergic to the space, whether it contains pathogens or not, whether you've been vaccinated against those pathogens. All those could be like real time, part of your cell phone network. We have the technology to do some of that slowly, but it's improving rapidly and exponentially.

LHL Is there a way to be able to tell when and where something is created that could be a threat to other life forms?

GC There's fairly good international agreement on diagnostics and especially on therapeutics, because they can really mess you up if they haven't gone through proper double blind, placebo controlled randomized clinical trials, the gold standard of the FDA and equivalents internationally, the EMA in Europe, and the CFDA in China, and so forth. They don't let you try out a new drug without going through the correct protocol, ideally with animal testing first. You can't even use new drugs on an individual basis, because they don't want people hurting themselves.

LHL And what about being able to track life formed through CRISPR editing? To understand on a global scale what exactly is being created and track these new living systems?

GC Well, CRISPR is not unique in any sense. It's not particularly more accessible than previous therapeutics. You know you can go out and get Oxycontin without a prescription. I mean it's illegal. But the law is hard to enforce. It's a numbers game. You're trying to keep the public health risk to a minimum. If you're not producing addictive drugs or harmful drugs, then the risk is lower. It still will be regulated. I think the key is coming up with drugs that are just as desirable as the ones that are illegal but safer and more effective. One of the goals of the FDA and other agencies worldwide is to come up with safer and more effective drugs. And then there's no motivation to use them any way other than the proper way.

LHL What kind of restrictions do you envision being put into place? How would they function?

GC There are restrictions on almost everything. If you alter an animal in the wild, you're actually restricted by three agencies in the United States; the FDA, the EPA (Environmental Protection Agency), and the U.S. Department of Agriculture. In some cases, they're looking out for the welfare of the engineered organism, which is a little odd when you're talking about mosquitos. You don't really care that much about the welfare of mosquitos. You want to make sure that the ecosystem doesn't depend on them in some way.

LHL I have been told that there are no regulations right now. Is that true?

GC It's regulated internationally. In fact, many of the proposals to engineer wild species with, say, gene drives, CRISPR gene drives, those will cross international borders. And when you know in advance they're going to do that, then you need to get international harmony on that topic beforehand. If you override that step, then there will probably be agencies that will reverse what you did, and hunt you down, and there are consequences.

LHL How do these regulations prevent the creation of new life forms?

GC You can certainly create them. You can't deploy them. As soon as you deploy them, it's detectable. And that's why I think surveillances should be one of our top priorities. The earlier we detect new life forms, the earlier we can start reversing them.

LHL Exactly how does this happen?

GC You have a sensor network, which can include animal, or plant sensors, mechanical, electrical sensors; if they're cheap enough, they can be distributed worldwide and they can have real time monitoring and you should be able to detect the very first instances of something that's unusual, and you have to know what you're looking for to some extent. But even any change in the natural frequencies of things could tip you off that something is happening.

LHL Well that's a relief. A lot of people I've talked to seem to not know about these systems of detection.

GC They are very primitive, but yes – the CDC has a network of stations and physicians, and samples, if they have an unusual patient. But that could be so much more cost effective and medically effective if every person had their own personal sensor, or maybe had several personal sensors, just like the average United States citizen has multiple electronic devices.

LHL I see. And what is the oversight of these sensor networks?

GC It's not absolutely uniform and absolutely enforced, but there's general agreement as to what the goals are. And furthermore, when you're talking about business, it is international. When Google decided it wanted to do Street View internationally, it had to get local permission to run its automated cameras up and down the streets of every country. Some allowed it, and some didn't. There was a whole patchwork of decisions. But for the most part, it's an international deliverable, and it's out there now: You can get Street View and Google Maps for almost every place in the world.

LHL All driven into being by optimists like you.

GC I would say it takes fairly minimal optimism to not be paralyzed by pessimism. And I would say that I've achieved that level. It's not that there are no solutions. There are just a lot of problems. In fact, the creative process in this case is being stimulated to work on solving problems... In fact, I would say I'm even pessimistic about the technologies because we often will launch five different technologies in a particular direction knowing that four of them will fail. If we were optimistic, we'd just say, "Oh, this is going to work, right." Super optimistic would be "I don't need to do anything, just leave it the way it is, let it evolve." Slightly more optimistic would be "Yeah, something is going to work, but not everything. So I have to try a lot of different things."

LHL When did you become interested in biological and computer interventions?

GC I've been interested in the intersection of biology and computers since I was ten years old. I worked first with crystallography of genetic material. So, it wasn't quite genetics, but it soon became obvious that the best use of skills and computer science and biology was going to be genetics. And that's both reading and writing DNA, and essentially reading and writing everything biological, from organs to ecosystems, to precision medicine.

LHL I think of this as the art form of our time.

GC Right. In fact, one of my post-docs describes his field as sculpting evolutions.

LHL I totally agree.

GC It's a four-dimensional sculpture that includes every part of our ecosystem.

LHL And time.

GC Right. That's the fourth dimension, time.

# Lynn Hershman Leeson in conversation with Sabine Himmelsbach



The conversation between Sabine Himmelsbach (SH) and Lynn Hershman Leeson (LHL) took place via e-mail in January and February 2019.

SH In your artistic carrier you always have been interested in current societal developments and technological innovation. Living in San Francisco, have you been inspired by the technological advancements and developments in Silicon Valley?

LHL I think in the Bay Area you cannot help but be aware of the dynamic shifts going on, changes that have migrated and affected the entire globe. Things like Connectivity and Uber and AirBnB, Google and Facebook. But even before, the history is there: In fact, television was invented in San Francisco so it really is in the subliminal consciousness of the region.

SH What triggered your interest in biotechnologies and when did you start to work on the topics evolving around it, like regenerative medicine, gene editing, etc.?

LHL In 2006 I began a quest to educate myself on this subject. It was shortly after the genome was programmed. But my research became more intense around 2011, after I finished *!W.A.R.* and *Strange Culture* and began to think about what really was important in the global strategies for survival. At that point I started directly interviewing scientists in creating the works that became *The Infinity Engine;* works that dynamically reshaped our idea of the self and identity, but from the inside out.

SH Your film *Strange Culture* is very political. It's dedicated to the true story of Steve Kurtz, a member of the Critical Art Ensemble, who has been detained by the FBI under suspicion of bioterrorism since his wife unexpectedly died in her sleep of heart failure. The petri dishes and scientific equipment that paramedics found in their home made them suspicious of him. The artists collective had been working with genetically modified food at that time to generate awareness among a broader public and help them understand the principles of the technology itself. Your film openly questions governmental policy and I think has also helped to support Steve Kurtz during his trial.

LHL Yes, I felt it was critical to do this, to help another artist. I did not know Steve at the time, but felt it was essential that we create a vehicle to tell this story to many people. Steve has himself said the film helped end his possible 23-year jail sentence.

SH In your work centered around biotechnologies you are also advocating for a better understanding of these technologies among the broader public – inviting them to look behind the usually closed doors of the scientific lab. Would you discuss the artistic form you chose for *The Infinity Engine*? I am thinking of the lab context, but also the appropriation of scientific materials, such as the wounded warrior poster that you found in a genetics lab or the bio printed nose that you received from Dr. Anthony Atala from the Wake Forest School of Regenerative Medicine.

LHL Yes, I like to use reality in the work because it is often more surreal than anything I could make up or fictionalize, and it gives a different edge.

SH In your exhibition *Anti-Bodies* at HeK (House of Electronic Arts Basel) you finalized your complex multi-room installation, *The Infinity Engine,* after years of working on it. Had you envisioned the concept for all eight rooms from the very beginning, or did it develop in the course of production?

LHL I always envisioned eight rooms in my original drawings. An "8" on its side is infinity and it is always the double helix, so one way or another I wanted all the information to be formatted that way.

Fortunately, we ended up with eight distinct elements, which was perfect.

SH Does the finalization of *The Infinity Engine* represent the conclusion of your interest in investigating biotechnologies as a subject for your work? Or is it still a frontier that needs more reflection and exploration?

LHL It's absolutely not the conclusion. I'm going to make a feature film about ramifications I discovered researching the installation, particularly genetic scarring or epigenetics.

SH Sounds like you are adding another layer to your work dealing with questions of identity! You coined the term "Anti-body" in connection with your work back in 1996, in your text "Romancing the Anti-Body: Lust and Longing in (Cyber) space." At that time you were relating to a fragmented body with experiences in the real and virtual space of the then new Cyberspace of the Internet. Now, for the exhibition at HeK, Dr. Thomas Huber, Senior Researcher at the NIBR – Novartis Institutes for BioMedical Research of the company Novartis Pharma AG, developed an antibody that bears your name in its molecular structure.

LHL Yes, I think LYNNHERSHMAN antibody and ERTA antibody are important, not only in the idea of identity but in identity from the inside out!

SH Your work has in many ways developed around the question of identity and now one could say a biological dimension has been added. In earlier works you "mutated" your persona yourself, as you described it in an interview. Now a pharmaceutical company has produced "your" antibody. Can you explain how the idea for this radical project developed and what it means to you that such an antibody exists?

LHL It means a lot because it inverts identity, it attaches from the inside out, it is not a body but a reframing of the biological essence of who we are, and is also a device to attack toxins in our environment, which essentially is what artists do anyway.

SH When we first met Dr. Thomas Huber we talked a lot about antibodies and their therapeutic function. I remember that he mentioned that an antibody is an illustrative example of how something like evolution takes place every day in our bodies. In your writing and work you claim that the antibody has a therapeutic quality for culture itself. Can you reflect on that?

LHL Yes, it is a motivation for artists to seek out the toxins that destroy culture; to neutralize the negative effects of repression. And this is done through art itself. Sometimes overtly, sometimes subtly. So doing this biologically gives it an even deeper resonance and meaning.

SH One room in *The Infinity Engine* is dedicated to the current state of biological surveillance. Surveillance has been an important topic throughout your work, moving from electronic surveillance in works like *CybeRoberta* from the mid 1990s, a biological surveillance enabled by facial-recognition systems, in which eyes have been replaced with cameras to *The Infinity Engine.* Can you talk a bit more about this work and the shift towards biological surveillance of our bodies?

LHL I think surveillance now takes place in the cellular level, where our histories can be accessed and detected via the archive of our DNA.

SH The eighth and last room of *The Infinity Engine* displays the LYNNHERSHMAN antibody in a glass vial behind the closed bars of a laboratory door. Next to it, visitors can find another glass vial that contains four nanograms of DNA with all the digital files of the show (images and videos) stored on DNA. Their digital code has been transformed into biological code. Can you explain the process and why you chose to transfer *The Infinity Engine* onto DNA?

LHL It was the logical thing to do. It was the poetic essence of the project, simmered into invisible archival storage. It had not only the files from the exhibition but also the electronic diary that is the archive of my life. This is the future, I believe, for manipulated life and archiving our histories. I loved that all the work from over a decade could be reduced to such a minute, intense size. To me, it was like a *haiku* of the universe.

SH *The Infinity Engine* covers a decade of research, as you say, and it follows biotechnological advances and developments. The installation enables the audience to get a deeper understanding of current scientific progress and also shows the ambivalence and concerns that one might have, including the ethical questions that need to be dealt with, etc. You show both sides, the dark and the light. In a short video that accompanies the presentation of the DNA and antibody you end with a clip from your earlier film, *Conceiving Ada,* in which you have Tilda Swinton as Ada Lovelace say: "The redeeming gift of humanity is the ability of each generation to recreate itself." It's a hopeful ending for *The Infinity Engine.* So would you describe yourself as an optimist?

LHL Totally. I think that is what artists are. Like antibodies themselves. finding toxins or dangers. And if successful, they use hope and optimism to cure them.

# Lynn Hershman Leeson LYNNHERSHMAN Antibody and ERTA Antibody Reveal

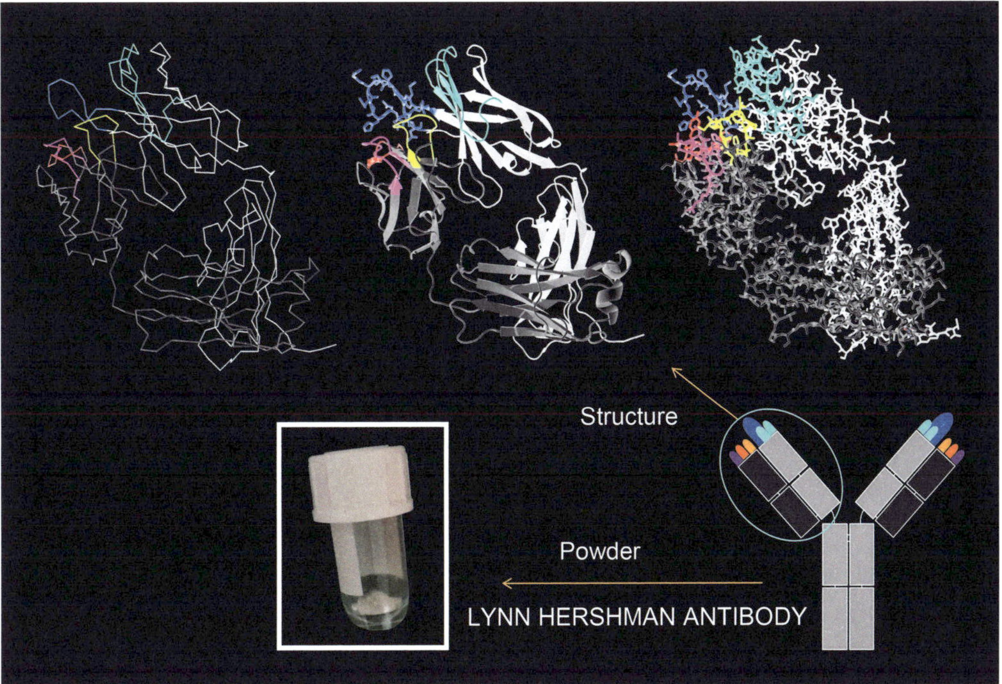


Fig. 1: Structure of the LYNNHERSHMAN Antibody visualized using PyMOL and presented as powder in a glass vial.

The Antibody Project was consummated in October, 2018 in a conceptual union between Dr. Thomas Huber, the therapeutic antibody research group leader at Novartis Labs, Basel, and the artist Lynn Hershman Leeson that would result in the production of an antibody inspired by leading scientific research to be featured in the final version of *The Infinity Engine,* an art installation about the state of DNA manipulation and the impact on society particularly the implications of how bioengineering is altering our concept of identity. Beside their widely known role as immune molecules and vaccines, antibodies have become a central tool for biotechnology and biomedicine. The Antibody Room would feature the development of an artificially engineered antibody that bears the name "Lynn Hershman" in its molecular structure. A second antibody, "ERTA", based on Hershman's identity based project Roberta Breitmore was simultaneously developed.[1]

Hershman notes that "Anti-bodies identify, expose and transform toxins in culture. These same issues have permeated my work for the past 50 years. An antibody is a basic representation of identity; a reactive molecule capable of being reactive against oneself, an inverted biological gesture that has as its goal healing from the inside out, a cyborgian dream of infiltrating the body itself in an attempt to create a radical and curative recovery." (Fig. 1)

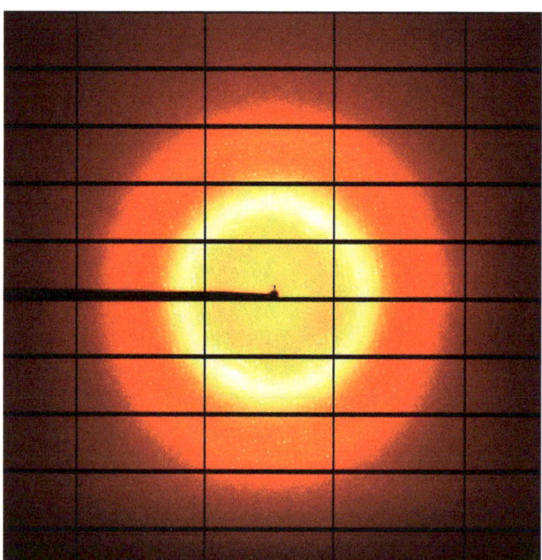

Fig. 2: X-ray diffraction pattern from a protein crystal. Bright spots are caused by diffracted x-rays that hit the detector surface.

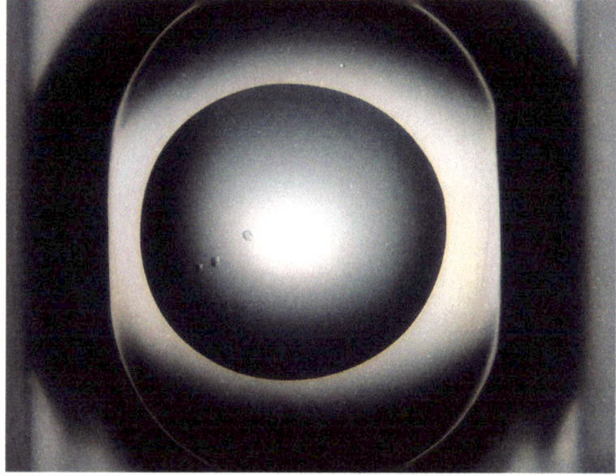

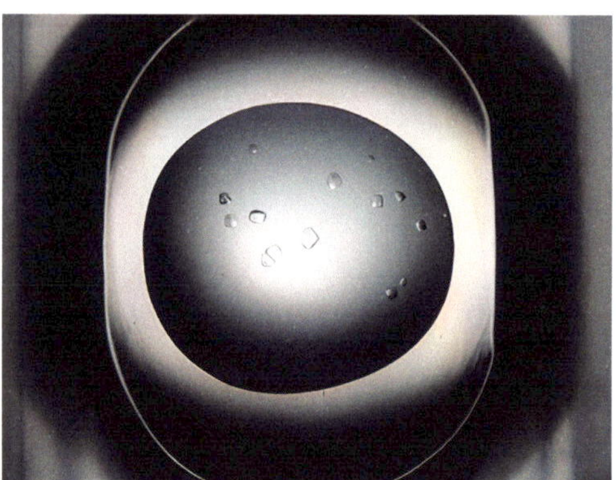

Fig. 3/4: Protein crystals at two different times of growth, after 1 hour and 16 hours.

After the antibody was designed it was subjected to a series of research experiments to discover its properties and potential therapeutic or research applications. The LYNNHERSHMAN antibody consists of four protein chains with a total of 1,334 amino acids. For the exhibition around sixty quadrillion molecules were produced, an unimaginably large number. Because antibodies are extremely small, this only amounts to about fifteen milligrams. Antibodies can't be seen with the naked eye or an optical microscope. The spatial structure of proteins is calculated by x-ray refraction. Harvesting both antibodies took four months. The properties were exposed through diffusion x-rays. (Fig. 2)

A few weeks before the "birth" of the antibodies, they were measured in time sequences exposing protein crystals used for x-ray structure analysis to derive a #D structure of the antibody-antigen interactions, taken by a robot camera at different time points that follow the actual growth of the antibody. (Fig. 3/4)

## Conclusion

Both the LYNNHERSHMAN antibody, and ERTA antibody could readily be produced and the biophysical properties were quite promising. LYNNHERSHMAN is quite strong (99%) and shows a lot of integrity. ERTA is even stronger, with even more integrity. LYNNHERSHMAN antibody was capable of binding to a broad variety of proteins (approximately 2600 out of 7000). In a stark contrast, the ERTA antibody shows superior production and biophysical properties but will NOT bind to any of the assessed 7000 proteins. It's inability to attach to anything is extremely unusual. This project will be uploaded online and be subjected to further tests for eventual functionality.

*The Infinity Engine* has been exhibited beginning May 3 at HeK (House of Electronic Arts Basel) and the Riga Biennial as of June 2, 2018 and the Guangzhou Triennial December 2018.

1 An antibody identifies toxins in culture and then attempts to neutralize or erase them. Roberta Breitmore and later Roberta's viralized representative multiples illuminated the rampant toxins of sexism in her 1970's era. By the mid 1980s antibody photographs appeared. See: Lynn Hershman Leeson, Romancing the Antibody, Lust and Longing in Cyberspace, exh. cat., Seattle Art Museum (Seattle, 1995).

Further reading: Thomas Huber, "Generation of the Lynn Hershman Leeson Antibody," www.diaphanes.net, April 10, 2018, https://www.diaphanes.net/titel/generation-of-the-lynn-Hershman-antibody-5613 (accessed February 13, 2019). Meritxell Rosell, "Lynn Hershman Leeson & Thomas Huber: anti-body or antibody?", CLOT Magazine (April 18, 2018), http://www.clotmag.com/lynn-hershman-leeson (accessed February 13, 2019).

# Lynn Hershman Leeson
# Artist biography



Lynn Hershman Leeson, born 1941 in Cleveland, Ohio, lives and works in San Francisco and New York. She studied at Case Western Reserve University and at San Francisco State University. Hershman Leeson is professor emeritus at the University of California and was A.D. White Professor at Cornell University.

With a keen sense of the key issues of our time, media artist and filmmaker Lynn Hershman Leeson investigates socially relevant issues such as the relationship between humans and technology, identity, surveillance, and the use of media as a tool of empowerment against censorship and political repression. Over the last forty years she has made pioneering contributions to the fields of photography, video, film, performance, installation and interactive as well as net-based media art. Since the 1970s, her works have been shown in over 200 international solo and group exhibitions, e.g. at the Berkeley Art Museum, the De Young Museum, San Francisco, The Museum of Modern Art, New York, The National Gallery of Canada, Ottawa, Kunsthalle Bremen, Lehmbruck Museum, Duisburg, The Cleveland Museum of Art, The Modern Art Oxford or KW Kunstwerke Berlin. In 2014–15, a comprehensive retrospective of her work from the mid-1960s to current productions was shown at the ZKM | Zentrum für Kunst und Medien in Karlsruhe. In 2017, the Yerba Buena Center for the Arts in San Francisco also hosted a major retrospective of her work.

Hershman Leeson published the groundbreaking documentary *!Women Art Revolution* in 2011, which has been shown internationally in many major museums and was recognized by the Museum of Modern Art as one of the three best documentaries of the year. Hershman Leeson wrote, directed and produced the feature films *Strange Culture, Conceiving Ada* and *Teknolust,* starring actress Tilda Swinton. Her are all in worldwide distribution and have screened at the Sundance Film Festival, Toronto Film Festival and The Berlin International Film Festival, among others.

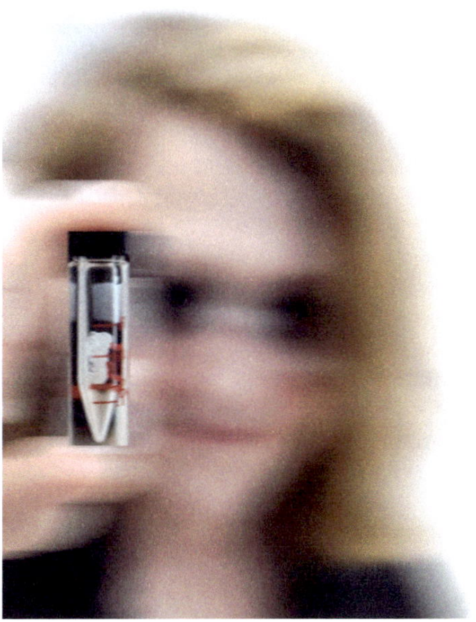

Lynn Hershman Leeson showing her antibody

She was awarded the Alfred P. Sloan Foundation Prize for writing and directing *Teknolust. !Women Art Revolution* received the Grand Prize Festival of Films on Art.

Lynn Hershman Leeson is a recipient of a SIGGRAPH Lifetime Achievement Award, Prix Ars Electronica Golden Nica, and a John Simon Guggenheim Memorial Foundation Fellowship. In 2017, she received a USA Artist Fellowship, the San Francisco Film Society's "Persistence of Vision" Award and will receive the College Art Association's Lifetime Achievement Award.

Artwork by Lynn Hershman Leeson is featured in the public collections of The Museum of Modern Art, The San Francisco Museum of Modern Art, the ZKM | Center for Art and Media, the Los Angeles County Museum of Art, The Tate Modern, The National Gallery of Canada, and the Walker Art Center in addition to many celebrated private collections.

See also: www.LYNNHERSHMAN.com

## George Church [1]

George Church is Professor of Genetics at Harvard Medical School and Director of PersonalGenomes.org, which provides the world's only open-access information on human Genomic, Environmental and Trait data (GET, see: http://www.getconference.org/). His 1984 Harvard PhD included the first methods for direct genome sequencing, molecular multiplexing and barcoding. These led to the first genome sequence (pathogen, *Helicobacter pylori)* in 1994. His innovations have contributed to nearly all "next generation" DNA sequencing methods and companies (CGI-BGI, Life, Illumina, Nanopore). This plus his lab's work on chip-DNA-synthesis, gene editing and stem cell engineering resulted in founding additional application-based companies spanning fields of medical diagnostics (Knome/PierianDx, Alacris, AbVitro/Juno, Genos, Veritas Genetics) and synthetic biology / therapeutics (Joule, Gen9, Editas, Egenesis, enEvolv, WarpDrive). He has also pioneered new privacy, biosafety, ELSI (ethical, legal, social implications), environmental and biosecurity policies. He is director of an IARPA BRAIN Project and NIH Center for Excellence in Genomic Science. His honors include election to NAS & NAE & Franklin Bower Laureate for Achievement in Science. He has coauthored over 500 papers, 143 patent publications and one book (see: Church, George, and Ed Regis. *Regenesis. How Synthetic Biology Will Reinvent Nature and Ourselves.* New York, 2014).

1 The biographical information comes from: George Church, genetics.hms.harvard.edu/, January 12, 2019, http://arep.med.harvard.edu/gmc/ (accessed March 3rd, 2019).

## Rudolph Frieling

Rudolf Frieling received an M.A. from the Free University of Berlin and a Ph.D. from the University Hildesheim, Germany. He was appointed Curator of Media Arts at the San Francisco Museum of Modern Art in 2006 where he curated major survey exhibitions such as *The Art of Participation: 1950 to Now* (2008–09) on the history of contemporary participatory practice and *Stage Presence: Theatricality in Art and Media* (2012) on the crossover between visual and performing arts. Most recently, he co-curated the retrospective *Bruce Conner: It's All True* (2016) which toured to the Museum of Modern Art, New York, and the National Museum Reina Sofia, Madrid, and *Soundtracks* (2017), SFMOMA's first large-scale exhibition dedicated to artists working with sound and space. He also co-curated the survey of *Rafael Lozano-Hemmer: Unstable Presence* (2018–20) and is a co- curator of the retrospective *Suzanne Lacy: We Are Here* (2019), a pioneer in the field of social practice. Prior to his tenure at SFMOMA, Frieling worked at ZKM | Center for Art and Media in Karlsruhe, Germany, as a curator and researcher from 1994 to 2006. He was project director and co-editor of a book and multimedia series on the history of media art *Media Art Action* (1997), *Media Art Interaction* (2000) and the online archive *Media Art Net* (2004–05) as well as the restoration/publication project *40yearsvideoart.de* (2006). Frieling is also an Adjunct Professor at the California College of Arts. He lives and works in San Francisco.

Sabine Himmelsbach

Since March 2012, Sabine Himmelsbach is the new director of HeK (House of Electronic Arts Basel). After studying art history in Munich she worked for galleries in Munich and Vienna from 1993–96 and later became project manager for exhibitions and conferences for the Steirischer Herbst Festival in Graz, Austria. In 1999 she became exhibition director at the ZKM | Center for Art and Media in Karlsruhe. From 2005–11 she was the artistic director of the Edith-Russ-House for Media Art in Oldenburg, Germany. Her exhibition projects include Fast Forward (2003); Coolhunters (2004); Ecomedia (2007); MyWar (2010) and Culture(s) of Copy (2011). 2011 she curated gateways. Art and Networked Culture for the Kumu Art Museum in Tallinn as part of the European Capital of Culture Tallinn 2011 program. Her exhibitions at HeK in Basel include Sensing Place (2012), Semiconductor: Let There be Light (2013), Ryoji Ikeda (2014), Poetics and Politics of Data (2015), Rafael Lozano-Hemmer: Preabsence (2016), unREAL (2017), Lynn Hershman Leeson: Anti-Bodies and Eco-Visionaries (2018). As a writer and lecturer she is dedicated to topics related to media art and digital culture.

Thomas Huber

Dr. Thomas Huber is a research group leader at Novartis NIBR Biologics Center in Basel. His current role is technology leader and co-project team leader for multispecific-antibody modalities. In 2012 to 2013, he was appointed project team leader at Respiratory Disease Center in Horsham, UK. Since he joined Novartis in 2007, he has established several global technology platforms in the field of therapeutic antibody and protein engineering. Dr. Huber received his PhD in the group of Prof. Andreas Plückthun at the Department of Biochemistry of the University of Zürich and holds a Master in Biochemistry and Immunology from the University of Zürich.

*The Infinity Engine*
(Lab Poster 1)
2014
Inkjet-Print
53,3 × 66 cm
Courtesy ZKM | Center for Art and Media

*The Infinity Engine*
(Lab Poster 2)
2014
Inkjet-Print
66 × 53,3 cm
Courtesy ZKM | Center for Art and Media

*The Infinity Engine*
(Lab Poster 3)
2014
Inkjet-Print
53,3 × 66 cm
Courtesy ZKM | Center for Art and Media

*The Infinity Engine*
(Photography of laboratory vessels)
2014
Inkjet-Print
28 × 21,5 cm
Courtesy ZKM | Center for Art and Media

*The Infinity Engine*
(Syringe)
2014/2018
2 channel video installation, loop
Courtesy Bridget Donahue Gallery, New York; Anglim Gilbert Gallery, San Francisco; Waldburger Wouters Gallery, Brussels; ShanghART, Shanghai/Beijing/Singapore and the artist

*The Infinity Engine*
(Bio Printing)
2014
Video
2:50 min
Courtesy the artist

*The Infinity Engine*
(Artifacts of Bio Printing)
2014
Plastic, glass, wood
67,5 × 125 × 15 cm
Courtesy ZKM | Center for Art and Media

*The Infinity Engine*
(3D-Printed Nose)
2014
Synthetic material
10,2 × 10,2 cm
Courtesy ZKM | Center for Art and Media

*The Infinity Engine*
(Jellyfish Feline)
2014
Color photograph
65,2 × 54,5 cm
Courtesy ZKM | Center for Art and Media

*The Infinity Engine*
(Crops/Animals/Labs)
2014
Wallpaper
290 × 1750 cm
Courtesy the artist

*The Infinity Engine*
(Aquarium Glowfish)
2015
Video
10 min
Courtesy ZKM | Center for Art and Media

*A Perfect Archive.*
George Church interviewed by Lynn Hershman Leeson
2017
Video
7:03 min
Courtesy the artist

*Facial Recognition System*
2018
Apple Mac mini, USB camera, mirror
Dimensions variable
Courtesy Bridget Donahue Gallery, New York; Anglim Gilbert Gallery, San Francisco; Waldburger Wouters Gallery, Brussels; ShanghART, Shanghai/Beijing/Singapore and the artist

*The Infinity Engine*
(Artifacts of Antibody Creation)
2018
Various laboratory tools
Courtesy Novartis Pharma AG and the artist

*Lynn Hershman Antibody*
2018
Antibody, glass vial
4,8 × 1,4 × 1,4 cm
Courtesy Novartis Pharma AG and the artist

*Lynn Hershman Data Storage*
2018
300 ng DNA, plastic vial
4,7 × 1,2 × 1,2 cm
Courtesy the artist

*Strange Culture*
2007
Video
74:54 min
Courtesy the artist

## Sabine Himmelsbach
## Vorwort

Vom 3. Mai bis zum 5. August 2018 wurde am HeK, Haus der elektronischen Künste Basel, die Ausstellung *Lynn Hershman Leeson: Anti-Bodies* gezeigt. Sie war einem aktuellen Werkzyklus der amerikanischen Künstlerin und Filmemacherin Lynn Hershman Leeson gewidmet: den Biotechnologien und deren Bedeutung für die Gesellschaft und den Menschen. In ihrer künstlerischen Laufbahn beschäftigtsich Hershman Leeson mit dem Zusammenspiel von Technologien, Medien und Identität und der sich verändernden Beziehung zwischen Körper und Technologie. Hershman Leesons Oeuvre umfasst Fotografie, Film, Video, Objekte und Installationen, Computer basierte Kunst, Software und Performance. Sie spürt in ihren Werken seit den 1960er Jahren den bahnbrechenden technologischen Entwicklungen und deren Auswirkungen auf unsere Vorstellungen von individueller Identität und Einzigartigkeit wie ein Seismograph nach. Schon zu Beginn ihrer Karriere thematisierte sie den Menschen als Cyborg, als ein Mischwesen, durchdrungen von Technologie. In den 1970er Jahren kreierte sie mit Roberta Breitmore eine fiktive Figur, die ihr als Alter Ego diente. 1984 schuf sie mit *Lorna* die erste interaktive Videodisk, die ein Eingreifen des Publikums in die Geschichte der Protagonistin Lorna ermöglichte. In den 1990er Jahren widmete sie sich in zahlreichen Werken den Veränderungen, die das World Wide Web mit sich brachte, beschäftigte sich mit Fragen der virtuellen Realität und gehörte zu den ersten, die sich bereits damals mit künstlicher Intelligenz auseinandersetzten. Anfangs der 1990er Jahre prägte Hershman Leeson in ihrem Werk den Begriff des »Anti-body«, der sich auf ihre Recherchen und Werke hinsichtlich einer virtuellen Identität im Cyberspace bezog. Tatsächlich brauchte es keinen physischen Körper mehr, wie noch bei Roberta Breitmore, um eine fiktive Identität im globalen Netzwerk anzunehmen. Hershman Leesons Anti-Körper verstand sich als virale Präsenz im Internet und manifestierte sich in künstlichen Intelligenzen wie ihrer Online-Persona *DiNA.*

Die rasanten Entwicklungen im Bereich der Biotechnologien sieht Hershman Leeson als die zentrale Herausforderung unserer Zeit. Diesen Entwicklungen spürt sie angefangen mit dem Film *Strange Culture* von 2007 seither in zahlreichen Werken nach. Die Ausstellung am HeK fokussierte auf diese Auseinandersetzung mit Biotechnologien. Seit mehreren Jahren schon arbeitete Hershman Leeson an ihrer komplexen Installation *The Infinity Engine,* in ihrer großen Retrospektive *Civic Radar* am ZKM | Zentrum für Kunst und Medien in Karlsruhe in Teilen erstmals zu sehen war und die in der Ausstellung am HeK zum Abschluss gebracht werden konnte.

Basel als Zentrum der Schweizer Pharmaindustrie erschien dabei als idealer Ort für dieses Themenfeld. Es war ein Glücksfall, als sich der Forscher Dr. Thomas Huber, Senior Investigator am NIBR Biologics Center der Novartis Pharma AG, zu einem Austausch mit Hershman Leeson bereit erklärte. Aus diesem künstlerisch wissenschaftlichen Austausch entstand ein eigenes Projekt, die Entwicklung des Antikörpers LYNNHERSHMAN durch die Forschungsgruppe von Dr. Thomas Huber. Die Entwicklung und Testphase des neuen Antikörpers nahm in der Ausstellung eine fundamentale Rolle ein und gehörte zu den zentralen neuen Räumen von *The Infinity Engine.* Wie Hershman Leeson oft betont, war der Abschluss ihrer komplexen Installation erst durch die neuesten biotechnologischen Entwicklungen der letzten Jahre möglich – von der Nutzung der DNA als biologischem Speicher bis hin zu einer individualisierten Medizin. Die Ausstellung zeigt diese Entwicklungen – ihre Chancen und ethischen Herausforderungen – anhand von zahlreichen Statements führender Wissenschaftlerinnen und Wissenschaftler auf. In der Inszenierung der acht Räume von *The Infinity Engine* gelingt es Hershman Leeson in ihrer künstlerischen Interpretation und Aneignung einen Blick hinter die Kulissen des wissenschaftlichen Labors als Ort der Wissensproduktion zu werfen. Sie führt vor Augen, wie sich die Grenzen zwischen natürlichem und künstlichem Leben im Zeitalter synthetischer Biologie zunehmend auflösen und Leben heute synthetisch geformt und manipuliert werden kann. Es liegt an uns, diese Zukunft im besten Sinne zu gestalten.

Dieses ambitionierte Projekt wäre nicht möglich gewesen ohne die Zusammenarbeit mit der Novartis Pharma AG. Ich möchte mich an dieser Stelle herzlich bei Dr. Thomas Huber und seinem Team bedanken. Durch ihre Aufgeschlossenheit und Bereitschaft konnten neue Wege beschritten und ein für beide Seiten inspirierender Dialog angestoßen werden. Bedanken möchte ich mich auch bei Sandra Schlüchter, Head NIBR Basel Communications, für die kommunikative Begleitung des Projekts. Durch eine großzügige finanzielle Unterstützung der Novartis Pharma AG wurde es möglich, die Ausstellung mit dieser Publikation zu dokumentieren. Ein Dank dafür geht an Martin Furler Bassand, Global Art Curator der Novartis Art Collection.

Ein weiterer Dank für die großzügige Unterstützung der Ausstellung geht an die Ernst und Olga Gubler-Hablützel Stiftung.

Danken möchte ich auch den Leihgebern der Werke, insbesondere dem ZKM | Zentrum für Kunst und Medien in Karlsruhe und den Galerien der Künstlerin,

Waldburger Wouters in Brüssel, Bridget Donahue in New York und Anglim Gilbert Gallery in San Francisco.

Ein besonderer Dank gilt aber Lynn Hershman Leeson für ihr großes Engagement und ihre Leidenschaft, mit der sie dieses Projekt vorangetrieben hat. Es war eine inspirierende und bereichernde Erfahrung, gemeinsam diese einzigartige Ausstellung entwickeln zu dürfen.

# Sabine Himmelsbach
# Lynn Hershman Leeson: Anti-Bodies

»I try to live in the present, because most people live in the past. If you live in the present, most people think you live in the future, because they don't know what happens in their own time.«
Lynn Hershman Leeson[1]

Die amerikanische Künstlerin und Filmmacherin Lynn Hershman Leeson wird zu Recht als Porträtistin des Informationszeitalters beschrieben, als eine aufmerksame Beobachterin der Protokolle und Institutionen, die unsere Vorstellungen von Identität und Individualität prägen werden.[2] Wie ein Seismograph reagiert sie in ihrer Kunst auf gesellschaftliche Entwicklungen und besonders auf Veränderungen, die mit dem technologischen Fortschritt einhergehen. Schon zu Beginn ihrer Karriere zeigte sie in den1960er-Jahren in ihren Cyborg-Zeichnungen und -aquarellen den Menschen als Zwitterwesen aus Mensch und Maschine. Persönliche Traumata und bahnbrechende technologische Entwicklungen prägten ihr Werk gleichermaßen in der unablässigen Auseinandersetzung nach dem Verständnis von Identität und Individualität. Die Auswirkungen von Medientechnologien und die mit ihnen einhergehenden neuen Möglichkeiten sozialer Interaktion wurden immer wieder Thema ihrer Werke. In ihrer Touch-Screen-Installation *Deep Contact* (1984) wurde der Screen zum Fenster in eine virtuelle Welt, die uns seither allgegenwärtig begleitet. Der zunehmenden Virtualisierung der Welt und unseren fiktionalen digitalen Identitäten spürte sie in ihren Arbeiten *Agent Ruby* (1996–2002) und *DiNA* (2004) nach. Diese und andere Werke reflektierten auch die Entstehung des World Wide Web und die damit einhergehende globale Konnektivität. Immer wieder gehörte Hershman Leeson zu den Pionierinnen der Kunst, die mit neuen Technologien experimentierten. So schuf sie mit *Lorna* (1984) die erste interaktive Video-Disk-Installation, in der die Betrachter_innen aktiv in den Handlungsverlauf eingreifen und die Geschichte der Protagonistin mitbestimmen konnten.

In den letzten Jahren beschäftigte sich Hershman Leeson aufs Neue mit den fundamentalen Auswirkungen des technologischen Fortschritts auf den Menschen. Die bahnbrechenden Entwicklungen der Biowissenschaften brachten radikale Veränderungen für unser Verständnis des Selbst mit sich, nachdem Leben gestaltbar wurde. Die Möglichkeiten, Chancen, aber auch ethischen Grenzen der Biowissenschaften lotet Hershman Leeson in ihren aktuellen Werken aus. Für die Planung der Ausstellung *Anti-Bodies* 2018 am HeK (Haus der elektronischen Künste Basel) war es also schlüssig, sich ganz auf diesen neuen Werkkomplex, der die regenerative Medizin, die Genforschung und die Antikörperforschung gleichermaßen umfasst, zu fokussieren.[3]

Als Anfangs- und Referenzpunkt der Ausstellung am HeK setzten wir den Film *Strange Culture* (2007), der auf einer wahren Begebenheit beruhte und Hershman Leesons intensives Interesse an den Biotechnologien weckte. Der inszenierte Dokumentarfilm *Strange Culture* war ein Plädoyer für künstlerische Freiheit und ein Statement der Unterstützung für einen Künstlerkollegen. Der Film basierte auf der Geschichte des Künstlers Steve Kurtz, einem Mitglied der Künstlergruppe *Critical Art Ensemble,* der nach dem unerwarteten Herzversagen und Tod seiner Frau unter Anklage wegen des Verdachts des Bioterrorismus geriet, weil in seinem Haus Petrischalen und andere wissenschaftliche Geräte gefunden wurden, die für die biologische Forschung verwendet werden. Hershman Leesons Film re-inszenierte die Geschichte dieser Begebenheiten mit Schauspieler_innen, ließ aber auch die Betroffenen in Interviews selbst zu Wort kommen. Ihr Film half Kurtz in seinem Gerichtsverfahren und zeigte auf, welche staatliche Paranoia im Umgang mit Biotechnologien nach den Anschlägen vom 11. September 2001 in den USA herrschten. In der künstlerischen Arbeit von Steve Kurtz, die der BioArt zuzuordnen ist, geht es darum, einer breiten Bevölkerung Zugang zu aktuellen Methoden und Praktiken der Biotechnologie zu vermitteln. Diese »Black Box« biotechnologischer Entwicklungen entwickelte sich auch für Hershman Leeson zum Gegenstand einer langjährigen Auseinandersetzung.

Angelpunkt der Ausstellung am HeK wurde die komplexe mehrräumige Installation *The Infinity Engine,* die sich mit Gentechnik, DNA-Manipulation, der Produktion transgener Organismen und der regenerativen Medizin befasst und nun mit der Reflexion zentraler neuer wissenschaftlicher Erkenntnisse ihren Abschluss fand. Das Projekt hatte seine Anfänge bereits 2014 in Hershman Leesons umfassender Retrospektive *Civic Radar* am ZKM | Zentrum für Kunst und Medien in Karlsruhe. Die ersten vier Räume der Installation wurden bereits dort gezeigt. In *The Infinity Engine* zeigt Hershman Leeson auf, wie sich die Grenzen zwischen natürlichem und künstlichem Leben im Zeitalter synthetischer Biologie zunehmend auflösen und Leben künstlich gestaltet werden kann. Oder wie der Medientheoretiker Peter Weibel im begleitenden Katalog zur Ausstellung *Civic Radar* schreibt, »Hershman Leeson's work redefines the nature of human identity in the Information Age.«[4]

Schon Gottfried Wilhelm Leibniz beschrieb den lebendigen Körper als eine »Maschine der Natur«.[5] Die Natur ist eine »Infinity Engine«, eine unendliche Maschine, die unzählige Variationen und Entwicklungen ermöglicht und deren evolutionärer Prozess täglich in unseren Körpern ausgetragen wird. Die modernen Biotechnologien erlauben nun, den Menschen selbst und seine evolutionären Prozesse aktiv zu gestalten.

Ihre langjährige Beschäftigung mit Fragen nach Identität und Individualität führt Hershman Leeson in ihrer aktuellsten Arbeit anhand der Biopolitik fort. In *The Infinity Engine* ahmt sie ein funktionsfähiges Genetiklabor nach und ermöglicht anhand von acht Räumen einen kritischen Blick auf die komplexen Entwicklungen der Biowissenschaften – von der regenerativen Medizin, den komplexen Verzweigungen des Experimentierens mit dem Genom bis hin zur Verwendung von DNA als biologischem Speichermedium.[6] Die Zahl »8« verweist auf Unendlichkeit und erinnert an die Doppelhelix, die gedrehten Stränge der DNA, der ›Software des Lebens‹[7]. Im Folgenden möchte ich kurz auf die acht Räume von *The Infinity Engine* eingehen.

Raum 1: Zugang zum Labor

Mit dem Betreten der Ausstellung wurden die Besucherinnen und Besucher eingeladen, einen Laborkittel anzuziehen und in die Rolle eines Wissenschaftlers zu schlüpfen, dem es erlaubt ist, die schwere Labortüre zu öffnen und hinter die sonst für Laien verborgenen Räume des wissenschaftlichen Labors zu treten. Den Eingangsbereich bildeten entsprechend immersive Projektionen, die eine Laborsituation inszenierten: Gänge und wissenschaftliche Produktionsstätten, die überall sein könnten und keinen Bezug auf einen speziellen Ort nehmen, sondern das Labor als den erkenntnistheoretischen Ursprung der modernen Life Sciences und den Ort heutiger Wissensproduktion definieren. Mit diesem »Ortswechsel«, der das Museum zum wissenschaftlichen Labor werden lässt, zeigt Hershman Leeson die Notwendigkeit auf, sich mit neuen Erkenntnistheorien und der Logik des technisch-wissenschaftlichen Regimes vertraut zu machen, wie die Kulturwissenschaftlerin Ingeborg Reichle in einem Text zu den ersten vier Räumen von *The Infinity Engine* schreibt.[8]

Raum 2: Bio Printing

Der wiederum erste Raum innerhalb des ›Labors‹ war den Techniken der regenerativen Medizin sowie der künstlichen Herstellung menschlicher Organe mittels 3D-Bioprinting gewidmet. Der Raum beinhaltete mehrere Gerätschaften, die in der regenerativen Medizin zum Einsatz kommen. Zu sehen war außerdem ein Videointerview, das Hershman Leeson mit Dr. Anthony Atala führte. Atala ist einer der Forscher, die die Methode des 3D-Bioprinting entwickeln haben. In dem Video werden zwei Fallstudien von Menschen vorgestellt, deren Lebensqualität durch das Bioprinting von Organen wesentlich verbessert wurden. Als zentrales Objekt war eine dreidimensionale Gewebe- und Zellstruktur in Form einer menschlichen Nase ausgestellt, die Hershman Leeson als wertvolles Museumsobjekt in einer Glasvitrine auf einem Sockel präsentiert.[9] Die Errungenschaften der regenerativen Medizin inszeniert Hershman Leeson in einer ganz eigenen Ästhetik, wobei sie sich bestehende Materialien aus der Wissenschaft wie »Readymades« aneignet und in den Kunstkontext überführt.

Die Möglichkeiten der regenerativen Medizin leiteten eine Entwicklung ein, an deren Ende der Mensch die Fähigkeit der Schöpfung selbst in die Hand genommen hat. Nicht mehr die Natur allein ist eine »infinity engine«, eine unendliche Maschine, sondern der Mensch wird zum Herrn über die Schöpfung, zum ›Homo Deus‹, wie der israelische Historiker Yuval Noah Harari schreibt.[10] Für diese Konstruierbarkeit von Leben schuf Hershman Leeson mit ihrer Videoinstallation *Infinity Engine (Syringe)* (2018) ein eindrückliches Bild, das sich auf das berühmte Fresco der Schöpfung von Michelangelo in der Sixtinischen Kapelle bezieht, in der Gottes Finger den Menschen berührt und ihm damit Leben einhaucht. In Hershman Leesons Version sind die Hände durch Injektionsnadeln ersetzt.

Raum 3: Gentechnik / CRISPR Mutationen

Ein weiterer Raum thematisierte die aktuellen spektakulären Entwicklungen, die mit der Manipulation des genetischen Erbguts möglich wurden.[11] 1953 stellt der amerikanische Biologe James D. Watson zusammen mit dem englischen Physiker Francis Crick die Struktur der DNA als Doppelhelix vor, wofür sie 1962 mit dem Nobelpreis ausgezeichnet wurden. Seit 2003 gilt das gesamte menschliche Genom als entschlüsselt. Inzwischen sind individuelle Genanalysen für wenig Geld per Internet-Bestellung möglich geworden. Diese Entwicklungen trugen dazu bei, dass Individualität oder das Selbst stärker als je zuvor auf die DNA zurückgeführt werden, wie der Schriftsteller Markus Jansen in seinem Buch *Digitale Herrschaft* schreibt.[12]

Mit der Entwicklung der sogenannten ›Genschere‹ CRISPR-Cas9 in den letzten Jahren wurde es möglich, das Erbgut jedes beliebigen Organismus auf einfache Art und Weise zu bearbeiten und zu verändern. Wie sehr unser Planet bereits von genmanipulierten Organismen bevölkert ist, zeigt Hershman Leeson auf, indem sie eine Wand vollständig mit einer Wandtapete, *Infinity Engine (Crops/Animals/Labs)* (2014), auskleidete, die eine Palette von Hybridkulturen und unzählige Bilder von genmanipulierten Tieren und Pflanzen und den Laboren, in denen diese produziert werden, enthält. Aufgelistet werden auch die Motivationen, die für die Produktion ausschlaggebend waren – von der Resistenz gegenüber Schädlingen bis hin zur erhöhten Nahrungsproduktion bei Getreide beispielsweise. Ein Video von transgenen leuchtenden Zebrafischen in einem Aquarium, *Infinity Engine (Aquarium Glowfish)* (2014) oder das Bild einer leuchtenden Katze, *Infinity Engine (Jellyfish Feline)* (2014), beide entstanden durch hinzugefügte Gene von Quallen, machten bewusst, wie umfassend die Errungenschaften der Gentechnik bereits eingesetzt werden. Organismen sind heute nichts anderes als digitale Information, bestehend aus einer vierstelligen »Software des Lebens«[13], die umgeschrieben und neu codiert werden kann. So bezeichnet der Transhumanist Ray Kurzweil DNA auch als den »Nano-Computer« der Natur.[14]

Raum 4: Ethik

Diese neuen Möglichkeiten bzw. Machbarkeiten gehen einher mit komplexen ethischen Fragen. Entsprechend widmete sich der anschließende Raum den ethischen Fragen hinsichtlich Genetik und Biopolitik. Besucherinnen und Besucher hatten hier die Möglichkeit, Hershman Leesons Sammlung juristischer Dokumente und Informationen zu genetischen Patenten nachzulesen, die in Zusammenhang mit der Gentechnik stehen und die die ethische Dimension des Themas verdeutlichen. So wird von der Künstlerin auch das moralische Dilemma angesprochen, vor dem wir heute stehen, wenn biotechnologische Entwicklungen einerseits neue Heilungsmethoden darstellen, andererseits aber auch für die Manipulation und genetische Überwachung des Menschen eingesetzt werden können. Hershman Leesons Inszenierung ist dabei niemals bewertend, sondern erlaubt uns einen vertieften Blick hinter die Kulissen wissenschaftlicher Produktion, um uns selbst ein profunderes Bild machen zu können. Ihr persönlicher Blick ist dabei stets ein positiver: »You have to be optimistic about the advantages of technology – I have a desire for utopia, and I hope that the technology is used in an inspired way. I may be naïve, but I think an awareness of both the dangers and the benefits can provide a method of survival in an enhanced and profound manner.«[15]

Raum 5: George Church

In ihrer komplexen Installation lässt Hershman Leeson immer wieder Wissenschaftlerinnen und Wissenschaftler in Interviews zu Wort kommen. So befragte sie auch George Church, Professor für Genetik an der Harvard Medical School und ein prominenter Vertreter der synthetischen Biologie, der in seinem Buch *Regenesis* die provozierende Frage stellte, wie die synthetische Biologie die Natur und den Menschen neu erschaffen wird und wir uns dabei möglicherweise zu einer neuen Spezies entwickeln.[16] In dem Videointerview von Hershman Leeson, *A Perfect Archive* (2018), spricht Church von den Möglichkeiten, DNA als biologischen Speicher zu nutzen. Eine revolutionäre neue Technik erlaubt es, DNA als Speichermedium zu verwenden. Dafür wird binärer digitaler Code basierend auf einer Abfolge von Nullen und Einsen mithilfe einer speziellen Software in eine Abfolge der Buchstaben A, C, G und T, den Basen des biologischen Codes der DNA umgewandelt. Das dabei erzeugte biologische Molekül kann mittels einer handelsüblichen DNA-Sequenziermaschine wieder in digitalen Code rückübersetzt werden. Bis zu 215 Petabyte an Daten passen auf ein Gramm DNA, das als biologisches Speichermedium extrem haltbar ist. Diese neue Technik verspricht eine Lösung für die langfristige Speicherung digitaler Daten zu sein, die täglich exponentiell anwachsen. Inkunabeln der Filmgeschichte wie George Méliès' *Le voyage dans la lune (Die Reise zum Mond)* von 1902 wurde bereits erfolgreich von Church und seinem Team in DNA gespeichert und wieder in digitalen Code rücküberführt. Hershman Leeson nutzte diese neue Technologie auch als Speicher ihres eigenen Werks, das im letzten Raum von *The Infinity Engine* zu sehen war.

Raum 6: Forensische Spuren

Zeigten die bisherigen Räume der Installation auf, wie DNA als Baustein des Lebens manipulier- und gestaltbar geworden ist, so verwies Raum 6 darauf, wie der Mensch auch anhand seiner biologischen Daten überwacht werden kann. In der interaktiven Videoinstallation *Infinity Engine (Facial Recognition Software)* (2018) wurden die Gesichter von Besucherinnen und Besuchern von einer Gesichtserkennungssoftware analysiert und interpretiert. Die Algorithmen versuchten, Geschlecht, Alter und anhand der Mimik auch die Emotionen einer Person zu identifizieren. Überwachung ist ein durchgängiges Thema und Motiv im Werk von Hershman Leeson. Diese findet mittlerweile auf der zellularen Ebene statt, wie sie selbst schreibt.[17] Angefangen mit der fiktiven Identität von *Roberta Breitmore* (1973–1978), deren Leben auf fingierten Daten basierte, hin zum maschinengesteuerten Blick von *CybeRoberta* (1996) zeigt die Künstlerin durch ihre neuen Werke, wie unsere Körper heute nicht mehr nur von außen mittels Kameras überwacht werden, sondern die Überwachung des menschlichen Körpers zunehmend bereits von innen heraus, basierend auf der Analyse unserer DNA, stattfindet.

Raum 7: Antikörper

Der nächste Raum, das titelgebende Herzstück der Ausstellung *Anti-Bodies,* war der Antikörperforschung gewidmet. In Zusammenarbeit mit Dr. Thomas Huber, Senior Investigator am NIBR Biologics Center der Novartis Pharma AG, und seinem Team wurde ein Antikörper entwickelt, der den Namen »Lynn Hershman« in seiner molekularen Struktur wiedergibt.

Antikörper sind spezielle Eiweiße (Proteine) und spielen eine wesentliche Rolle in der natürlichen Immunabwehr, weshalb sie auch für therapeutische Zwecke in der Forschung entwickelt werden. Sie erkennen körperfremde oder veränderte körpereigene Strukturen (sogenannte Antigene) und markieren sie, sodass sie für andere Bestandteile des Immunsystems, die für die Abwehr zuständig sind, gut erkennbar sind und eliminiert werden können. So werden sie gezielt zur Behandlung von bestimmten Krankheiten eingesetzt – beispielsweise in der Krebstherapie. Hierfür werden künstliche, mittels gentechnischer Verfahren im Labor hergestellte Antikörper entwickelt, die gezielt auf die Erkennung bestimmter Strukturen hin produziert werden können.

Der LYNNHERSHMAN Antikörper wurde von Dr. Thomas Huber und seinem Team auf seine Eigenschaften und Einsatzmöglichkeiten hin wissenschaftlich erforscht und dokumentiert. Der gesamte Arbeitsprozess wurde dokumentiert und in der Ausstellung anhand von digitalen Animationen und mikroskopischen Aufnahmen anschaulich gemacht. Weiterhin enthielt der Raum diverse Elemente und Gerätschaften, die zur Produktion eines Antikörpers verwendet werden und zeigte die Entwicklung hin zu einer personalisierten Medizin auf.[18]

Der LYNNHERSHMAN Antikörper erwies sich in seiner Struktur als enorm vielseitig. Der gleichzeitig hergestellte Antikörper ERTA, der in seiner Aminosäurenstruktur auf das Alter Ego von Lynn Hershmans fiktiver Figur ›Roberta Breitmore‹[19] Bezug nimmt, konnte dagegen kaum Verbindungen zu Antigenen herstellen. Diese überraschenden Ergebnisse wurden von Hershman Leeson als konsequente Entsprechungen ihrer eigenen künstlerischen Praxis interpretiert.[20] Mit der Herstellung ihres Antikörpers wurden Hershman Leesons Auseinandersetzungen mit Fragen nach Identität und Einzigartigkeit um eine neue biologische Dimension erweitert.

Raum 8: DNA

Der abschließende achte Raum von *The Infinity Engine* war nicht begehbar, sondern konnte nur durch das schmale Glasfenster einer verschlossenen Labortüre betrachtet werden. Der Raum war in ein intensives Blau getaucht. In seiner Mitte befand sich ein Sockel, auf dem eine Spiegelbox mit zwei Glasfläschchen platziert war, die sich darin in einer schier unendlichen Tiefe spiegelten. Ein Fläschchen enthielt das Pulver des LYNNHERSHMAN Antikörpers, im anderen befanden sich 300 Nanogramm DNA, die alle digitalen Dokumente der Ausstellung, Videos und Bildmaterial sowie die Videotagebücher *The Electronic Diaries* (1986–1994) der Künstlerin in niedriger Auflösung in sich trugen. Das amerikanische Labor Twist Biology speicherte die binären Datenpakete in den biologischen Code der DNA. Wie Rudolf Frieling so wunderbar in seinem Essay in dieser Publikation schreibt, wurde Raum 8 damit zur Kulmination des gesamten Werks von Hershman Leeson. Der Künstlerin gelang es, Fragmente ihres Werks, ihr künstlerisches Vermächtnis in einem biologischen Speicher der Nachwelt dauerhaft zur Verfügung zu stellen.

Bereits anfangs der 1990er-Jahre prägte Hershman Leeson in ihrem Werk den Begriff des »Anti-body« für ihre Recherchen und Werke, die Identität und Individualität ausloteten bis hin zu einer virtuellen Identität im Cyberspace, bei der es keinen physischen Körper mehr braucht, um eine fiktive Identität im globalen Netzwerk anzunehmen.[21] In der Ausstellung *Anti-Bodies* wurde diese Suche nicht mehr auf den biologischen Körper selbst und seine virtuellen Repräsentationen fokussiert, sondern auf unsere biologische Essenz: »While the search for antibodies exists in all of my works, identifying the antibody moves inwards with this project and becomes an inverted biological gesture that has as its goal healing from the inside out, a cyborgian dream of infiltrating the body itself and thereby attempts to create a radical and curative recovery of individual culture.«[22] Die Ausstellung *Anti-Bodies* brachte einerseits die langjährige

Auseinandersetzung Hershman Leesons mit den aktuellen Entwicklungen in den Biowissenschaften zu einem vorläufigen Abschluss, andererseits generierte sie eine Essenz der Ausstellung selbst, der sie mit den Videotagebüchern auch zentrale Aspekte ihres Lebens hinzufügte – für immer verwahrt im biologischen Speicher der DNA.

1 Lynn Hershman Leeson in einem Interview in: *die tageszeitung,* 2014.
2 Dr. Pamela Lee auf der Website von Lynn Hershman Leeson: http://www.LYNNHERSHMAN.com/current/ (aufgerufen am 7. April 2019).
3 Die Ausstellung *Lynn Hershman Leeson: Anti-Bodies* wurde vom 3. Mai bis 5. August 2018 am HeK, Haus der elektronischen Künste Basel, gezeigt.
4 Peter Weibel, »The Work of Lynn Hershman Leeson: A Panoply of Identities«, in: *Lynn Hershman Leeson: Civic Radar,* hrsg. von Peter Weibel, Ausst.-Kat. ZKM | Zentrum für Kunst und Medien, Ostfildern 2015, S. 55.
5 Gottfried Wilhelm Leibniz, *Monadologie und andere metaphysische Schriften* (1714), herausgegeben und übersetzt von Ulrich Johannes Schneider, Hamburg 2002, zit. nach Markus Jansen, *Digitale Herrschaft. Über das Zeitalter der globalen Kontrolle und wie Transhumanismus und Synthetische Biologie das Leben neu definieren,* Stuttgart 2015, S. 197.
6 Für die Trennung der einzelnen Räume arbeiteten wir mit Farbcodierungen, die sich an der üblichen Farbgebung für die Darstellung der Bausteine der Doppelhelix der DNA orientierten.
7 Craig Venter, *Life at the Speed of Light. From the Double Helix to the Dawn of Digital Life,* London 2013, S. 7.
8 Ingeborg Reichle, »The Infinity Engine«, in: *Lynn Hershman Leeson: Civic Radar,* hrsg. von Peter Weibel, Ausst.-Kat. ZKM | Zentrum für Kunst und Medien, Ostfildern 2015, S. 335.
9 Das Objekt ist ein Geschenk des amerikanischen Wissenschaftlers Dr. Anthony Atala von der Wake Forest School of Regenerative Medicine an die Künstlerin.
10 Yuval Noah Harari, *Homo Deus. Eine Geschichte von Morgen,* München 2018.
11 Der Raum enthielt zudem mehrere Interviews mit Wissenschaftler_innen, die die beschriebenen Entwicklungen vertiefen und weitere Informationen boten.
12 Jansen 2015 (wie Anm. 5), S. 127.
13 Venter 2013 (wie Anm. 7), S. 7.
14 Ray Kurzweil, *The singularity is near. When Humans Transcend Biology,* New York 2006, S. 117.
15 Lynn Hershman Leeson interviewed by Hou Hanru, in: *Lynn Hershman Leeson: Civic Radar,* hrsg. von Peter Weibel, Ausst-Kat. ZKM | Zentrum für Kunst und Medien, Ostfildern 2015, S. 177.
16 George M. Church und Ed Regis, *Regenesis. How Synthetic Biology Will Reinvent Nature and Ourselves,* New York 2012.
17 Siehe das Interview mit Lynn Hershman Leeson in dieser Publikation.
18 So wurde auch die Geschichte von Emily Whitehead in einem Video gezeigt. Emily Whitehead, ein sieben Jahre altes amerikanisches Mädchen, litt an akuter lymphoblastischer Leukämie und hatte kaum mehr Hoffnung zu überleben. Sie war 2012 das erste Kind, das mit einer experimentellen Methode behandelt wurde, die unter dem Begriff CAR-T für Schlagzeilen sorgte und von Novartis getestet wurde. Seit ihrer Behandlung ist Emily Whitehead krebsfrei.
19 Siehe auch den Text von Rudolf Frieling in dieser Publikation.
20 Siehe den Text *Antibody Reveal* von Lynn Hershman Leeson in dieser Publikation.
21 Lynn Hershman Leeson (Hg.), *Clicking In: Hot Links to a Digital Culture,* Seattle 1996, S. 325–337.
22 Lynn Hershman Leeson in einer E-Mail an die Autorin.

## Rudolf Frieling
## LYNNHERSHMAN – Eine Frage ins Blaue

»Hallo, mein Name ist Lynn Hershman. Komm' und besuch' mich im Chelsea Hotel.«[1]

Einen guten Ausgangspunkt, um tiefer in die Arbeit von Lynn Hershman einzutauchen, bietet der oben zitierte TV-Spot, in dem derselbe Satz von fünf verschiedenen Personen gesprochen wird, wobei aber nur die erste die »echte« Lynn Hershman ist.[2] Ein Name ist lediglich ein Name und kann selbstverständlich auch von anderen verwendet oder anderen zugewiesen werden. Die beunruhigende Verbindung zwischen fünf Gesichtern und einem einzigen Namen verbirgt jedoch, dass mit einem Namen vor allem »die archivierbare, bürokratische und damit politische Kennzeichnung von Identität« einhergeht, wie die Künstlerin es ausdrückt.[3] Ein Name ist also eine Festlegung und die Vervielfältigung der Identität der Künstlerin in diesem »Drama« verweist bewusst und kritisch darauf, solche Identifizierungsprozesse aufmerksam zu beobachten, die eigenen Spuren zu verwischen, Zweifel zu säen und einen präskriptiven und beschränkenden Begriff von Identität spielerisch zu vermeiden. In der Kunst wie im öffentlichen Leben steht ein Name zugleich auch für die Wahrnehmung eines kontinuierlichen und identifizierbaren Werkes, das als Signatur eines Künstlers oder einer Künstlerin bezeichnet werden kann. In diesem Sinn hat sich Lynn Hershman einen »Namen« gemacht, der für eine kritische Auseinandersetzung mit sich verändernden Identitäten steht, wobei sie sich hierbei selbst immer wieder aufs Neue herausgefordert und dies oft mit der Erforschung neuer Technologien verbunden hat. Die Beantwortung der Frage, wofür ein Name steht, muss bei der Betrachtung von Hershmans jüngster Arbeit – *Room #8* (2018) – allerdings auf ganz andere Weise erfolgen, denn hier bildet der Name der Künstlerin buchstäblich das physische Zentrum der Arbeit. Entsprechend entwickelt dieser Text einen Gedankengang, der sich mit der radikalsten Wende in Lynn Hershmans Werk befasst: der direkten Verkörperung ihres Namens als Antikörper, wodurch sich die Frage »Wer ist Lynn Hershman?« in Form der Frage »Was ist LYNNHERSHMAN?« ganz neu stellt.

Beginnen wir mit der einfacheren Frage: Was im Werk der Künstlerin rechtfertigt diesen besonderen Fokus auf ihren Namen? Beim genaueren Blick auf die vielen Meilensteinen in ihrer Karriere, angefangen in den 1960er Jahren mit frühen reaktiven Maschinen – einer Reihe von Masken, die die Anwesenheit eines Besuchers zum Auslösen eines Klanges erfordern – über die erste interaktive Erzählung in *Lorna* (1983) oder den frühen Einstieg in Künstliche Intelligenz in *Agent Ruby* (1999–2002) und *DiNA* (2004), haben mich Fragen fasziniert, die während eines Gesprächs mit der Künstlerin über *Room #8* und dessen spezifischen Bestandteil der Antikörper auftauchten. Ich habe mich gefragt, ob Hershmans jüngste Arbeit tatsächlich der Höhepunkt ihrer gesamten Karriere sein könnte. Ihre kurze Antwort auf diese Frage lautete, dass es nicht viel gäbe, mit dem diese sich in Verbindung bringen ließe, und dass ihre neue Arbeit eher einzigartig sei. Ich habe ihr Atelier in San Francisco jedoch mit zwei Gefühlen verlassen, die mich nach einer anderen und etwas längeren Antwort haben suchen lassen. Das erste war die etwas unheimliche Beobachtung, dass Lynn Hershman bereits über ihr Erbe nachdenkt, darüber, was von ihrem Werk bleiben wird. Sie stellt sich der Frage der Sterblichkeit also nicht nur als menschliches Wesen wie wir alle, sondern auch als »Künstlerin« oder »Persona«. Das zweite Gefühl war meine Überraschung, als sie die Installation des »Antikörpers« von *Room #8,* den sie in ihrer viel umfassenderen Ausstellung der *Infinity Engine* auch mit *Room ∞* oder als das mathematische Symbol für Unendlichkeit übersetzt, als »Haiku« der Ausstellung bezeichnete. Von dieser Referenz überrascht, habe ich mich gefragt, ob die politischen Bezüge ihres Werks, ihr wegweisender Einsatz von Performance und Technologie, ihre Poetik oft überschattet haben könnten. Lassen sich ihre früheren Arbeiten nutzen, um eine poetische Transformation und Abstraktion des »Selbst« hervorzuheben, die für ihre jüngste Arbeit wesentlich ist? Was folgt, ist ein Versuch, meinen beiden Eindrücken mit Blick auf Hershmans künstlerische Entwicklung nachzugehen, von der Erschaffung eines Namens und einer Identität bis hin zum heutigen Anliegen, die biologischen Essenzen unserer Existenz als Spezies zu konstruieren oder künstlich zu entwickeln.

Wenn in allen Identitätskonstruktionen von Lynn Hershman ein Name hervorsticht, dann ist es der von Roberta Breitmore, ihrer legendären Performance als fingierter Charakter in den 1970er-Jahren, die 1978 mit einem »Exorzismus« in der Krypta von Lucrezia Borgia in Rom endete. Robertas Name fungiert als lose Anspielung auf einen praktizierenden Alchemisten: »Der Name Roberta bezog sich auf den Begründer der Alchemie [die Künstlerin spielt hier vermutlich auf Robert Fludd an, der als einer der großen westlichen Alchemisten gilt] und ihr Leben war tatsächlich alchemistisch. Es ging um Prozess, Veränderung und Transformation und um das androgyne Doppel.«[4] Die Serie der Manifestationen von Roberta Breitmore mit dem Begriff der Alchemie zu verknüpfen, liegt nahe angesichts einiger früher Kommentare von der Künstlerin und Arturo Schwartz anlässlich der ersten öffentlichen Erwähnung des Namens in der Ausstellung *Roberta Breitmore: An Alchemical Portrait Begun in 1975 (Ein alchemistisches Porträt, begonnen 1975).* Der Kunsthistoriker Arturo Schwartz war, so die Künstlerin, in diesem Bereich ihr Lehrer und dachte mit ihr über ein »alchemistisches Opus« nach.[5] Im Gegensatz zur Variabilität von Cindy Shermans Selbstporträts als eine jeweils andere Person mit ihren streng kontrollierten Evokationen medialisierter Historien- oder Genrebildern, ist in Hershmans Werk der Parameter der Identität, ihre materielle Manifestation, ein offener Prozess und eher generativ statt repräsentativ. Indem sich die Roberta Breitmore-Serie auf das reale Leben ausgewirkt hat, hat sie Unterschiede verwischt. Nachdem Hershman fünf Jahre lang mit einem anderen »Ich« gelebt und sogar Breitmores Persönlichkeit auf mehrere Körper verteilt und drei »Klone« engagiert hat, die sie in der Öffentlichkeit repräsentierten, hatte das Projekt seinen Zweck erfüllt und sie genug über die »Randbereiche ihres Lebens« erfahren. Hershman beendet das Projekt in der Hoffnung auf die therapeutische Wirkung eines Exorzismus' für ihr eigenes Leben.

Das Ende in eine Krypta zu verlegen, einen Ort, der Körper eingeschlossen hält, ist mehr als eine symbolische Geste. In Hershmans künstlerischer Entwicklung verschiebt es die bisherige Entwicklung von Arbeiten mit Masken in Vitrinen hin zu ortsspezifischen Eingriffen mit Masken in öffentlichen Räumen wie Hotels (*Dante Hotel,* 1972, *Forming of Sculpture Drama in Manhattan,* 1974) in die Privatsphäre eines abgeschlossenen Raums, um fotografisch zu dokumentieren, wie eine von Roberta Breitmores *Construction Charts* zu Asche verbrannt wurde. Lynn Hershman hat Spuren ihrer Arbeit verbrannt und die Gruft mit einem Gefäß voll Asche verlassen, die letztendlich jedoch in den Windungen ihrer Karriere verloren ging. Was heute noch übrig ist, sind Fotografien, Archivunterlagen und -dokumente sowie der Name. Ihre ikonische Kleidung tauchte anlässlich von *Civic Radar* (2016), der Retrospektive der Künstlerin im Yerba Buena Center for the Arts in San Francisco, von mehreren Personen getragen wieder auf – eine zeitgenössische Nachstellung oder Wiederaufführung. Roberta Breitmore wurde als Hommage von Freunden und Mitarbeitern von den Toten auferweckt.

Die Retrospektive hat Breitmores Ephemera in Vitrinen und Rahmen ausgestellt, wodurch sich das »Wer« und das »Was« der Künstlerin und ihres Werkes identifizieren und eine detaillierte wie umfassende Antwort auf unsere Frage »Wer ist Lynn Hershman?« finden lässt. Ungeachtet von kuratorischen Entscheidungen, wie das Erbe der Künstlerin und ihres simulierten Charakters öffentlich präsentiert werden kann, hat Hershman im Haus der elektronischen Künste Basel, wo *Room #8* zuerst ausgestellt wurde, versucht, sowohl ihren Namen als auch Robertas Erbe in ihrem neuen Werk unter der Rubrik »Antikörper« wieder auferstehen zu lassen. Vor der Eröffnung hat sie mir ein Bild von sich geschickt, unscharf, eine Hand mit einer Phiole ausgestreckt, auf die die Kamera fokussiert ist. Die Betreffzeile fungierte als Bildunterschrift und lautete, ohne weitere Erklärung: »This is Lynn« (»Das ist Lynn«). Wenn »Lynn« ein etikettiertes Fläschchen mit archivierbarem Inhaltsstoff ist, bin ich versucht zu fragen: Was ist »Lynn«, abgesehen von ihrem Vornamen? Können wir überprüfen, was sich in der Ampulle befindet und wie »Lynn« dort hineingelangte? Oder sollten wir einfach die Körperlichkeit der Phiole und ihren Inhalt der Sphäre konzeptueller Kunst zuordnen, bei der nicht die Materie zählt, sondern allein die Idee – »Lynn« wäre dann ein Denkspiel und das Fläschchen könnte alles enthalten, was wir uns vorstellen oder was die Künstlerin behauptet.

Dieser Gedankengang erscheint zwar plausibel, dennoch erscheint die Interpretation eher unwahrscheinlich. Die Karriere von Lynn Hershman manifestiert sich als fortlaufende Untersuchung unseres gegenwärtigen, realen Lebens, als Konversation mit alternativen Identitäten, die auf sehr realen Erfahrungen beruht. Hershman ist ebenso sehr eine konzeptionelle Denkerin und Performerin wie eine Materialistin auf der Suche nach realen Verkörperungen. Und der Beginn ihrer Karriere liefert hier wieder einen wertvollen Hinweis. Das am engsten mit ihrer frühesten bedeutenden Arbeit verbundene Material ist Wachs, eine formbare Substanz, die sich unter Einwirkung von Wärme verwandelt. *Conversation* (1966) verbindet beispielsweise in drei Kammern einer Plexiglasvitrine zwei aus Wachs gefertigte Gesichtsfragmente mithilfe eines Gewirrs aus farbigen Drähten. Eine verwandte Arbeit, *Genealogy* (1968), zeigt acht lebensgroße Mundfragmente nebeneinander. Beide Arbeiten belegen, dass die zuverlässigsten Fakten in Hershmans künstlerischer Praxis Spuren oder Teile des Körpers der Künstlerin sind. In einem bewussten Versuch, jede biografische Spur zu verwischen, kombinierte sie den Abdruck ihres realen Körpers mit der Maskierung ihres Gesichts – ähnlich auch in *Self-Portrait as Another Person* (1965), in der das Gesicht schwarz und, wie oft von ihr bevorzugt, halb unter einer Perücke versteckt ist. Das Tragen einer Maske hat alle möglichen psychologischen, sozialen und kulturellen Traditionen und Konnotationen, aber in diesem Fall interessiert mich primär der Umstand, dass diese Formbarkeit von Körperteilen das Ergebnis traumatischer Erlebnisse war, bei denen die Künstlerin in einem Krankenhaus unter einem Sauerstoffzelt immobilisiert war, wo Zeichnen ausgeschlossen und nur der eigene Körper immer in Reichweite war. Einige dieser frühen Masken heißen »Atemmaschinen«. Sie verfügen über Sensoren, die sie bei der Annäherung einer anderen Person »animieren«. Sie sind Automaten und dennoch authentische Nachbildungen des Gesichts der Künstlerin. Wenn man so will, werden sie nur durch die Co-Präsenz eines anderen lebendig und beziehen ihre Faszination auf heutige Besucher aus ihrer dramatischen Abkapslung. Die Maschinen sind gesprächig, schließen einen Dialog jedoch aus. Einige Masken atmen einfach nur, andere haben etwas zu sagen, aber keine von ihnen gibt eine Rückmeldung. Ein oder Aus ist die einzige Option. Sie sind fest umschlossen, von Haaren bedeckt und »leben« in einem transparenten Würfel. Diese Spannung, so meine Argumentation, zieht sich tief durch Hershmans gesamte Karriere, in der jede spezifische Verkörperung und Verstrickung einer Arbeit mit der materiellen Realität einen Beweis für einen Kampf nicht nur um einen Namen, sondern auch um eine menschliche Bindung darstellt – wie Agent Ruby 2002 in ihrem »e-dream portal« sagt: »Verbinden wir uns.« Was mich in der Vergangenheit fasziniert hat, war Hershmans oft durchdachte und überraschende Weise, in verschiedenen Medien diskursive Bindungen durch Gespräche aufrechtzuerhalten, vom KI-Bot bis hin zum realen Leben und zurück oder auch durch direkte Ansprache der Betrachterin oder des Betrachters in ihrer Videoserie *Electronic Diaries* (1984–1994). Angesichts dieser langjährigen Auseinandersetzung mit dem »Realen« scheint es weit hergeholt, die Epiphanie eines poetischen Satzes oder eine visuelle Anspielung auf ein Haiku zu beschwören, wie es die Künstlerin in unserem Gespräch getan hat. Lynn Hershman, so schien es mir immer, war zu sehr in die philosophischen, aber auch politischen Implikationen ihrer Werke involviert, um eine formalistische Reduktion und eine poetische Verdichtung zu suchen. Und dennoch spricht Hershman bei ihrer Installation *Room #8* von einem Haiku und einer kunsthistorischen Strömung, die ihre künstlerische DNA tief durchzieht.

Um dieser Disjunktion nachzugehen, entnehmen wir dem Wissensfundus des bekannten Merriam Webster Dictionary einen ersten Hinweis: »Haiku: eine ungereimte japanische Versform aus drei Zeilen mit jeweils fünf, sieben und fünf Silben.«[6]
Eine durch minimalistischen Code erzeugte Szene evoziert bei jedem Leser und bei jeder Leserin andere Vorstellungen und einen weitergefassten Kontext als die Beschreibung eines Ereignisses im natürlichen Umfeld. Wenn wir einem Haiku Farbe zuordnen, fiel die Wahl wahrscheinlich auf eine monochromatische oder vielleicht das vorsichtige Nebeneinander von nur zwei Farben. *Room #8* arbeitet mit genau dieser Logik. Es ist ein abgeschlossener Raum in blauem Licht und konnotiert damit die Farbe von Unendlichkeit oder Ewigkeit – siehe das Blau von Yves Klein, das coole Design in Stanley Kubricks Science-Fiction-Klassiker *2001: Odyssee im Weltraum* (1968) mit seinem schwarzen Monolith oder auch eines jener immateriellen, immersiven Environments von James Turrell. Dieser blaue Raum hier liegt jedoch unzugänglich hinter einer verschlossenen Labortür mit kleinem Fenster und robustem Schließmechanismus. Die Besucherinnen und Besucher blicken durch dieses Fenster, um ein auf einem Sockel ausgestelltes Objekt zu betrachten, eine verspiegelte Box mit zwei Phiolen. Sie sehen die Aura eines kostbaren Objekts in tiefblauer Leere.

Yves Klein ist hier von großer Bedeutung – man denke nur an sein berühmtes Blau-Pigment oder sein fotografisches »Haiku« über den Sprung in die Leere sowie seine Ausstellung von 1958 *La spécialisation de la sensibilité à l'état matière première en sensibilité picturale stabilisée, Le Vide.* Diese Werke stellen für Hershman wichtige Parameter kunsthistorischer Referenzen dar. Sie benennt ebenso den Einfluss von Marcel Duchamp auf ihr Denken, insbesondere in Form der berühmten Installation *Etant donnés : 1° la chute d'eau, 2° le gaz d'éclairage* von 1946–1966,[7] heute im Philadelphia Museum of Art, auf die sich *Room #8* mit der Verwendung einer geschlossenen Umgebung mit Tür und Gucklöchern zur Kontrolle des Blicks auf das ausgestellte Objekt oder Raums bezieht. Der Körper in Duchamps Installation, provozierend sexualisiert in der Darstellung eines weiblichen Aktes, ist in Hershmans Installation offensichtlich nicht vorhanden, sondern wird von zwei unauffälligen Ready-Mades ersetzt, wissenschaftlichen Phiolen außer Reichweite, was sie – je nach Disposition des Betrachters – entweder um so geheimnisvoller oder begehrenswerter macht. Wenn wir der Duchamp-Analogie weiter folgen, vor allem anhand der Werke *Boîte en valise* und *Boîte alerte (Emergency Box)* von 1959, die einen broschierten Katalog, Ephemera, Postkarten, Notizen, Umschläge, ein Portfolio von Künstlerabzügen, gedruckte Nylonstrümpfe und eine Schallplatte mit 45 U/min. enthalten, erkennen wir den Mechanismus, etwas Unerreichbares und Entferntes zu zeigen, dies jedoch in unmittelbarer Nähe. In *Etant donnés* ist dieser Strategie die Darstellung eines sexualisierten Körpers hinzugefügt, womöglich begehrenswert, mit Sicherheit aber in einem Mausoleum verschlossen. Und dennoch, indem man durch die Gucklöcher schaut, kommt etwas Essenzielles von Verführung ins Spiel.[8] Duchamp hätte das Foto des Exorzismus' von Roberta Breitmore, ausgestreckt neben einem Sarg in der Krypta von Lucrezia Borgia, in eine »Boîte«, eine Kiste mit Erinnerungen und Blaupausen für Repliken und Kopien, hinzugefügt. Hershman kommentiert ihre Erfahrung angesichts dieses berühmten Kunstwerks: »Man konnte darüber nur spekulieren, es gab [...] nichts, um das man herumlaufen hätte können, nichts, das man hätte bedienen können, es sagte automatisch Nein, ein Nicht-Eingang, wie der Tod, nicht-interaktiv.« Für sie ist die Darstellung von Ephemera oder die symbolische Darstellung eines Körpers nur sekundär. Das Hauptziel besteht darin, eine

Arbeit als produktiv, generativ und aktiv zu gestalten. Wie hat sie dies in *Room #8* erreicht?

*Room #8* enthält folgende Bestandteile: Labortür mit Hardware, Infinity Mirror Box, Phiole mit LYNNHERSHMAN Antibody (hergestellt von Novartis), Phiole mit DNA (hergestellt von Twist Biology), blaues Licht sowie zusätzliche kontextabhängige Informationen, die bei einer Ausstellung von *Room #8* optional hinzugefügt werden können.[9] Die gespiegelte Box zieht den Blick der Betrachtenden auf sich. Der glänzende und endlos spiegelnde Behälter für zwei Phiolen ist die Essenz dieses Raumes: eine Phiole mit dem Archiv von *The Complete Electronic Diaries,* als DNA gespeichert, und eine zweite Phiole mit der weißen Pulveressenz eines tatsächlichen Antikörpers, der auf den Buchstaben des Namens LYNNHERSHMAN basiert.[10] Die verschlossene Labortür entzieht der Betrachterin und dem Betrachter das Objekt und agiert wie eine Tresortür für die Spiegelbox mit ihrer auffallend reflektierenden Leuchtkraft, verstärkt durch das tiefblaue Licht des umgebenden Raums. Indem dabei vage mythologische oder märchenhafte Konnotationen hervorgerufen werden – wie zum Beispiel das Bild eines Glassargs und eines scheinbar in der Zeit erstarrten Moments, einem Traum von unendlicher Schönheit und Jugend nicht unähnlich –, nutzt es eine Bildsprache, die ewiges Leben durch eine zukünftige Aktion verspricht: die Zerstörung des Glassargs. Hershmans Streben nach menschlicher Berührung durch die Medien wird hier mit einer Umgebung gekoppelt, in der ein zukünftiges Leben und eine zukünftige Aktion aus einem Tiefspeicher entstehen, aus dem Lebenswerk der Künstlerin in einem DNA-Fläschchen gespeichert, und dem Leben echter Antikörper, die darauf warten, in der Zukunft als Katalysatoren oder Immunisierungsmittel zu dienen. Beeindruckend finde ich, wie die romantische Bildsprache hier Transparenz mit Unzugänglichkeit verbindet – einen Sarg, dem die Hoffnung auf Wiedergeburt und Transformation innewohnt.

Hershmans *Room #8* darf jedoch nicht auf ein romantisches Bild oder eine kunsthistorische Antwort auf Duchamps Mise en Scène des Spektakels des Blicks reduziert werden. Ihr Raum ist ebenso weit entfernt von ihren eigenen Wachsskulpturen der 1960er-Jahre, die Rituale des Todes und der Museologie beschwören, wie zum Beispiel in Madame Tussauds Prominentenkabinett. *Room #8* zeichnet sich dadurch aus, dass er zwei deutlich unterschiedliche Einflüsse verbindet: Er ist eindeutig Yves Kleins Ästhetik der Nicht-Repräsentation verbunden, entlehnt seine architektonischen Parameter jedoch der Realität der funktionalen Technoästhetik eines generischen wissenschaftlichen Labors. Die neutrale äußere Erscheinung eines Labors, eine Ästhetik des Anti-Spektakels, bildet den Rahmen für ein Interieur, das nicht nur eine Hommage an Kleins Blau und einen Akt wesentlicher Reduktion darstellt. Für Hershman ist das Haiku *Room #8* »die Essenz eines Gedankens. Und es ist dies sowohl eine physische wie auch spirituelle und intellektuelle Essenz der Erforschung von genetischer Manipulation.« Dem Betrachter und der Betrachterin, die eine Beschreibung der Genese des Projekts gelesen haben, wird allmählich klar, dass es sich hier um die Ästhetik für einen Schatz handelt, der sich in einem Kabinett von Spiegeln endlos reflektiert. Mit anderen Worten, die Ampullen sind Dokumente einer Form von Transformation – Film in DNA und Buchstaben in Antikörper – und der Inhalt der Ampullen beginnt sich in der Vorstellung des Betrachters zu entfalten. Wie kann man einen Film aus DNA rückübersetzen und wie werden die Antikörper in der Zukunft agieren? Das luxuriöse blaue Design um diesen Miniatur-Spiegelsaal – eine passende Architektur für das für die Ewigkeit verwahrte Werk und den Namen der Künstlerin – bedeutet angesichts der Vergeblichkeit von Konservierung für die Ewigkeit Dramatik und Ironie gleichermaßen.

Was ist LYNNHERSHMAN dann also? LYNNHERSHMAN ist der buchstäbliche Entwurf für den molekularen Code, mit dem ein echter Antikörper zusammengesetzt wurde. Die chemische Struktur der Aminosäuren und ihrer Symbole entspricht genau dem Namen der Künstlerin.[11] Der LYNNHERSHMAN Antibody, so erzählt uns Thomas Huber, Wissenschaftler bei Novartis, ist reaktionsfähig und aktiv, während das konzeptionelle Gegenstück, ein zweites Antikörper-Experiment namens ERTA, kurz für Roberta [Breitmore], in der Tat »tot« oder zumindest inaktiv ist, da die Buchstaben R und O keinem Aminosäuresymbol entsprechen. Die »Künstlerin« lebt, während der exorzierte simulierte Charakter tot ist. Die Künstlerin interpretiert dieses ungesehene und beispiellose Experiment halb im Scherz mit einer biografischen Parallele: »Roberta war die Manifestation eines Traumas. Und die Kreation von Roberta erlaubte ihrer Schöpferin Heilung. Und genau das ermöglichen Antikörper. In gewissem Sinne können sie Traumata heilen. [...] Der Hershman Antibody wird nicht wirklich verwendet, weil er sich an mit allem verbindet. Der Roberta-Antikörper bindet sich an nichts und sie [Novartis] verwenden ihn nicht. Der Hershman Antikörper mag alles. Sie [Novartis] hatten nie einen Antikörper, der alles mochte. Er kann sich an jeden Zustand anpassen, während Roberta das Gegenteil ist. Sie kann sich mit nichts verbinden, was irgendwie interessant ist. Robertas Beziehung und Bindung beschränkten sich in gewisser Weise auf Treffen mit Menschen, mit denen sie keine Bindung eingehen würde. Und ich mag zu viel, ich mache zu viel.« Während wir gleichermaßen unsicher sind, was die schwer zu messenden Auswirkungen von Kunst auf die reale Welt angeht, ist die Künstlerin mit dem Namen Lynn Hershman stolz auf die Tatsache, dass der Antikörper LYNNHERSHMAN reaktiv ist, auch wenn er kein medizinisch-alchemistisches Gold oder das Heilmittel für Krebs ist, auf das sie gehofft hatte. In ihrer Interpretation ist »Bonding« ein Schlüsselbegriff – er verspricht einen Prozess des Heilens und zwar obwohl die Künstlerin gleichzeitig zu viel Bindung proklamiert? Ich zögere, hinsichtlich der zukünftigen Verwendung des Antikörpers LYNNHERSHMAN von Heilung oder Heilen zu sprechen, aber es lässt sich nicht leugnen, dass er reaktiv und interaktionsfähig ist und damit metaphorisch gesehen ein vielversprechendes Kunstwerk im wirklichen Leben.

Und ERTA, der nicht-reaktive Antikörper? ERTA ist, figurativ gesagt, der letzte Nagel im Sarg der fiktiven Namen, die spielerisch als Umweg genutzt wurden, um auf ihre Umwelt einzuwirken und sie kritisch zu reflektieren: von Juris Prudence, Herbert Goode, Gay Abandon, Lynn Hershmans ersten spielerischen Pseudonymen als Kunstkritiker, die ihr nichtsdesto trotz halfen, sich einen Ruf als Künstlerin zu erarbeiten, bis hin zu den fiktiven, identischen Charakteren von Ruby, Olive und Marine in *Teknolust,* Repliken von DNA und Personifikationen der drei Farben Rot, Grün und Blau des elektronischen Bildspektrums, drei virtuelle »Kobolde, die auf Selbstverwirklichung jenseits der Agenda ihrer Schöpferin abzielen.«[12] Diese simulierten Charaktere verblassen alle im Vergleich zur realen molekularen Existenz von LYNNHERSHMAN. Technisch gesehen wurde dieser wissenschaftlich hergestellte Antikörper nicht von der Künstlerin Lynn Hershman erschaffen, sondern im Labor des Schweizer Chemieriesen Novartis, der an diesem Experiment zur Herstellung einer »Medizin« mitgearbeitet hat, ohne zu wissen, was diese heilen könnte. Die Lösung sucht somit noch nach einem von ihr zu lösenden Problem, ähnlich wie eine Künstlerin, die ein Werk produziert, ohne zu wissen, ob es überhaupt für die Öffentlichkeit von Bedeutung sein oder eine Wirkung haben wird. Das ist es, was Lynn Hershman an LYNNHERSHMAN mag. Der Name ist im realen Leben aktiv.

Wir zukünftige Bürgerinnen oder Wissenschaftler können *Room #8* und seine Bestandteile in noch unbekannten Verkörperungen dekodieren. Die archivierte DNA und die molekularen Substanzen sind dabei unerlässlich. Sie existieren im realen Leben und sind keine rein künstlerische Geste. Die *Infinity Engine DNA* ist die fortschrittlichste Form der Speicherung und Aufbewahrung von Informationen für die Zukunft, während die Antikörper ein generatives Programm für noch unbekannte zukünftige Bindungsprozesse sind, Wirkstoffe mit unbekannten Auswirkungen. Diese beiden Komponenten des Bio-Engineering garantieren der Künstlerin ein aktives Leben nach dem Tod. Antikörper und Hershmans frühe responsive Sound-Skulpturen aus den 1960er-Jahren »werden nur dann zum Leben erweckt, wenn es angebracht erscheint. Sie befinden sich bis zu ihrer Aktivierung in einem Trägheitszustand. Sie sind nicht immer aktiv. Sie brauchen die richtigen Bedingungen«. Vorausgesetzt, dass die beiden Antikörper in einem sicheren wissenschaftlichen oder musealen Umfeld ordnungsgemäß geschützt und aufbewahrt werden, wird der reaktive LYNNHERSHMAN Antibody weiterhin ein Katalysator für ökologische, soziale und politische Anliegen sein, die aus der Tiefe des Blaus von *Room #8* ausstrahlen. Und mit einiger Wahrscheinlichkeit wird LYNNHERSHMAN sich wie Ruby, Olive und Marine in *Teknolust* verhalten, wenn diese auf Selbstverwirklichung abzielen und über die Agenda ihrer Schöpferin hinausgehen. Die aktive Bindung kann sich als Segen erweisen – vielleicht nicht für die Künstlerin, aber für die künftigen Hüter der Phiole.

Eingedenk eines letztlich romantischen Verlangens in dieser utopischen Inszenierung[13] erinnere ich mich an die zentrale Szene in Andrey Tarkovskys Film *Stalker* (1979), in der die drei Protagonisten das Zentrum der »Zone« erreicht haben und nicht in der Lage sind, in eine Weite aus Sanddünen innerhalb eines Gebäudes einzutreten. In diesem gewölbten endlosen Raum gibt es nichts als Sand, aber er ist eine Epiphanie des Endes ihrer Reise. Es bleibt unklar, wie sich die drei Protagonisten nach dieser Reise wieder dem »echten Leben« zuwenden können, und es bleibt vielleicht unklar, wie der blaue *Room #8* und die zukünftige Anwendung des LYNNHERSHMAN Antibody nützlich sein können, beide Male sind es jedoch poetische Darstellungen einer Reise in Richtung Bewusstsein und Heilung. In Anbetracht dessen, dass Hershman sich selbst als Zeugin von Ereignissen bezeichnet hat, die von Roberta Breitmore ausgelöst wurden – »Oft überlebt man ein Trauma, indem man sich selbst zum Zeugen des Geschehens macht, quasi eine Überlebensstrategie.«[14] –, kulminiert Hershmans Karriere in einer Feier von aktivem Engagement, Ermächtigung (Agency) und Konnektivität. Ein bewusster Verlust von Kontrolle, der sowohl bei Roberta Breitmore als auch dem LYNNHERSHMAN Antibody von zentraler Bedeutung ist, bleibt ein Schlüsselelement ihrer ästhetischen Praxis.

*Room #8* ist keine Krypta, obwohl Besucherinnen und Besucher nur hinschauen dürfen und nur wenige Personen (Familienmitglieder für ihre Gruft und im Museum Konservatoren für die Installation) einen Schlüssel haben, um ihr Inneres zu eröffnen. Auf Friedhöfen wirken beeindruckende Monumente und Fassaden von Krypten oft so, als würden ihre Türen niemals mehr geöffnet, wenn sie nach einer Beerdigung geschlossen wurden. Die Leichen sind für immer eingeschlossen. Der Grabstein an einer Krypta tut, was er tun soll, nämlich die Toten an der Rückkehr hindern. *Room #8* ist jedoch kein Mausoleum, in dem eine einbalsamierte Leiche für die Öffentlichkeit erhalten bleibt – es gibt hier schließlich keinen Körper, nur einen Antikörper. Lynn Hershman sagt über ihre Installation hinter einer verschlossenen Tür: »*Room #8* ist ein Raum, den man nicht betreten kann. Als Künstlerinnen schauen wir immer auf diese Eintritts-/Austrittsmatrix. [...] Er lässt sich als Performance in der Zeit betrachten, da die eingekapselten Antikörper in 20 Jahren wiederbelebt werden könnten. Es ist ein Konservierungsmittel mit der Option zurückzukehren. Es besteht die Möglichkeit für einen weiteren Eintritt.« Wir, die zukünftigen Wissenschaftlerinnen oder Konservatoren, würden dann mit ihr interagieren und es ihr damit ermöglichen, am Leben zu bleiben.

Die Künstlerin hat diesen Gedankengang mit der Kunst verknüpft und eine weitere logische Schlussfolgerung gezogen: »Ich glaube, Kunst ist ein optimistischer Prozess, ein Prozess des Glaubens.«[15] Die ästhetische Morphologie von Lynn Hershman – ein Begriff, den sie schon früh für ihre Methodik reklamiert hatte – ist im Wesentlichen die Kunst, Systeme von Immunität gegen zukünftige Toxine zu produzieren.[16] In *Room #8* erfahren wir, dass es Heilung für uns, aber auch für die Künstlerin geben könnte. Ihren eigenen Namen aufzubewahren, für eine spätere Wiederkehr zu sorgen – dieses Kunstwerk ist Projektion und Wirklichkeit zugleich: die Verdichtung einer ganzen Karriere künstlerischen Experimentierens zum Realen hin, faszinierend wie die Wahrhaftigkeit von evozierten Bilder in einem Haiku. Das poetische Bild materialisiert sich in einer Phiole aus Glas, nominell selbst ein flüssiges Material, das das trockene körnige Pulver eines Namens enthält. Der gesamte *Room #8* ist damit ein Haiku über die ultimative alchemistische Transformation, in der eine Phiole geöffnet wird und das Leben wie Phönix aus der Asche entspringt. *Room #8* liefert diese utopische wie spirituelle Transformation vom Tod bis zur Wiedergeburt als wirklichen Vorgang dank Agent LYNNHERSHMAN. Die Künstlerin legt den Grundstein für ihre künftige Wiederkehr – mag es möglicherweise auch vergeblich sein, aber es ist zu gut, um nicht daran zu glauben. Unter diesem Gesichtspunkt wird die Frage »Was ist LYNNHERSHMAN?« nicht nur zur Frage, *wer,* sondern auch *was* in Zukunft eigenmächtig handeln können wird. Den Tod auf diese Weise zu überwinden, ist sicher nicht das schlechteste Ergebnis.

1 TV-Spot für ihre ortsspezifische Installation *Forming a Sculpture Drama* in Manhattan (1974). Alle Zitate von Lynn Hershman stammen, sofern nicht mit einer Fußnote zitiert, aus einer nicht veröffentlichten Interviewaufnahme des Autors im Atelier der Künstlerin in San Francisco am 22. Februar 2019.

2 Die Künstlerin hat 1992 ihren Namen in Lynn Hershman Leeson geändert, ich habe mich jedoch entschieden, ihren ursprünglichen Namen zu verwenden, um die Kontinuität mit ihrer neuesten künstlerischen Arbeit *LYNNHERSHMAN Antibody* (2018) zu betonen.

3 Vorstellung von LYNNHERSHMAN Antibody and ERTA Antibody am 24. April 2018.

4 Lynn Hershman (1992) zitiert in Lynn Hershman: Civic Radar, hrsg. von Peter Weibel, Ausst.-Kat. ZKM | Zentrum für Kunst und Medien Karlsruhe, Ostfildern 2016, S. 110.

5 Siehe auch die Arbeit *Roberta Breitmore: An Alchemical Portrait Begun in 1975, a cartoon,* die 1978 von Spain Rodrigues in Auftrag gegeben wurde, sowie ihr Abendessen für Arturo Schwartz, *The Alchemical Machination or The Bird Striped Bare with Herb Batchlors, Even* (sic!), eine auch orthografische Parodie auf Duchamps berühmtes Werk *The Bride Stripped Bare by Her Bachelors, Even.*

6 Siehe: »haiku«, Merriam Webster's dictionary, https://www.merriam-webster.com/dictionary/haiku (aufgerufen am 11. April 2019).

7 Siehe die ausführliche Medienbeschreibung des Museums: »Mixed Media Assemblage: (Außen) Holztür, Eisennägel, Ziegel und Stuck; (Innen) Ziegelsteine, Samt, Holz, Pergament über einer Armierung aus Blei, Stahl, Messing, synthetischen Spachteln und Klebstoffen, Aluminiumblech, geschweißtem Stahldrahtsieb und Holz; Werkzeugbrett, Haar, Ölfarbe, Kunststoff, Stahlbindeklammern, Kunststoffwäscheklammern, Zweige, Blätter, Glas, Sperrholz, Messingscharnier, Nägel, Schrauben, Watte, Collotypie, Acryllack, Kreide, Graphit, Papier, Pappe, Klebeband, Stifttinte, elektrische Leuchten, Gaslampe (Bec Auer-Typ), Schaumgummi, Kork, Elektromotor, Keksdose und Linoleum. Philadelphia Museum of Art, https://www.philamuseum.org/collections/permanent/65633.html?mulR=884479142|5 (aufgerufen am 11. April 2019).

8 Siehe die fotografische Collage Seduction (1988) und ein Video mit dem Titel Seduction of a Cyborg (1994), eine poetische Allegorie über die Invasion des Körpers durch die Technologie und die Zerstörung des Immunsystems.

9 Es handelt sich hierbei um ein zweiminütiges Video, die Datei des »Antibody Wallpaper« und sechs digitale Archivfotografien, die von der jeweiligen Kuratorin oder dem Kurator auszuwählen sind.

10 »Ich habe alle relevanten Informationen der Infinity Engine [und] meines ›Archivs‹«, also The Electronic Diary, zusammengenommen, aber in extrem niedrige Auflösung gebracht, um diesen Vorgang überhaupt finanzieren zu können. In der Information von Infinity Engine bilden jedes JPG und jeder Text einen einzelnen Frame auf

der Zeitleiste. Die Kosten eines solchen Vorgangs belaufen sich aktuell auf 20.000 Dollar pro Sekunde. Daher musste ich bei der Realisierung auf großzügige Menschen und eine niedrige Auflösung vertrauen, damit das Projekt konzeptionell solide wird. [...] Ich habe darauf bestanden, dass es sowohl konzeptionell solide ist als auch den Umwandlungs- und Umwandlungsprozess durchläuft, was vier Monate in Anspruch genommen hat.« Lynn Hershman in einer E-Mail an den Autor vom 25. März 2019.

11 Die 20 natürlichen Aminosäuren, die die Grammatik von Antikörpern oder Immunglobulinen bilden, werden üblicherweise mit Buchstaben abgekürzt, sodass der LYNNHERSMAN Antibody der folgenden Aminosäuresequenz entspricht, den Bausteinen des Proteins: L (Leucin) – Y (Tyrosin) – N (Asparagin) – N (Asparagin) – H (Histidin) – E (Glutaminsäure) – R (Arginin) – S (Serin) – H (Histidin) – M (Methionin) – A (Alanin) – N (Asparagin).

12 *Ruby Rich* in *Civic Radar* 2016 (siehe Anm. 4), S. 259.

13 Lynn Hershman verfasste einen Aufsatz mit dem Titel *Romancing the Anti-body: Lust and Longing in (Cyber)space (Die Romantisierung des Anti-Körpers: Lust und Sehnsucht im (Cyber-)Raum),* der erstmals 1994 im Cameraworks Magazine veröffentlicht wurde und sich mit der digitalen Konstruktion von Körpern befasste.

14 Lynn Hershman verfasste einen Aufsatz mit dem Titel *Romancing the Anti-body: Lust and Longing in (Cyber)space (Die Romantisierung des Anti-Körpers: Lust und Sehnsucht im (Cyber-)Raum),* der erstmals 1994 im Cameraworks Magazine veröffentlicht wurde und sich mit der digitalen Konstruktion von Körpern befasste.

15 *Civic Radar* 2016 (siehe Anm. 4), S. 175.

16 *Civic Radar* 2016 (siehe Anm. 4), S. 177.

17 Vor kurzem hat Hershman den *Alchemist Wand for the 21st Century (Alchemistischer Zauberstab für das 21. Jahrhundert)* (2011) geschaffen – einen hölzernen Besen, dessen Bürsten in 24-Karat-Gold getaucht und so modifiziert wurden, dass sie unsichtbare Toxine in lokalen Umgebungen erkennen. Die Messwerte werden auf einen Bildschirm in der Nähe übertragen, sodass Benutzerinnen und Benutzer die unsichtbare Toxizität ihres Standorts beheben können.

# Thomas Huber
# Die Generation des LYNNHERSHMAN-Antikörpers

## Abwehrmechanismen unseres Körpers

Unser Immunsystem schützt uns vor Krankheitserregern und hilft, Malignitäten wie Krebs, die aus veränderten Körperzellen entstehen, zu erkennen und zu bekämpfen. Antikörper sind eine wichtige Komponente des Immunsystems und ermöglichen es unserem Körper, unbekannte Gefahren zu erkennen. Das ist eine außergewöhnliche Fähigkeit. Wir sind dazu in der Lage, täglich eine unglaublich große Anzahl neuer und verschiedener Antikörper zu produzieren. Das Immunsystem selektioniert Antikörper, die fremde Pathogene neutralisieren. Nicht funktionale oder gefährliche Antikörper werden vernichtet. Dieser komplexe Prozess bereitet uns optimal auf neue Gefahren vor und kann mit der Theorie der natürlichen Selektion, wie von Charles Darwin und Alfred Russel Wallace beschrieben, verglichen werden – und er findet jeden Tag in unserem Körper statt. Meistens bemerken wir davon gar nichts. Fehler hingegen, die während dieses Prozesses entstehen, können jedoch ernsthafte Konsequenzen haben – Beispiele dafür sind Autoimmunerkrankungen und Krebs.

## Die Eigenschaften von Antikörpern

Antikörper sind Proteine, die sich aus Aminosäureketten aufbauen. Es gibt 20 verschiedene natürliche Aminosäuren, die in der Regel mit einem einzelnen Buchstaben abgekürzt werden. »L« steht zum Beispiel für Leucin (für weitere Abkürzungen siehe Abbildung 1). Vier Ketten mit insgesamt etwa 1330 Aminosäuren bilden einen Antikörper. Diese Ketten haben eine komplexe räumliche 3D-Struktur, werden aber häufig vereinfacht als »Y« dargestellt. In großen Teilen sind Antikörper gleich. Antikörper unterscheiden sich lediglich in einem kleinen, aber sehr wichtigen Bereich an der Spitze des »Y«. Dieser winzige Teil wird auch als »HCDR3« bezeichnet und ist an der Bindung zum Pathogen beteiligt (siehe Abbildung 2). Jeder Antikörper enthält einen definierten Aminosäurestrang. Dieser Prozess ist nicht vollkommen willkürlich, gewisse Aminosäuren kommen häufiger vor als andere. Die natürliche Verteilung der Aminosäuren in der »HCDR3«-Region korreliert mit der Buchstabengröße, wie Abbildung 3 zeigt. Die Aminosäuresequenz in dieser Region stattet jeden Antikörper mit seiner individuellen Funktionalität aus. Nennen wir sie ihre Persönlichkeit.

## Die Idee für den LYNNHERSHMAN-Antikörper

Als wir während Lynns Besuchs des Novartis Instituts für Bio-Medical Research (NIBR) über natürliche Antikörpergenerationen und Antikörperpersönlichkeiten diskutierten, kam uns die Idee für einen personalisierten Antikörper. Wir definieren die Aminosäuresequenz der »HCDR3«-Region so, dass die Abkürzungen der Aminosäuren den Namen LYNN HERSHMAN ergeben. Dadurch erhalten wir den »LYNNHERSHMAN-Antikörper«. Theoretisch besteht die Möglichkeit – zugegebenermaßen mit einer extrem geringen Wahrscheinlichkeit – dass jemand von uns, oder selbst Lynn, diese Antikörpersequenz bereits einmal im Körper hergestellt hat. Was wäre die Funktion des Antikörpers gewesen? Hat er unsere Lebensqualität verbessert?

Lynns Name bietet den Vorteil, dass jeder Buchstabe als Abkürzung der 20 natürlichen Aminosäuren vorliegt. Scrabble-spielenden wird auffallen, dass sechs Buchstaben des Alphabets, nämlich B-J-O-Q-U-X-Z, nicht als Abkürzung natürlicher Aminosäuren verwendet werden und dass es leider keinen Aminosäurestrang für ROBERTA BREITMORE, THOMAS HUBER oder SABINE HIMMELSBACH gibt. Sollten wir mit Spitznamen arbeiten? So kam es, dass wir uns schließlich ERTA für Roberta ausgedacht haben. Auf diese Weise entstand der »ERTA-Antikörper«.

## Herstellung eines Antikörpers

Unser Immunsystem ist clever und speichert den Bauplan eines jeden nützlichen Antikörpers. Dies beschleunigt die Immunantwort auf Krankheitserreger, mit denen wir uns zum zweiten Mal infizieren. Wir werden wahrscheinlich nicht mehr krank, weil wir »immun« gegen den Erreger geworden sind.

Die DNA ist der Bauplan der Antikörper. Spezialisierte B- oder Plasmazellen in unserem Körper können nach solchen Bauplänen große Mengen an Antikörpern herstellen. Technische Fortschritte machen es möglich, einen Bauplan chemisch zu synthetisieren. Immortalisierte Zell-Linien wie CHO-Zellen (Chinesische Hamster-Ovarialzellen) oder HEK-Zellen (humane embryonale Nierenzellen) werden genutzt, um Antikörper rekombinant außerhalb des Körpers »in vitro« zu produzieren.

Diesen Vorgang, wie in Abbildung 4 dargestellt, nutzten wir für die LYNNHERSHMAN- und ERTA-Antikörper. In Zellkulturflaschen züchteten wir einen Liter HEK-Zellen, die insgesamt sechzig Billiarden (60.000.000.000.000.000) Antikörpermoleküle in sieben Tagen produzierten. Dank ihres sehr geringen Gewichts von nur 0,000.000.000.000.000.000.25 Gramm manifestiert sich diese unglaublich hohe Anzahl von Molekülen in nur ungefähr 0,015 Gramm reinem Antikörper.

## Antikörperstruktur

Antikörper können weder mit dem bloßen Auge noch mit Hilfe eines Mikroskops gesehen werden. Ein Molekül ist weniger als 0,000.005 Millimeter groß. Mit komplexen Technologien wie der Röntgenstrukturanalyse kann man die Struktur sichtbar machen. Es ist uns gelungen, Kristalle aus dem Antikörpergerüst der LYNNHERSHMAN- und ERTA-Antikörper zu züchten und sie einem Röntgenstrahl auszusetzen. Mit einer mathematischen Prozedur konnten wir die Struktur des Antikörpers aus dem Röntgenbeugungsmuster rekonstruieren. Die »HCDR«-Regionen mit der LYNNHERSHMAN- oder ERTA-Aminosäure Sequenz wurden mithilfe einer Software in die Struktur so modelliert, dass sie eine realistische dreidimensionale Struktur im Kontext des ganzen Antikörpergerüsts widerspiegelt (Abbildung 5–8).

Das Experiment

Die beiden Schleifen LYNNHERSHMAN und ERTA unterscheiden sich sehr in ihrer Länge. Welche Persönlichkeiten haben sie und welche Funktionen? Bedenkt man, welchen winzigen Teil des Antikörpers wir verändert haben, stellt sich die Frage, ob überhaupt ein Unterschied nachgewiesen wurde? Die Antwort darauf muss in einem Experiment gefunden werden. Die Bindung ist die Hauptfunktion eines Antikörpers. Er muss Erreger binden und neutralisieren. Wir gaben etwa 7000 verschiedene Proteine auf einen kleinen Chip und testeten, welches davon von den Antikörpern gebunden wird. Therapeutische Antikörper, die Krankheiten behandeln, binden genau ein Antigen. Solche Antikörper werden über ihre Funktion selektioniert. Die Aminosäuresequenz ist zunächst unbekannt und wird im wahrsten Sinne des Wortes während des Prozesses »entdeckt«. Das Design des LYNNHERSHMAN-Antikörpers reflektiert gewissermaßen den umgekehrten Prozess. Umso spannender wäre es, wenn das Design eine besondere Funktion aufweisen würde.

Das Ergebnis

Die beiden Persönlichkeiten hätten nicht unterschiedlicher sein können. Der LYNNHERSHMAN-Antikörper bindet eine Vielzahl, genaugenommen 2500 der 7000 getesteten Proteine, während der ERTA-Antikörper nicht ein einziges bindet. Auf dem Protein-Chip in Abbildung 9 sieht man nur die Kontrollpunkte für ERTA. Das ist wirklich außergewöhnlich, denn es ist nicht einfach, einen Antikörper zu designen, der überhaupt keine Funktionen hat – dies eindeutig zu beweisen, wird zu einer eher philosophischen Aufgabe. Analog dazu ein Gedanke: Schwierig ist es das Glück zu finden, aber es fällt uns leicht einzusehen, was uns unglücklich macht. Trotz der interessanten Beobachtungen sind beide Antikörper von keinem therapeutischen Nutzen. Möglicherweise könnte man den ERTA-Antikörper als Negativkontrolle in Experimenten während der Entdeckung therapeutischer Antikörper verwenden.

Die Generation der LYNNHERSHMAN- und ERTA-Antikörper verdeutlicht trotzdem den gesamten Prozess und auch, welchen Unterschied in der Persönlichkeit eine kleine »HCDR3« Region bewirken kann. Lynns Frage, ob Antikörper intelligent sind, können wir mit ja beantworten. Nicht nur der evolutionäre Prozess, der uns vor neuen Krankheiten schützt, ist clever, sondern auch die Architektur des Antikörpers selbst. Die Variation nur weniger Aminosäure-Schleifen liefert auf höchst ressourcenschonende Weise eine lebensrettende Vielfalt von Antikörperpersönlichkeiten.

Am LYNNHERSHMAN-Antikörperprojekt war eine Vielzahl von Spezialistinnen und Spezialisten beteiligt, denen ich für Ihre Unterstützung danken möchte:

Sandra Schlüchter [1], Lionello Ruggeri [1], Ting Zhou [1], Agostino Cirillo [1], Xavier Leber [1], Barbara Brannetti [1], Brendan Kerins [1], Brigitte Menary [1], Regis Cebe [1], Remi Boeuf [1], Meike Scharenberg [1], Mauro Zurini [1], Frederic Villard [1], Christian Schleberger [1], Claude Logel [1], Adriano Marra [1], Jean-Michel Rondeau [1]
Lynn Hershman Leeson [2], Boris Magrini [3] and Sabine Himmelsbach [3]

1 Novartis Pharma AG, Basel, Schweiz
2 LYNNHERSHMAN.com, San Francisco
3 HeK, Haus der elektronischen Künste, hek.ch

Abbildungen

Abb. 1: Aufstellung aller Aminosäuren und ihrer Abkürzungen mit einem Buchstaben.

Abb. 2: Schematische Darstellung eines Antikörpers in typischer Y-Form. Symmetrisches Molekül aus 2 kürzeren (hellgrau) und 2 längeren Peptid-Ketten (dunkelgrau). Die HCDR3-Schleifen an den Spitzen des Y sind orange dargestellt, sie sind an der Pathogenbildung beteiligt. Die DNA (Antikörper-Blaupause), die die HCDR3-Aminosäuresequenz des Template-Antikörpers (grau) kodiert, wurde durch DNA ersetzt, die die Aminosäuresequenz LYNNHERSHMAN (orange) kodiert. Auf gleiche Weise stellten wir einen Antikörper her, der die Aminosäuresequenz ERTA als HCDR3 enthält.

Abb. 3, oberes Bild: Vorkommen von natürlicher Aminosäure im HCDR3-Loop im Einzelbuchstabencode. Die Größe des Buchstabens spiegelt die Wahrscheinlichkeit der Aminosäure wider, die an dieser Stelle zu finden ist. Unteres Bild: Lynn Hershman Aminosäure-String für HCDR3.

Abb. 4: Antikörperproduzierende Säugetierzelle. Die Expressionsplasmid-DNA (Antikörper-Blaupause) wird in den Zellkern eines Säugetiers übertragen. Mithilfe des zelleigenen Mechanismus werden Antikörper produziert und in die Nährmedien abgesondert.

Abb. 5: Schematische Abbildung des Vorgangs, um die 3D-Struktur eines Antikörpers zu erhalten. Die Synchroton-Lichtquelle ist eine sehr stabile und leistungsstarke Quelle des Röntgenstrahls. Wenn der Strahl auf den Kristall trifft, wird er geteilt. Basierend auf dem Beugungsmuster kann die Struktur des Antikörpers mathematisch rekonstruiert werden.

Abb. 6: Beugungsmuster eines Röntgenstrahls, der auf einen Proteinkristall trifft. Der Kristall wird mit einem Halter in den Strahl gebracht (weiße Linie von links). Aus der Position und Intensität der kleinen dunklen Flecken wird die 3D-Struktur des Proteins berechnet. Der Detektor besteht aus verschiedenen Segmenten.

Abb. 7/8: In ihrer natürlichen Umgebung sind Antikörperstrukturen nicht starr, sondern durchlaufen Konformationsbewegungen. Diese Bewegungen können durch molekulardynamische Berechnungen simuliert werden. Solche Berechnungen werden von Supercomputer-Clustern durchgeführt. Es kann Wochen dauern, um 1 Millisekunde der Konformationsbewegung der Antikörperstruktur zu simulieren. Die lange LYNN-HERSHMAN-Schleife hat eine sehr hohe Konformationsflexibilität, während die Vergleichsschleife ERTA praktisch starr ist. (von Ting Zhou)

Abb. 9: Proteinbindungsbewertung durch Protein-CHIP. Das Bild zeigt einen repräsentativen Teil des gesamten Proteins CHIP. Proteinbindungsprofil des LYNNHERSHMAN-Antikörpers (links) und des ERTA-Antikörpers (rechts).

Abb. 10: Ampulle mit dem Bauplan des LYNNHERSHMAN Antikörpers.

Abb. 11: E.coli Bakterienkolonien. Erweiterung des Blueprints.

Abb. 12: Säugetierzellen wurden mit dem Bauplan transfiziert.

Abb. 13: Kultivierung von transfizierten Säugetierzellen, die LYNNHERSHMAN Antikörper produzieren. Antikörper können aus den Nährmedien gereinigt werden.

# George Church im Interview mit der Künstlerin

Das Interview mit George Church, Professor für Genetik an der Harvard Medical School und Professor für Gesundheitswissenschaft und -technologie in Harvard und am MIT (Massachusetts Institute of Technology) führte Lynn Hershman Leeson am 23. März 2017 an der Harvard Medical School in Boston, Massachusetts. Die Diskussion kreiste um das Thema Regeneration und die Archivierung von Material auf der DNA.

Lynn Hershman Leeson: Was genau tun Sie?

George Church: Die meiste Zeit meiner beruflichen Laufbahn habe ich damit verbracht, sich exponentiell verbessernde Technologien zu entwickeln, mit denen DNA gelesen und geschrieben werden kann. 2012 kam es uns wie eine logische Schlussfolgerung vor, dass wir einen Weg finden müssten, um sie zusammen in ein Archivierungssystem mit digitaler und analoger Information zu hinterlegen. Speicherung von Information ist entweder in biologischen oder in komplett nicht-biologischen Systemen möglich, in denen sie einfach nur archiviert wird. Wenn sie auf letztere Art gespeichert werden, kann die Information ungefähr eine Million Jahre aufgehoben werden. Im trockenen Zustand ändert sich nichts. Wenn sie in biologischen Systemen gespeichert werden, ist in der Regel eine sehr viel kürzeren Speicherung vorgesehen, die sich mit komplexen Systemen wie dem Hirn oder medizinischen Systemen verbinden soll oder wie eine Black-Box-Speicherung funktioniert. In diesem Fall ist es uns egal, wie lange sie haltbar sind, so lange sie den physiologischen Zustand als eine zeitliche Funktion akkurat anzeigen.

LHL: Stimmt es, dass Sie Filmmaterial archivieren, indem Sie es in DNA verwandeln?

GC: Ja. Mein Labor, Microsoft und Technicolor haben eine ganze Reihe Videos auf DNA gespeichert. Wir haben sogar einen Film von 1902 erst digitalisiert und dann die digitalen Nullen und Einsen auf die As, Cs, Gs und Ts übertragen. Nullen und Einsen sind im Grunde sehr leicht auf As, Cs, Gs und Ts mappbar, aber wir können auch analoge Daten direkt auf die DNA übertragen.

LHL: Und wie kann er vorgeführt oder zurückkonvertiert werden?

GC: Man kann ihn genau so zeigen wie einen digitalen Film. Bei digitalen Filmen gibt es keine Photonen im Disc-Laufwerk. Die DNA wird rekonvertiert, damit sie vom Disc-Laufwerk gelesen und dann auf eine Leinwand projiziert oder auf einem Monitor gezeigt werden kann.

LHL: Welche Filme haben Sie auf diese Art restauriert?

GC: Den erwähnten Film von 1902, *Die Reise zum Mond,* haben wir in digitale Nullen und Einsen konvertiert und dann in DNA, dann wieder zurück in Nullen und Einsen und zurück in einen zeigbaren Film. Man bemerkt keinen Unterschied. Es sind genau die gleichen Farben, der gleiche Ton und so weiter.

LHL: Warum gerade dieser Film?

GC: Technicolor hat ihn ausgewählt. Wahrscheinlich, weil es einer ihrer kostbarsten Filme ist. Der Regisseur und Produzent des Films, Georges Méliès, war zum Ende seines Lebens hin sehr enttäuscht und versuchte, alle seine Filme zu zerstören. Man glaubte, dass er auch diesen Klassiker zerstört hatte, der der erste kolorierte Film überhaupt war. Jedes Bild wurde einzeln von Hand mit transparenten Farben koloriert. Schließlich wurde eine Kopie gefunden, die allerdings in schlechtem Zustand war und von Hand mit viel Arbeit restauriert wurde. Davon wurden digitale Sicherungskopien gemacht, aber die befinden sich in normalen Archiven. Allerdings wollten sie diesen Film so dauerhaft wie möglich archivieren. Und so lange wir eine Lebensform sind, die auf Grundlage einer DNA funktioniert, so lange werden wir in der Lage sein, DNA zu lesen. Das ist die Idee dahinter.

LHL: Eine solche Arbeit ist ziemlich utopisch. Betrachten Sie sich selbst als Optimisten?

GC: Ja. Manches davon hat eine optimistische und eine pessimistische Seite. Die Vorstellung, dass man etwas in einer Form speichern muss, die Millionen von Jahre überdauert, setzt ja irgendwie voraus, dass wir unsere derzeitige Technologie oder auch unsere Zivilisation verlieren werden und wiederherstellen müssen. Das ist das Negativszenario, das uns motiviert. Das Gleiche gilt für Operationen im All: Sie entstammen der Notwendigkeit, dass wir von unserem Planeten runtermüssen, weil wir wie Kaninchen vor der Schlange Asteroiden und Supervulkane anstarren, wenn wir alle auf unserem Planeten bleiben wollen. Positiv kann man dagegen betrachten, dass diese Arbeit viele Möglichkeiten eröffnet hat. Wenn wir den Planeten verlassen, dann könnte das mit einer Gruppe Menschen geschehen, die klein genug und ausreichend finanziert ist, dass es machbar sein könnte, alle krankheitserregenden Mikroorganismen oder vielleicht sogar alle Mikroorganismen zu eliminieren. Es könnte außerdem notwendig und möglich sein, ihre Strahlungsempfindlichkeit, ihre Empfindlichkeit gegenüber der Schwerkraft und vielleicht sogar ihre Schmerzempfindlichkeit zu verringern, zumindest für eine kurze Zeit. Man kann also den Schmerz an- und abstellen, und zwar ohne benommen zu werden, was eine Nebenwirkung der üblichen Anästhetika und Opiate ist. Es gibt einen bekannten genetischen Mechanismus, nach dem Menschen unempfindlich gegenüber Schmerz geboren werden. Natürlich ist es ein Risikofaktor, wenn man immer schmerzunempfindlich ist. Aber andererseits könnte man eine Operation ohne Betäubung, ohne Antibiotika und ohne Sterilisierung durchführen, man könnte einfach in seinen normalen Klamotten kommen und aufgeschnitten werden, man könnte sich sogar selbst aufschneiden. Dies alles sind interessante Möglichkeiten, wenn man über die Notwendigkeit, diesen Planeten verlassen zu müssen, nachdenkt. Welche Möglichkeiten haben wir, uns selbst zu verändern, wenn wir an unsere Bedürfnisse in der Zukunft nachdenken?

LHL: Glauben Sie, dass es notwendig sein wird, auf einen unverschmutzten Planeten zu ziehen, einen, der zukunftsfähig ist?

GC: Ich glaube, die Motivation von diesem Planeten wegzukommen liegt nicht unbedingt in der Vermeidung von Umweltverschmutzung. Verschmutzung ist ein Merkmal von Leben, nicht nur von menschlichem Leben. Wenn man weit genug zurückblickt, enthielt die Atmosphäre ursprünglich gar keinen Sauerstoff. Photosynthese betreibende Organismen verschmutzten die Atmosphäre, bis sie 21 Prozent Sauerstoff enthielt, was für viele, viele Lebensformen giftig ist. Das war in den Anfangstagen des Lebens Umweltverschmutzung im großen Stil. Menschen werden ziemlich sicher auch nachfolgende Planeten verschmutzen, denn die Bevölkerung wächst. Wenn die Bevölkerung wächst, dann verschmutzen wir den Planeten zumindest mit Menschen, selbst dann, wenn wir ihn nicht mit Kohlenwasserstoffen und giftiger Atmosphäre und so weiter verschmutzen. Ich bin nicht deshalb der Meinung, dass wir den Planeten verlassen sollten. Wir sollten dies tun, weil der Planet von einem Asteroiden oder einem Supervulkan zerstört werden wird, der all die Arbeit, die wir in unsere Intelligenz und Zivilisation gesteckt haben, zunichte machen wird. Deshalb brauchen wir überall Kolonien. Je weiter weg desto besser.

LHL: Was sind weitere Gefahren für diesen Planeten?

GC: In der Vergangenheit war die Erde bereits von verschiedenen Vulkanausbrüchen und Asteroideneinschlägen betroffen. Dadurch wurde das Licht, das auf den Planeten fällt, verdunkelt und viele Arten starben aus. Wenn die Photosynthese verhindert wird, werden fast alle Nahrungsquellen gekappt. Die Zivilisation wäre also zumindest in Gefahr, im schlimmsten Fall wäre eine komplette biologische Vernichtung die Folge.

LHL: Sie nehmen also an, dass eine unbekannte Größe dazu führen könnte, dass es zu einer Massenvernichtung kommt und es notwendig wird, die Erde zu verlassen?

GC: Unbekannt – das ist genau der Knackpunkt. Es könnte in tausenden von Jahre geschehen, aber es könnte auch morgen geschehen. Wir hatten vor Kurzem gerade eine recht nahe Begegnung mit einem unerwarteten Asteroiden. Er war alarmierend lange unentdeckt geblieben. Er war klein und weit entfernt, aber trotzdem besorgniserregend. Wie schnell kämen wir von der Erde runter? Ich glaube, wir haben Prioritäten. Wenn wir uns auf die Krankheiten in den Entwicklungsländern konzentrieren und den Lebensstandard aller erhöhen, können wir mehr dafür ausgeben und sind nicht mehr in einer Wettbewerbssituation wie heute. Es würde mich aber nicht überraschen, wenn wir innerhalb des nächsten Jahrhunderts den Planeten verlassen könnten und lebensfähige, zukunftsfähige Kolonien hätten, von wo die Menschen nicht zurückkommen würden. Das könnte auch schon früher der Fall sein.

LHL: Glauben Sie, dass die Natur des Menschen der Grund für viele der Zerstörungen ist, insbesondere der Klimazerstörung und der Luftverschmutzung, die wir gerade erleben?

GC: Die Natur des Menschen hat sich verändert. Größtenteils nicht genetisch. Ich ziehe keine klare Grenze zwischen genetischer und nichtgenetischer Vererbung. Wir erben Dinge, wie zum Beispiel unsere Fähigkeit, mit Flugzeugen zu reisen, ins Weltall zu fliegen, Computer zu nutzen, und so weiter. Das ist genauso vererbt wie unsere Augenfarbe. In manchen Fällen sogar ein bisschen besser vererbt. Das Erbe durchdringt uns mehr. Wir werden uns weiter verändern. Die schnellste Weiterentwicklung mit den meisten Folgen ist heute die kulturelle Entwicklung, und zu dieser Kultur gehört auch die Technologie. Und zur Technologie gehört auch die Genetik. Unsere Genetik könnte das Tempo und die Auswirkungen der Kultur annehmen, denn sie ist heutzutage Teil der Kultur. Zum ersten Mal in der Geschichte können wir eine gute Idee durch das Internet in einem Tag verbreiten. Wenn es um die Herstellung von Dingen geht, verbreitet sie sich durch das Internet und andere Ressourcen innerhalb eines Jahres. DNA kann sich durch Fortpflanzung nicht so schnell verbreiten. Jeder Erneuerungszyklus benötigt 20 Jahre.

LHL: Was sehen Sie als unsere Möglichkeiten?

GC: Es ist wichtig, jede neue Technologie mit Bildung und Dialog zu begleiten. Es ist keine Einbahnstraße. Zuhören und Kommunikation sind notwendig, wenn man den Menschen die Verfügbarkeit einer Technologie vermitteln will. Die Technologie kann dadurch radikal im Preis gesenkt werden. Das haben wir bereits bei Mobiltelefonen, Computern, Internetsuchen und beim Lesen und Schreiben der DNA gesehen. All diese Dinge erreichen einen Punkt, an dem sie fast umsonst sind. Dafür werden sie von Werbung oder ähnlichem begleitet. Die Menschen müssen die Vorteile und Risiken kennen.

LHL: Wie werden diese Entscheidungen getroffen? Wer kontrolliert sie?

GC: Entscheidungen darüber werden in der üblichen Kraut-und-Rüben-Mischung der Entscheidungsfindung aus Politik und Wirtschaft getroffen. Hauptsächlich wird sie von den Kräften des Markts beeinflusst. Wenn ein findiger Unternehmer sich eine Begründung dafür ausdenken kann, warum die Menschen sieben Milliarden Handys brauchen, wird es eben sieben Milliarden Handys geben. Das gleiche gilt für die DNA. Wenn jemand eine Begründung findet, warum sieben Milliarden Menschen davon profitieren können, ob sie es sich leisten können oder nicht, dann wird, sofern ein finanzieller Vorteil winkt, irgendwer im System eine Möglichkeit finden, es unter die Leute zu bringen. Ich glaube, dass Entscheidungen in Wirklichkeit auf diese Weise getroffen werden. Ob eine Region, ein Land oder die Vereinten Nationen eine Entscheidung treffen oder nicht ist weniger vorhersehbar als die ökonomischen Bedürfnisse und Wünsche der Menschen.

LHL: Wie können wir Kultur fassen und archivieren?

GC: Ich finde es sehr wichtig, dass wir Geschichte in einem archivarischen, einem lebendigen Sinn bewahren. Es mag nicht ganz oben auf der Prioritätenliste stehen, aber es ist einer der Gründe für Wiederbelebung, einer der Gründe für eingefrorene Zoos. Es ist besser, wenn wir es als intaktes Ökosystem bewahren können, denn wir wissen zu wenig über Ökosysteme, um sie aus Tiefkühllagerung wiederzubeleben, und vielleicht möchten wir es auch nicht. Aber damit wir in vollem Umfang historische Versionen neben lebendigen Versionen von allem, Kulturen, Sprachen bewahren können, müssen wir unseren technologischen Fortschritt, unsere Refugien und Archive aufbewahren.

LHL: Optimisten sehen Risiken und finden Lösungen für potenzielle Gefahren, oder?

GC: Naja, ich mache mir über alles Sorgen, deshalb ich würde mich nicht als ausgewiesenen Optimisten bezeichnen. Wenn ich ein absoluter Optimist wäre, würde ich gar keinen Grund für Technologie erkennen können, da alles geregelt ist! Es ist kein Problem, wenn neun Milliarden Menschen auf dem Planeten leben, deshalb brauchen wir auch nichts zu tun. Ausbrechende Krankheiten sind kein Problem. Es gibt keine Probleme mit Zivilisationskrankheiten. Was dies alles angeht, bin ich Pessimist, deshalb glaube ich, dass Nichtstun keine gute Lösung ist.

LHL: Genau das würde ein Optimist sagen.

GC: Ich mache mir nicht nur wegen allem Sorgen, ich versuche auch, alle anderen dazu zu bringen, sich deswegen Sorgen zu machen. Es ist eine Art, die Menschen anzusprechen, wenn auch keine besonders gute, aber es ist wichtig, dass sie darüber Bescheid wissen. Als Technologinnen und Technologen haben wir eine bessere Sicht auf diese Dinge. Manche Wissenschaftlerinnen und Wissenschaftler halten es nicht für nötig, diese Sicht zu vermitteln. Ich schon. Ich glaube, es ist wichtig, es so schnell wie möglich zu tun. Im Vorfeld zu sehr vor Problemen zu warnen, ist immer noch besser als zu wenig davor zu warnen. Zum Beispiel wurde vorhergesagt, dass es sechzig Jahre dauern würden, bis wir das menschliche Genom für hunderte von Dollar lesen können würden. Stattdessen hat es sechs Jahre gedauert. Ich glaube, dass es viele solche Dinge geben kann, die uns bedrohen. Ich mache mir Sorgen wegen natürlicher Probleme wie zum Beispiel Supervulkane. Ich mache mir Sorgen wegen unnatürlicher Probleme, die momentan nicht viel mit Technologie zu tun haben, wie die Größe der Weltbevölkerung. Sie hat ihre Wurzeln in der Technologie; die grüne Revolution ermöglichte es uns, die bisherige Bevölkerungsgrenze zu verdoppeln. Und ich mache mir Sorgen wegen

Basistechnologien, die normalen Menschen oder sehr kleinen Bevölkerungsgruppen eine Macht ermöglichen, die in der Vergangenheit nur Nationen vorbehalten war, vielleicht sogar niemandem. Es war immer so, dass ein Mensch allein nicht viel Schaden anrichten konnte, aber heute, mit Atom-, Bio- und Chemiewaffen, kann eine einzelne Person viel anrichten. Das gilt insbesondere für Biowaffen, die können sich aus einer einzigen Zelle verbreiten, oder als einzelnes Virus, und eine Einzelperson kann etwas erfinden, das von globaler Bedeutung ist. Auch hier glaube ich, dass Nichtstun keine Option ist. Wir müssen proaktiv sein. Wir müssen gute Technologien zur Überwachung entwickeln, die einige der psychologischen und sozialen Motivationen für den Missbrauch existierender Technologien eliminieren können.

LHL: Und wie soll das geschehen?

GC: Diagnosen sind sicherlich eine Art der Überwachung, doch die Überwachung, von der ich mit einem pessimistischen Ausblick spreche, ist die Überwachung der Umwelt in Hinblick auf neu entstehende Krankheiten. Wir sollten alle Forscherinnen und Forscher und das, was sie tun, überwachen, offiziell oder inoffiziell, ob sie das wollen oder nicht. Niemand hat das Recht, mit der Synthetischen Biologie zu tun, was ihm oder ihr gefällt. Sie alle sollten überwacht werden. Aber es gibt viele positive Aspekte der Überwachung. Ich glaube, wir entwickeln uns immer weiter und werden dezentralisierte Überwachung in unseren Körpern haben, die vorhersieht und uns damit in der Präventivmedizin hilft.

LHL: Das ist genau meine Meinung: Es handelt sich um ein inneres biologisches Überwachungssystem, das Informationen liest, die normalerweise nicht erkannt werden. Wird das mit Zellen oder Sensoren durchgeführt?

GC: Besonders Sensoren, die neue Infektionserreger auslesen, können uns dabei helfen, Epidemien bereits bei Patient Null zu stoppen. Wir müssen nicht mehr warten, bis eine Million Menschen mit Flugzeugen ihre Seuche verteilen. Wir können sie in dem Moment aufhalten, in dem wir sie entdecken.

LHL: Das wäre ein beachtlicher Fortschritt.

GC: Diagnoseverfahren werden ein bisschen besser. Im Moment haben wir die paradoxe Situation, dass die Technologie viel besser in Sachen Diagnose ist, in der medizinischen Standardpraxis, zum Beispiel bei Erkältungskrankheiten, aber nur behandelt und nicht diagnostiziert wird. Das hat mit den gefühlten Realitäten und den relativen Kosten von Diagnose und Behandlung zu tun.

LHL: Wie kann man sich das konkret vorstellen?

GC: Einige der aktuellen Sensoren können ein bisschen Spucke durch einen DNA-Sequenzierer laufen lassen und alle Viren und Bakterien im Mund, jedem anderen Körperteil oder auch in der Luft auslesen. Das ist noch recht langsam, wird aber immer schneller. Diese Auslesung könnte man theoretisch auch sehen, wenn man einen Raum betritt: Man kann sehen, ob man auf den Raum allergisch reagiert, ob er Erreger enthält und ob man möglicherweise dagegen geimpft ist. Das könnte alles in Echtzeit geschehen, in unserem Handynetzwerk. Wir haben die Technologie, das langsam zu machen, aber sie verbessert sich schnell und exponentiell.

LHL: Gibt es eine Möglichkeit, sagen zu können, wann und wo etwas entsteht, das eine Bedrohung für andere Lebensformen darstellen könnte?

GC: Es gibt ziemlich gute internationale Abkommen zu Diagnosen und insbesondere zu Therapien, denn die können echten Schaden anrichten, wenn sie nicht eine ordentliche placebokontrollierte randomisierte Doppelblindstudie durchlaufen haben. Das ist der Goldstandard der FDA (Food and Drug Administration) in den USA und ihren weltweiten Entsprechungen, der EMA in Europa und der CFDA in China und so weiter. Ein neues Medikament darf nicht ausprobiert werden, ohne das korrekte Verfahren durchlaufen zu haben, idealerweise zuerst mit Tierversuchen. Neue Medikamente dürfen nicht einmal von Individuen selbst getestet werden, weil man verhindern möchte, dass Menschen sich selbst schaden.

LHL: Was ist mit der Nachverfolgung von Leben, das durch CRISPR-Behandlung verändert wurde? Um weltweit zu verstehen, was genau geändert wurde und um dieses neuen Systeme zurückzuverfolgen?

GC: CRISPR ist keinesfalls einzigartig. Es ist auch nicht viel zugänglicher als vorherige Therapien. Man kann Oxytocin ohne Rezept bekommen. Das ist zwar illegal, aber das Recht ist schwer durchzusetzen. Es ist ein Zahlenspiel. Man versucht, das öffentliche Gesundheitsrisiko bei einem Minimum zu halten. Wenn keine süchtig machenden oder schädlichen Medikamente verkauft werden, ist das Risiko geringer. Trotzdem wird es reguliert. Ich glaube, der Schlüssel liegt darin, Medikamente zu entwickeln, die genauso attraktiv sind wie die illegalen, dafür aber sicherer und effektiver. Eines der Ziele der FDA und der Agenturen auf der ganzen Welt ist es, sicherere und effektivere Medikamente zu entwickeln. Und dann gibt es keine Gründe mehr, sie auf andere Art als die gewünschte zu nutzen.

LHL: Welche Arten von Restriktionen sollten verordnet werden? Wie würden sie wirken?

GC: Es gibt Restriktionen für fast alles. Wenn man ein freilebendes Tier verändern möchte, dann hindern einen sogar drei Agenturen in den USA daran: die FDA, die EPA (Environmental Protection Agency) und die US-amerikanische Landwirtschaftsbehörde. In manchen Fällen geht es ihnen um das Wohlergehen des veränderten

Organismus, was ein bisschen seltsam ist, wenn es um Mücken geht. Man schert sich ja eigentlich nicht so sehr um das Wohlergehen von Mücken. Man möchte sicherstellen, dass das Ökosystem nicht auf eine Weise von ihnen abhängig ist.

LHL: Ich habe gehört, dass es im Moment keine Regulierungen gibt. Stimmt das?

GC: Es ist international geregelt. Viele der Anträge auf Veränderung wilder Arten beispielsweise mit Gene Drive, CRISPR Gene Drive, werden internationale Grenzen überschreiten. Und wenn man das vorher weiß, dann muss man vorher internationale Einigkeit zu diesem Thema schaffen. Wenn man diesen Schritt auslässt, dann werden Agenturen das wahrscheinlich wieder rückgängig machen, verfolgen und Konsequenzen einleiten.

LHL: Wie verhindern diese Regulierungen die Schaffung neuer Lebensformen?

GC: Man kann sie sicherlich erschaffen, aber man kann sie nicht aussetzen. Sobald sie ausgesetzt sind, ist das nachverfolgbar. Deshalb finde ich, dass Überwachung einer unserer Hauptschwerpunkte sein sollte. Je früher wir neue Lebensformen entdecken, desto schneller können wir anfangen, sie rückgängig zu machen.

LHL: Wie genau geht das?

GC: Man braucht ein Sensorennetzwerk, das Tier- oder Pflanzensensoren beinhalten kann, mechanische oder elektronische Sensoren. Wenn sie billig genug sind, können sie weltweit angewendet werden und in Echtzeit überwachen. Dann sollte man in der Lage sein, die ersten Anzeichen von etwas Ungewöhnlichem zu entdecken, man sollte aber ungefähr wissen, wonach man sucht. Aber sogar Veränderungen in der natürlichen Häufigkeit könnte einen darauf stoßen, dass etwas vor sich geht.

LHL: Das ist erleichternd. Viele Menschen, mit denen ich gesprochen habe, scheinen von solchen Erkennungssystemen nichts zu wissen.

GC: Sie sind sehr einfach, aber ja – das DCD hat ein Netzwerk von Stationen, Ärztinnen und Ärzten und nimmt Proben, wenn sie einen ungewöhnlichen Patienten haben. Aber das System könnte viel kosteneffektiver und medizinisch effektiver sein, wenn jeder Mensch seinen eigenen Sensor hätte, oder vielleicht verschiedene persönliche Sensoren, so wie jede US-amerikanische Bürgerin und jeder US-amerikanischer Bürger auch mehrere Elektrogeräte hat.

LHL: Und wie funktioniert die Aufsicht über diese Sensorennetzwerke?

GC: Es ist nicht ganz vereinheitlicht und in Kraft gesetzt, aber es gibt einen Rahmenvertrag, was die Ziele sind. Und wenn man über die Wirtschaft spricht, ist es international. Als Google beschloss, Street View international zu machen, musste es sich vor Ort die Erlaubnis einholen, mit automatisierten Kameras die Straßen eines jeden Landes abzufahren. Manche gaben die Erlaubnis, andere nicht. Es war ein Flickenteppich der Entscheidungen. Aber größtenteils ist es international verfügbar, es ist draußen: Man kann Street View und Google Maps für fast jeden Ort auf der Welt einsehen.

LHL: Ins Leben gerufen von Optimisten wie Ihnen.

GC: Ich würde sagen, dass man nur ein kleines bisschen Optimismus braucht, um nicht gelähmt vom Pessimismus zu sein. Ich glaube, dass ich diese Stufe erreicht habe. Es ist nicht so, dass es keine Lösungen gäbe. Es gibt nur so viele Probleme. Der kreative Prozess in diesem Fall wird von der Arbeit an der Problemlösung angeregt... Ich würde sogar sagen, dass ich pessimistisch bin, was die Technologien angeht. Oft entwickeln wir fünf verschiedene Technologien, die alle in die gleiche Richtung gehen und wissen, dass vier davon scheitern werden. Wären wir optimistisch, würden wir sagen: »Oh, das wird klappen!« Superoptimisten würden sagen: »Ich brauche nichts zu tun, ich lasse es einfach wie es ist, es wird sich entwickeln.« Ein bisschen optimistischer wäre: »Ja, irgendwas wird funktionieren, aber nicht alles. Deshalb muss ich viele verschiedene Dinge ausprobieren.«

LHL: Seit wann interessieren Sie sich für Bio- und Computererfindungen?

GC: Ich interessiere mich für die Schnittstelle zwischen Biologie und Computern, seit ich zehn Jahre alt bin. Zunächst habe ich mit Kristallographie von Genmaterial gearbeitet. Das war noch nicht gerade Genetik, aber mir wurde schnell klar, dass sich die besten Möglichkeiten für meine Fähigkeiten in der Biologie und mit Computern in der Genetik boten. Das beinhaltet beides, das Lesen und Schreiben von DNA, und grundsätzlich das Lesen und Schreiben von allem Biologischen, von Organen über Ökosysteme bis hin zur Präzisionsmedizin.

LHL: Ich glaube, das ist die Kunstform unserer Zeit.

GC: Ja. Tatsächlich beschreibt eine meiner Post-Doc-Arbeiten dieses Feld als Modellieren von Evolutionen.

LHL: Da stimme ich total zu.

GC: Es ist vierdimensionales Modellieren, das jeden Teil unseres Ökosystems einschließt.

LHL: Und Zeit.

GC: Genau. Zeit ist die vierte Dimension.

## Sabine Himmelsbach
## Interview mit Lynn Hershman Leeson

Das Gespräch fand per E-Mail im Januar und Februar 2019 statt.

Sabine Himmelsbach: Als Künstlerin warst Du immer auch an aktuellen gesellschaftlichen Entwicklungen und technologischen Erneuerungen interessiert. Du lebst in San Francisco; haben die technischen Fortschritte und Entwicklungen des Silicon Valley Dich inspiriert?

Lynn Hershman Leeson: In der Bay Area kann man gar nicht anders, als die dynamischen Verlagerungen wahrzunehmen, Veränderungen, die von hier aus die ganze Welt beeinflusst haben. Dinge wie Connectivity, Uber, AirBnB, Google und Facebook. Aber historisch war das schon gegeben: Tatsächlich wurde das Fernsehen in San Francisco erfunden, das Thema steckt also wirklich im Unterbewusstsein der Region.

SH: Was weckte Dein Interesse an Biotechnologien? Wann begannst Du, mit damit verbundenen Themen wie regenerativer Medizin und Genom-Editierung zu arbeiten?

LHL: 2006 fing ich an, mich mit diesem Thema zu beschäftigen. Das war kurz nachdem das Genom programmiert worden war. 2011, nachdem ich *!W.A.R.* und *Strange Culture* beendet hatte, beschäftigte ich mich intensiver mit dem Thema und begann darüber nachzudenken, was in der globalen Überlebensstrategie wirklich wichtig ist. Damals begann ich, Forscherinnen und Forscher zu interviewen und machte damit Arbeiten wie *The Infinity Engine;* Arbeiten, die auf dynamische Weise unsere Ideen von uns selbst und unserer Identität umformen, allerdings von innen nach außen.

SH: Dein Film *Strange Culture* ist sehr politisch. Er widmet sich der wahren Geschichte von Steve Kurtz, einem Mitglied des Critical Art Ensemble, der vom FBI unter dem Verdacht des Bioterrorismus festgenommen wurde, nachdem seine Frau unerwartet im Schlaf an Herzversagen gestorben war. Die Petrischalen und die wissenschaftlichen Geräte, die die Rettungskräfte in ihrem Haus fanden, machten ihn verdächtig. Das Künstlerkollektiv arbeitete damals mit genveränderten Lebensmitteln, um bei einem breiteren Publikum ein Bewusstsein dafür zu schaffen und es den Menschen möglich zu machen, die Prinzipien der Technologie selbst zu verstehen. Dein Film stellt offen die Politik der Regierung in Frage und hat, soweit ich weiß, auch dabei geholfen, Steve Kurtz während seines Prozesses durch erneute Aufmerksamkeit auf den Fall zu unterstützen.

LHL: Ja, es war mir wichtig, einem anderen Künstler zu helfen. Ich kannte Steve zu der Zeit nicht, aber ich hielt es für wichtig, dass wir eine Möglichkeit schaffen, um seine Geschichte vielen Menschen zu erzählen. Steve selbst sagte, dass der Film ihm dabei half, einer drohenden 23-jährigen Haftstrafe zu entkommen.

SH: In Deinen Arbeiten über Biotechnologien wirbst Du auch für ein besseres Verständnis dieser Technologien bei einer breiteren Bevölkerungsschicht. Du lädst Menschen ein, einen Blick hinter normalerweise geschlossene Türen wissenschaftlicher Labore zu werfen. Könntest Du uns etwas über die künstlerische Form, für die Du Dich bei *The Infinity Engine* entschieden hast, erzählen? Ich denke an den Labor-Kontext, aber auch an die Aneignung wissenschaftlichen Materials, so wie das Poster des verwundeten Soldaten, das Du in einem Genlabor gefunden hast oder die mit einem Bioprinter hergestellte Nase, die Du von Dr. Anthony Atala von der Wake Forest School of Regenerative Medicine erhalten hast.

LHL: Ja, ich nutze in meiner Arbeit gerne die Wirklichkeit, denn sie ist oft surrealer als alles, was ich mir ausdenken könnte, und es gibt den Dingen eine andere Richtung.

SH: Mit Deiner Ausstellung *Anti-Bodies* im HeK (Haus der elektronischen Künste Basel) hast Du Deine komplexe, mehrere Räume umfassende Installation *The Infinity Engine* nach Jahren der Arbeit abgeschlossen. Hattest Du von Anfang an eine Vorstellung der acht Räume oder hat sich das im Laufe der Arbeit so ergeben?

LHL: In meinen ersten Zeichnungen hatte ich bereits acht Räume vorgesehen. Eine Acht ist liegend die Unendlichkeit und außerdem die Doppelhelix, deshalb wollte ich, dass die Information so formatiert wird. Zum Glück kamen am Ende acht einzelne Elemente heraus, das war perfekt.

SH: Stellt die Vollendung von *The Infinity Engine* eine Zusammenfassung Deines Interesses, die Biotechnologie als Thema für Deine Arbeit zu untersuchen, dar? Oder ist das Thema immer noch eines, das zusätzlicher Reflexionen und Erkundungen bedarf?

LHL: Es ist auf keinen Fall ein Abschluss. Ich werde einen Spielfilm über die Tragweite der Dinge machen, die ich erforscht habe, als ich an der Installation gearbeitet habe, insbesondere über genetische Narben oder Epigenetik.

SH: Das hört sich danach an, als würdest Du Deine Arbeit über die Frage nach der Identität eine weitere Schicht hinzufügen! Du hast 1996 mit Deinem Text »Romancing the Anti-Body: Lust and Longing in (Cyber)Space« den Begriff »Anti-Body« geprägt. Damals bezogst Du Dich auf einen fragmentierten Körper, der Erfahrungen in der wirklichen Welt und im virtuellen Raum des damals neuen Cyberspace des Internets hatte.

Für die Ausstellung im HeK hat Dr. Thomas Huber, Senior Researcher bei den NIBR, den Novartis Institutes for BioMedical Research der Novartis Pharma AG, einen Antikörper entwickelt, der in seiner molekularen Struktur Deinen Namen trägt.

LHL: Ja, ich glaube, die Antikörper LYNNHERSHMAN und ERTA sind wichtig, nicht nur, wenn es um die Vorstellung der Identität geht, sondern auch um die Identität von Innen heraus.

SH: Deine Arbeit hat sich auf vielfältige Weise rund um die Frage der Identität entwickelt, und man könnte sagen, dass dem nun eine biologische Komponente hinzugefügt wurde. In früheren Arbeiten »mutiertest« Du Deine Rolle selbst, wie Du in einem Interview beschriebst. Nun hat ein Pharmakonzern »Deinen« Antikörper hergestellt. Könntest Du uns erzählen, wie die Idee für dieses radikale Projekt zustande kam und was es für Dich bedeutet, dass solch ein Antikörper existiert?

LHL: Es bedeutet mir viel, denn es kehrt Identität um, es heftet sich innen an und kommt so nach außen, es ist kein Körper, sondern eine Restrukturierung der biologischen Essenz dessen, was wir sind, und es ist auch ein Mittel, um Gifte in der Umwelt anzugreifen, etwas, das im Grunde jeder künstlerischen Arbeit zugrunde liegt.

SH: Als wir Dr. Thomas Huber das erste Mal trafen, sprachen wir viel über Antikörper und ihre therapeutische Funktion. Ich erinnere mich daran, dass er sagte, dass ein Antikörper ein anschauliches Beispiel dafür ist, wie etwas wie die Evolution jeden Tag in unseren Körpern stattfindet. In Deinen Texten behauptest Du, dass der Antikörper einen therapeutischen Nutzen für die Kultur selbst hat. Könntest Du das erläutern?

LHL: Ja. Es ist eine Motivation für Künstlerinnen und Künstler, nach dem Gift, das die Kultur zerstört, zu suchen, seine negativen Verdrängungseffekte zu neutralisieren. Dies geschieht durch die Kunst. Manchmal offensichtlich, manchmal subtil. Indem man dies biologisch tut, bekommt es eine noch tiefere Bedeutung.

SH: Ein Raum in *The Infinity Engine* ist dem derzeitigen Stand der biologischen Überwachung gewidmet. Überwachung ist in Deiner Arbeit ein wichtiges und wiederkehrendes Thema, von der elektronischen Überwachung in Arbeiten wie *CybeRoberta* von Mitte der 1990er über Arbeiten über biologische Überwachung durch Gesichtserkennungssysteme, bei denen die Augen durch Kameras ersetzt wurden bis hin zu *The Infinity Engine.* Könntest Du ein bisschen über diese Arbeit und die thematische Verlagerung zur biologischen Überwachung unserer Körper erzählen?

LHL: Ich glaube, dass Überwachung heute auf der Ebene der Zellen stattfindet, auf der man über das Archiv der DNA Zugang zu unserer Geschichte hat.

SH: Der achte und letzte Raum von *The Infinity Engine* zeigt den LYNNHERSHMAN-Antikörper in einem Glasfläschchen hinter geschlossenen Labortüren. Daneben sehen Besucherinnen und Besucher ein weiteres Glasfläschchen, in denen sich vier Nanogramm DNA befinden, auf der sich alle digitalen Dokumente der Ausstellung, also Bilder und Videos, befinden. Ihr digitaler Code wurde in biologischen Code umgewandelt. Könntest Du den Prozess erklären und auch, warum Du beschlossen hast, *The Infinity Engine* auf DNA zu übertragen?

LHL: Das war die logische Konsequenz. Es war die poetische Essenz des Projekts, eingedampft in unsichtbares Archivmaterial. Es beinhaltet nicht nur die Dokumente der Ausstellung, sondern auch das elektronische Tagebuch, das das Archiv meines Lebens darstellt. Ich glaube, dass dies die Zukunft für manipuliertes Leben und die Archivierung unserer Geschichte ist. Mir gefällt es, dass alle die Arbeit von über einem Jahrzehnt auf so eine winzige, konzentrierte Größe reduziert werden konnte. Für mich war es wie ein *Haiku* des Universums.

SH: *The Infinity Engine* umfasst ein Jahrzehnt an Recherche und untersucht biotechnologische Vorteile und Entwicklungen. Die Installation ermöglicht es den Besucherinnen und Besuchern, ein tieferes Verständnis des aktuellen wissenschaftlichen Fortschritts zu bekommen und zeigt zugleich die Ambivalenzen und Bedenken, die man haben kann, darunter ethische Fragen, die verhandelt werden müssen.

Du zeigst beide Seiten, die dunkle und die helle. In einem kurzen Video, dass neben der DNA und dem Antikörper zu sehen ist, endest Du mit einem Ausschnitt aus Ihrem Film *Conceiving Ada,* in dem Du Tilda Swinton als Ada Lovelace sagen lässt: »Das erlösende Geschenk der Menschheit ist die Fähigkeit, sich in jeder Generation neu zu erschaffen.« Das ist ein hoffnungsvolles Ende für *The Infinity Engine.* Würdest Du Dich selbst als Optimistin bezeichnen?

LHL: Unbedingt. Ich glaube, das ist es, was Künstlerinnen und Künstler sind. Genau wie Antikörper. Sie finden gefährliche Gifte. Und wenn sie erfolgreich sind, nutzen sie Hoffnung und Optimismus, um sie unschädlich zu machen.

# Lynn Hershman Leeson
# Die Veröffentlichung der Antikörper LYNNHERSHMAN und ERTA

Das Antikörper-Projekt wurde im Oktober 2018 vollendet. Die konzeptuelle Zusammenarbeit von Dr. Thomas Huber, dem Gruppenleiter für therapeutische Antikörperforschung der Novartis Labs in Basel und der Künstlerin Lynn Hershman Leeson resultierte in der Produktion eines Antikörpers, inspiriert von der wissenschaftlichen Forschung, die in der letzten Version der Kunstinstallation *The Infinity Engine* dargestellt wurde. Sie befasst sich mit DNA-Manipulationen und deren Auswirkungen auf die Gesellschaft, insbesondere damit, wie das Bioengineering unser Konzept von Identität verändert. Neben ihrer allseits bekannten Rolle als Immunmoleküle und Impfstoffe sind Antikörper ein zentrales Werkzeug für die Biotechnologie und Biomedizin geworden. *The Antibody Room* stellte die Entwicklung eines künstlich hergestellten Antikörpers dar, das den Namen »Lynn Hershman« in seiner Molekülstruktur trägt. Eine zweiter Antikörper mit dem Namen ERTA, der sich auf Lynn Hershmans Identitäts-Projekt »Roberta Breitmore« bezieht, wurde gleichzeitig entwickelt.[1]

Hershman bemerkt: »Anti-Körper identifizieren, entlarven und neutralisieren Toxine in der Kultur. Diese Themen durchdringen meine Arbeit der letzten 50 Jahre. Ein Antikörper ist die grundlegende Darstellung von Identität; ein reaktives Molekül, das in der Lage ist, gegen sich selbst reaktiv zu sein, eine umgekehrte biologische Geste, deren Ziel die Heilung von Innen heraus ist, ein cyborgartiger Traum davon, den Körper selbst mit dem Versuch der Schaffung einer radikalen und kurierenden Genesung zu unterwandern.« (Abbildung 1).

Nachdem der Antikörper entwickelt wurde, durchlief er eine Reihe von Experimenten, um seine Eigenschaften und potenzielle therapeutische und wissenschaftliche Anwendungen zu erforschen. Der LYNNHERSHMAN-Antikörper besteht aus vier Proteinketten mit insgesamt 1.334 Aminosäuren. Für die Ausstellung wurden etwa sechzig Billiarden Moleküle produziert, eine unvorstellbar große Zahl.

Da Antikörper sehr klein sind, wiegt diese Anzahl nur etwa 15 Milligramm. Antikörper sind mit dem bloßen Auge oder einem Lichtmikroskop nicht zu erkennen. Ihre räumliche Struktur wird mit Röntgen-Refraktur berechnet. Die Züchtung der beiden Antikörper dauerte vier Monate. Ihre Eigenschaften wurden mit Röntgen-Diffusion dargestellt (Abbildung 2).

Einige Wochen vor der »Geburt« der Antikörper wurden sie in Zeitsequenzen gemessen, indem Proteinkristalle für die Röntgen-Strukturanalyse genutzt wurden, um eine #D-Struktur der Antikörper-Antigen-Interaktionen zu erhalten. Eine robotergeführte Kamera machte zu unterschiedlichen Zeitpunkten Aufnahmen, die das Wachstum des Antikörpers darstellen (Abbildungen 3+4). [Bildunterschrift Abbildung 3: eine Stunde, Bildunterschrift Abbildung 4: 18 Stunden]

Fazit

Beide Antikörper, LYNNHERSHMAN und ERTA, konnten problemlos produziert werden und ihre biophysikalischen Eigenschaften waren ziemlich vielversprechend. LYNNHERSHMAN ist recht stark und weist eine weitgehende Integrität auf. ERTA ist sogar noch stärker und weist noch höhere Integrität auf. Der LYNNHERSHMAN-Antikörper war in der Lage, sich mit einer breiten Anzahl von Proteinen zu verbinden (ungefähr 2.600 von 7.000). Im scharfen Kontrast dazu weist der ERTA-Antikörper bessere Produktionseigenschaften und biophysikalische Eigenschaften auf, verband sich aber mit KEINEM der geprüften 7.000 Proteine. Sein Unvermögen, sich mit irgendetwas zu verbinden, ist sehr ungewöhnlich.

Das Projekt wird online einsehbar sein und in weiteren Tests auf mögliche Funktionsfähigkeit geprüft.

*The Infinity Engine* wurde vom 2. Mai bis 5. August 2018 im HeK (Haus der elektronischen Künste Basel) und der Riga Biennale vom 2. Juni bis 28. Oktober 2018 sowie der Guangzhou Triennale im Dezember 2018 ausgestellt.

Weiterführende Literatur:
Thomas Huber, »Generation of the Lynn Hershman Leeson Antibody«, *www.diaphanes.net,* 10. April 2018, https://www.diaphanes.net/titel/generation-of-the-lynn-Hershman-antibody-5613 (aufgerufen am 13. Februar 2019).
Meritxell Rosell, »Lynn Hershman Leeson & Thomas Huber: anti-body or antibody?«, *CLOT Magazine* (18. April 2018), http://www.clotmag.com/lynn-hershman-leeson (aufgerufen am 13. Februar 2019).

1 Ein Antikörper identifiziert Toxine in Kulturen und versucht dann, sie zu neutralisieren oder zu entfernen. Roberta Breitmore und später Robertas viralisierte Vervielfachungen beleuchteten die ungehemmten Toxine des Sexismus zu ihrer Zeit in den 1970ern. Mitte der 1980er erschienen Fotografien von Antikörpern. Dazu: Lynn Hershman Leeson, *Romancing the Antibody, Lust and Longing in Cyberspace,* exh. cat., Seattle Art Museum (Seattle, 1995).

# Künstlerbiografie Lynn Hershman Leeson

Lynn Hershman Leeson, geboren 1941 in Cleveland, Ohio, lebt und arbeitet in San Francisco und New York. Sie studierte an der Case Western Reserve University sowie der San Francisco State University. Hershman Leeson ist Professorin Emeritus an der University of California, Davis und war A.D. White Professorin an der Cornell University.

Mit großem Gespür für Schlüsselthemen unserer Zeit verbindet die Künstlerin und Filmemacherin Lynn Hershman Leeson in ihren Werken neue Technologien mit Fragen nach Identität, Privatsphäre in einer Ära der Überwachung, Schnittstellen zwischen Menschen und Medien oder der Beziehung zwischen realen und virtuellen Welten. Seit den 1970er Jahren waren ihre Arbeiten in über 200 internationalen Einzel- und Gruppenausstellungen zu sehen, u.a. im Berkeley Art Museum, dem De Young Museum in San Francisco, dem Museum of Modern Art in New York, der National Gallery of Canada in Ottawa, der Kunsthalle Bremen, dem Lehmbruck Museum in Duisburg, dem Cleveland Museum of Art, der Modern Art Oxford oder den KW Kunstwerke Berlin. 2014–15 war am ZKM | Zentrum für Kunst und Medien in Karlsruhe eine umfassende Retrospektive ihres Werks von Mitte der 1960er Jahre bis zu aktuellen Produktionen zu sehen. 2017 richtete das Yerba Buena Center for the Arts in San Francisco ebenfalls eine große Retrospektive ihres Werks aus.

Hershman Leeson veröffentlichte 2011 den bahnbrechenden Dokumentarfilm *!Women Art Revolution,* der international in vielen großen Museen gezeigt und vom Museum of Modern Art als eine der drei besten Dokumentationen des Jahres ausgezeichnet wurde. Hershman Leeson schrieb, inszenierte und produzierte die Spielfilme *Strange Culture, Conceiving Ada* und *Teknolust* mit der Schauspielerin Tilda Swinton in der Hauptrolle. Ihre Filme wurden auf dem Sundance Film Festival, dem Toronto International Film Festival und der Berlinale gezeigt, bevor sie international vertrieben wurden.

Die Künstlerin erhielt zahlreiche Stipendien und Auszeichnungen, u.a. den Siemens Medienkunstpreis; den d.velop digital art award (d.daa) für ihr Lebenswerk im Bereich Neue Medien; den Prix Ars Electronica des renommierten gleichnamigen Medienkunstfestivals; eine Auszeichnung für ihr Lebenswerk des SIGGRAPH Festivals oder auch eine Auszeichnung der Alfred P. Sloan Foundation für ihr Schreiben und ihre Regie.
Ihre Arbeiten sind in vielen öffentlichen Sammlungen vertreten, beispielsweise des Museum of Modern Art in New York, des Wilhelm Lehmbruck Museums in Duisburg, der Tate Modern in London, des Los Angeles County Museum of Art in Los Angeles, der National Gallery of Canada, des Walker Art Center in Minneapolis, der Whitworth Art Gallery in Manchester oder des University Art Museum in Berkeley und weiteren berühmten privaten Sammlungen.
Siehe auch:
www.LYNNHERSHMAN.com

# Biographien

George Church [1]

George Church ist Professor für Genetik an der Harvard Medical School und Leiter von PersonalGenomes.org, das als einzige Plattform freien Zugang zu Informationen über menschliche Genomik-, Umwelt- und genetische Merkmalsdaten zur Verfügung stellt (GET, Abkürzuung für Genomic, Environental and Trait data, http://www.getconference.org).

Seine PhD-Arbeit im Jahr 1984 beinhaltete die ersten Methoden für direkte Genomsequenzierung, molekulare Multiplexverfahren und Barcoding. Dies führte zur ersten Genomsequenz (pathogen, *Helicobacter pylori)* im Jahr 1994. Seine Forschungen haben zu fast allen DNA-Sequenz-Methoden und -Unternehmen der »nächsten Generation« beigetragen (CGI-BGI, Life, Illumina, Nanopore). Dies und die Arbeit seines Labors an DNA-Chip-Synthese, Genom-Editing und Stammzellen-Engineering führten zur Gründung weiterer anwendungsbasierter Firmen im Bereich der medizinischen Diagnostik (Knome/PierianDx, Alacris, AbVitro/Juno, Genos, Veritas Genetics) und der synthetischen Biologie und Therapie (Joule, Gen9, Editas, Egenesis, enEvolv, WarpDrive). Er ist Vorreiter bei den Themen neue Privatsphäre, Biosicherheit und ELSI (ethische, legale und soziale Implikationen) und im Bereich der Richtlinien für Umwelt- und Biosicherheit.

Er ist Leiter eines IARPA BRAIN-Projekts und des NIH Center for Excellence in Genomic Science. Ausgezeichnet wurde er unter anderem als Preisträger von NAS & NAE & Franklin Bower für seine Errungenschaften in der Wissenschaft. Er ist Mitautor von über 500 wissenschaftlichen Aufsätzen, 143 Patentveröffentlichungen und eines Buchs (Church, George und Regis, Ed: *Regenesis. How Synthetic Biology Will Reinvent Nature and Ourselves.* New York, 2014).

Rudolf Frieling

Rudolf Frieling studierte an der Freien Universität Berlin und promovierte an der Universität Hildesheim. Im Jahr 2006 wurde er zum Kurator für Medienkunst am San Francisco Museum of Modern Arts (SFMOMA) ernannt. Seitdem kuratierte er dort große Überblicksausstellungen wie *The Art of Participation: 1950 to Now* (2008–09) über die Geschichte zeitgenössischer partizipativer Praxis und *Stage Presence: Theatricality in Art and Media* (2012) über die Überschneidungen von visueller und darstellender Kunst. Zuletzt ko-kuratierte er die Retrospektive *Bruce Conner: It's All True* (2016), die auch im Museum of Modern Art in New York und im Museo Reina Sofia in Madrid gezeigt wurde, und *Soundtracks* (2017), die erste große Ausstellung des SFMOMA, die Künstlerinnen und Künstlern gewidmet ist, die sich mit Klang und Raum auseinandersetzen. Außerdem ko-kuratierte er die Werkschau von *Rafael Lozano-Hemmer: Unstable Presence* (2018–20) und ist Ko-Kurator der Retrospektive *Suzanne Lacy: We Are Here* (2019) über die Pionierin im Bereich der sozialen Praxis. Vor seiner Tätigkeit am SFMOMA arbeitete Frieling von 1994 bis 2006 als Kurator und Wissenschaftler beim Zentrum für Kunst und Medien in Karlsruhe. Er war Projektleiter und Mitherausgeber der Buch- und Multimediaserien über die Geschichte der Medienkunst *Media Art Action* (1997) und *Media Art Interaction* (2000) und des Onlinearchivs *Media Art Net* (2004–05) sowie des Wiederherstellungs-/Veröffentlichungsprojekts *40yearsvideoart.de* (2006). Frieling ist außerdem Lehrbeauftragter am California College of Arts. Er lebt und arbeitet in San Francisco.

Sabine Himmelsbach

Seit März 2012 ist Sabine Himmelsbach Direktorin des HeK (Haus der elektronischen Künste Basel). Nach einem Kunstgeschichtsstudium in München arbeitete sie von 1993–96 für Galerien in München und Wien und wurde anschließend Projektleiterin für Ausstellungen und begleitende Symposien beim Steirischen Herbst Festival in Graz. 1999 übernahm sie die Ausstellungsleitung am ZKM | Zentrum für Kunst und Medien in Karlsruhe. Von 2005–11 leitete sie das Edith-Russ-Haus für Medienkunst in Oldenburg. Zu ihren Ausstellungsprojekten gehören unter anderem *Fast Forward* (2003); *Coolhunters* (2004); *Ökomedien* (2007); *MyWar* (2010) und *Culture(s) of Copy* (2011). 2011 kuratierte sie *gateways. Kunst und vernetzte Kultur* für das Kumu Kunstmuseum in Tallinn, Estland, im Rahmen der Europäischen Kulturhauptstadt Tallinn 2011. Zu ihren Ausstellungsprojekten am HeK in Basel gehören *Sensing Place* (2012), *Semiconductor: Let There Be Light* (2013), *Ryoji Ikeda* (2014), *Poetics and Politics of Data* (2015), *Rafael Lozano-Hemmer: Preabsence* (2016) und *unREAL* (2017), *Lynn Hershman Leeson: Anti-Bodies* und *Eco-Visionaries* (2018). In Vorträgen und Texten arbeitet sie zu Themen der Medienkunst und digitalen Kultur.

Thomas Huber

Dr. Thomas Huber ist Forschungsgruppenleiter beim Novartis NIBR Biologics Center in Basel. Er ist technologischer Leiter und Co-Projektteamleiter für multispezifische Antikörpermodalitäten. 2012 und 2013 war er Projektteamleiter am Zentrum für Atemwegserkrankungen (Respiratory Disease Center) in Horsham in Großbritannien. Seit er 2007 zu Novartis kam, etablierte er verschiedene weltweite Technologieplattformen im Bereich des therapeutischen Antikörper- und Protein-Engineering. Dr. Huber erlangte seinen PhD in der Gruppe von Prof. Andreas Plückthun am Institut für Biochemie an der Universität Zürich und seinen Masterabschluss in Biochemie und Immunologie an der Universität Zürich.

1 Die biografischen Angaben stammen von: George Church, *genetics.hms.harvard.edu/*, 12. Januar 2019, http://arep.med.harvard.edu/gmc/ (zugegriffen am 3. März 2019).

## Acknowledgements / Dank

To the artist / An die Künstlerin.
To the authors / An die Autorinnen und Autoren.
To all who had part in building the project / An alle, die zum Erfolg des Projekts beigetragen haben.

To the financial supporters of HeK / An die Subventionsgeber des HeK:

Schweizerische Eidgenossenschaft
Confédération suisse
Confederazione Svizzera
Confederaziun svizra

Swiss Confederation

Eidgenössisches Departement des Innern EDI
Département fédéral de l'intérieur DFI
Dipartimento federale dell'interno DFI
Departament federal da l'intern DFI
Federal Department of Home Affairs FDHA
**Bundesamt für Kultur BAK**
**Office fédéral de la culture OFC**
**Ufficio federale della cultura UFC**
**Uffizi federal da cultura UFC**
**Federal Office of Culture FOC**

**cms**
**Christoph Merian Stiftung**

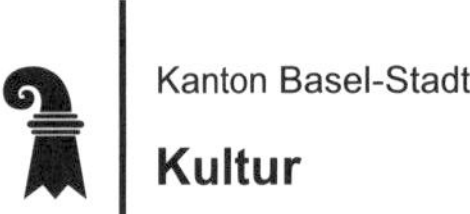


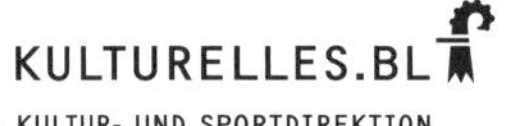


The publication is supported by / Die Publikation wird unterstützt von:

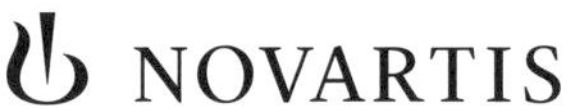

Publication accompanying the exhibition / Diese Publikation erscheint anlässlich der Ausstellung

Lynn Hershman Leeson: Anti-Bodies

An exhibition by HeK (House of Electronic Arts Basel) / Eine Ausstellung des HeK (Haus der elektronischen Künste Basel) May 3 – August 5, 2018 / 3. Mai – 5. August 2018

Published by / Erschienen im
Hatje Cantz Verlag GmbH
Mommsenstraße 27
10629 Berlin
Germany / Deutschland
www.hatjecantz.com

Ein Unternehmen der Ganske Verlagsgruppe
A Ganske Publishing Group Company



Editor / Herausgeber:
Sabine Himmelsbach for / für HeK (House of Electronic Arts Basel / Haus der elektronischen Künste Basel)

Contributions by / Beiträge von: George Church, Rudolf Frieling, Lynn Hershman Leeson, Sabine Himmelsbach, Thomas Huber

Proofreading / Korrektorat:
Leonie Häsler

Translation / Übersetzung [Rudolf Frieling]: Sybille Weber (English – German / Englisch – Deutsch)
Translation / Übersetzung [Sabine Himmelsbach]: Toby Axelrod (German – English / Deutsch – Englisch)
Translation / Übersetzung [Thomas Huber, George Church, Lynn Hershman Leeson]: Janna Düringer, Pingpong Translation (English – German / Englisch – Deutsch)

Graphic design / Gestaltung:
Hauser Schwarz, Basel

Production / Herstellung:
Janine Lattich, Hatje Cantz

Printing, binding, and reproductions / Druck, Bindung und Reproduktionen:
DZA Druckerei zu Altenburg GmbH, Altenburg

Typeface / Schrift:
Neue Haas Grotesk

Paper / Papier: Olin regular high white, Profigloss

ISBN 978-3-7757-4611-3

Printed in Germany

Image credits / Bildnachweis:
Lynn Hershman Leeson (pp./S. 14, 18–19, 22–23, 26–27, 30, 38, 40, 55–57); Lynn Hershman Leeson, Thomas Huber, Novartis Pharma AG (pp./S. 83–84); Thomas Huber, Novartis Pharma AG (pp./S. 32, 64–67); Laurids Jensen, Novartis Pharma AG (pp./S. 68–69, 87); Franz Wamhof (pp./S. 10–13, 16–17, 20–21, 24–25, 28–29, 31, 33, 34–37, 39, 44, 46, 49–50, 59); ZKM | Zentrum für Kunst und Medien (p./S. 15)

Cover illustration / Umschlagabbildung: Franz Wamhof

Cover inside / Umschlaginnenseite: Lynn Hershman Leeson